CAMBRIDGE TEXTS IN THE
HISTORY OF PHILOSOPHY

━━

CICERO
On Moral Ends

CAMBRIDGE TEXTS IN THE HISTORY OF PHILOSOPHY

Series editors
KARL AMERIKS
Professor of Philosophy at the University of Notre Dame
DESMOND M. CLARKE
Professor of Philosophy at University College Cork

The main objective of Cambridge Texts in the History of Philosophy is to expand the range, variety and quality of texts in the history of philosophy which are available in English. The series includes texts by familiar names (such as Descartes and Kant) and also by less well-known authors. Wherever possible, texts are published in complete and unabridged form, and translations are specially commissioned for the series. Each volume contains a critical introduction together with a guide to further reading and any necessary glossaries and textual apparatus. The volumes are designed for student use at undergraduate and postgraduate level and will be of interest not only to students of philosophy, but also to a wider audience of readers in the history of science, the history of theology and the history of ideas.

For a list of titles published in the series, please see end of book.

CICERO

On Moral Ends

EDITED BY
JULIA ANNAS
University of Arizona

TRANSLATED BY
RAPHAEL WOOLF
Harvard University

CAMBRIDGE
UNIVERSITY PRESS

CAMBRIDGE
UNIVERSITY PRESS

University Printing House, Cambridge CB2 8BS, United Kingdom

One Liberty Plaza, 20th Floor, New York, NY 10006, USA

477 Williamstown Road, Port Melbourne, VIC 3207, Australia

314-321, 3rd Floor, Plot 3, Splendor Forum, Jasola District Centre, New Delhi-110025, India

79 Anson Road, #06-04/06, Singapore 079906

Cambridge University Press is part of the University of Cambridge.

It furthers the University's mission by disseminating knowledge in the pursuit of education, learning and research at the highest international levels of excellence.

www.cambridge.org
Information on this title: www.cambridge.org/9780521669016

© Cambridge University Press 2001

First published 2001
7th printing 2011

A catalogue record for this publication is available from the British Library

ISBN 978-0-521-66061-7 Hardback
ISBN 978-0-521-66901-6 Paperback

Cambridge University Press has no responsibility for the persistence or accuracy of URLs for external or third-party internet websites referred to in this publication, and does not guarantee that any content on such websites is, or will remain, accurate or appropriate. Information regarding prices, travel timetables, and other factual information given in this work is correct at the time of first printing but Cambridge University Press does not guarantee the accuracy of such information thereafter.

Contents

Preface

For helpful comments on the Introduction and notes I am very grateful to Desmond Clarke, Hilary Gaskin, Raphael Woolf, Daniel Russell and Alison Futrell. I am especially grateful to Alison Futrell, my colleague in Roman History, for help with a number of Roman issues, from the Voconian law to the excess, in this work, of members of the Licinius Crassus family called Marcus. I also owe thanks to all the students, graduate and undergraduate, to whom I have taught this work in my courses on ancient ethics, and who have helped me come to see the difficulties it presents for a modern reader. I am grateful for the work of scholars who have, in the last decades, produced new translations of important texts from the Hellenistic or post-Aristotelian period of ancient philosophy, and have helped in the process of making the theories of the Stoics, Epicureans and even eclectics like Antiochus part of the normal syllabus in ancient philosophy. I hope that this new translation and edition will make Cicero's text more accessible to a wide audience interested in ancient ethics.

It has been a pleasure to work with Raphael Woolf, who has produced a translation which is not only philosophically accurate but also stylish in Cicero's manner without expanding the English to twice the length of the Latin. In writing the Introduction and notes I have also been helped by older editions and translations, particularly the older edition of Madvig, and the translations and comments in the Budé and Loeb editions. I have aimed to introduce the work to readers who need some help with the Greco-Roman cultural background that Cicero takes for granted, and who also need, fully to appreciate the arguments, some orientation as to the philosophical background to the debates which Cicero develops. Since the audience for this book will be diverse – people interested in some or all of philosophy, ethics, history, the classical world and the history of ideas – the help I have provided will inevitably be too much for some and too little for others. I hope, however, that it will at least help many people to begin their own engagement with Cicero's debates. Cicero thinks through the arguments that he sets out in order to help the reader, and himself, find the right answer to the major issue in ethics: how we should live. It is an issue that still deserves our attention today.

JULIA ANNAS

vii

Introduction

In June 45[1] Marcus Tullius Cicero composed *On Moral Ends*, a treatment in three dialogues, over five books, of fundamental issues of moral philosophy. The sixty-one year old Cicero, a Roman statesman with an eventful and distinguished career, had gone into political retirement during the ascendancy to supreme power of Julius Caesar after a turbulent period of civil war, in which Cicero had ended up on the losing side. His personal life had also fallen apart. In 46 he divorced Terentia, his wife of thirty years, and married his young ward Publilia. The marriage broke up less than a year later, partly because of Cicero's extreme sorrow at the death in childbirth of his much-loved daughter Tullia, together with her baby, in February 45. A productive writer, he decided to use his enforced and grief-stricken leisure to introduce educated Romans to major parts of the subject of philosophy in their own language, rather than leaving them to read the originals in Greek.[2] *On Moral Ends* is the most theoretical of the works on moral philosophy, accompanied by more specialized discussions in *On Duties* and *Tusculan Disputations* and the more 'applied' *Friendship, Old Age* and *Reputation*.

On Moral Ends is a substantial work of moral philosophy. There have been periods when it has been an influential part of the discourse of moral theory, and it has always been a valuable source for the three moral theories it discusses, those of Epicurus, the Stoics and Antiochus (the last a hybrid influenced by Aristotle). The modern reader, however, will probably find some aspects of the work puzzling, and an introduction to it is usefully framed round answering three questions which are likely to occur to us.

(1) Why is a work on moral theory in dialogue form, specifically in three dialogues, in each of which a theory is first put forward and then attacked?

(2) Why does a work on moral theory focus on our ends or goals (the title *De Finibus* is often translated 'final ends') rather than, say, right action or duty?

---

[1] All dates are BC unless otherwise noted.

[2] In the introduction to the second book of *On Divination*, one of these works of philosophy, he discusses the carrying-out of this plan.

(3) Why these theories? And, given that Cicero aims to cover the most important theories, where are Plato and Aristotle?

The sceptical method of ethics

Modern books do not typically introduce you to ethics by arguing for and then against theories. Cicero, however, aims to introduce his readers not just to the content of three ethical theories but to thinking about them philosophically, and for him this involves arguing for *and against* them. This is because he writes as an Academic Sceptic – a sceptic, that is, from Plato's Academy.

Plato pointedly refrains from presenting philosophical ideas in the form of treatises which give doctrines to be absorbed by the reader; he writes dialogues, in which ideas are discussed rather than presented on authority. The major figure in his dialogues, Socrates, sometimes puts forward positive claims of his own, and sometimes argues against the positions of others; when he does the latter, the arguments are always *ad hominem* – not in the modern sense of attacking the person rather than the position, but in the sense of using only premises accepted by the interlocutor, and showing him that his position has problems which are internal to it, and do not depend on accepting any of Socrates' own claims. Socrates' arguments against the positions of others reveal how far they are from having adequate rational support for their claims, and how ill-advised they are to hold them confidently. The positive ideas that Plato gives to Socrates and others[3] are put forward as ideas which should themselves be subject to the same kind of probing; in the *Parmenides* this happens in the dialogue, while elsewhere this task is left to the reader to take up.

Plato's legacy has been a divided one, with some thinkers focussing on the positive ideas and systematizing them, taking the resulting doctrines to be 'Plato's philosophy', while others have taken up the project, identified with Socrates, of philosophy as the activity of searching for truth by questioning the positions of people who claim to have found it.

Plato's immediate successors, later grouped together as the 'Old Academy', were apparently as interested in developing their own ideas as in studying Plato's. His nephew Speusippus and his successor Xenocrates developed mathematized metaphysical systems; the figure of most importance for later moral philosophy was Polemon, about whose ideas we know little directly, but who was influential in holding that nature was in some way a basis for ethics – and meaning by that, *human* nature.

In 265 there was a radical change, mentioned by Cicero in book II, 2 (cf. book V, 10). The Academy was taken over by a new head, Arcesilaus, who brought in the idea that philosophizing in the spirit of Plato was doing what

---

[3] In many dialogues Socrates becomes a recessive figure, and it is left to figures like the Visitor from Elea or an anonymous Athenian to lay out positive claims.

Socrates is represented as doing, namely questioning others on their own grounds rather than putting forward positive ideas of your own. In his teaching methods Arcesilaus went back to Socrates, refusing to hold forth himself and always questioning others. The Sceptical[4] (or 'New') Academy flourished; its targets were contemporary ones just as those of Socrates had been, and its best-known debates were with the Stoics, the most sophisticated philosophical school holding positive and systematic doctrines. Arcesilaus' most distinguished successor was Carneades (214–129/8), a powerful arguer who classified and systematized arguments and positions (*On Moral Ends* is indebted to his classification of moral theories and to many of his arguments). Like Socrates, the Sceptical Academics wrote nothing; one of Carneades' pupils, Cleitomachus, recorded 200 books of his arguments, but claimed to know nothing of the positions, if any, that Carneades committed himself to.

The last head of the Sceptical Academy, Philo of Larisa, moved from Athens to Rome about 88. Athens was undergoing violent political upheavals, and changed sides, committing itself to the anti-Roman side in the war involving King Mithridates of Pontus. In 86 the ruthless Roman general Lucius Cornelius Sulla punished this betrayal by sacking and plundering Athens, carrying off huge amounts of booty. Scholars generally agree that in this general state of ruin the philosophical schools, including those of Plato and Aristotle, came to an end as institutions. Their philosophy continued to be taught, but the successions of heads going back to the founders were broken.[5] Cicero thinks of the Sceptical Academy as a philosophy one can learn and teach anywhere, not as an institution specific to Athens.

From an early age Cicero was interested in philosophy as well as the rhetorical skills necessary for success in Roman politics. Around 88 he went to lectures in Rome by the Epicurean Phaedrus as well as the Academic Sceptic Philo of Larisa. In 79 he spent time in Athens (depicted at the start of book v) attending lectures by Antiochus of Ascalon (to whom we shall return). He was taught by a Stoic, Diodotus, who lived in his household until he died in 60. Cicero's knowledge of philosophy is thorough, and based on having worked through the arguments, not on superficial acquaintance with the ideas.

From his encounter with Philo of Larisa onwards Cicero identified himself as an Academic Sceptic; that is, to him philosophy consists essentially in the activity of seeking truth by discussing and arguing against the positions of others, rather than by thinking up your own position to hold or adopting someone else's. In ethics, this involves familiarizing yourself with

---

[4] 'Sceptical' here retains the idea of philosophy as investigating or inquiring (the meaning of the Greek verb *skeptesthai*) rather than a dogmatically negative denial of various positive claims, as the modern notion of scepticism implies.

[5] J. Glucker, *Antiochus and the Late Academy* (*Hypomnemata* 56), Göttingen 1978; J. Lynch, *Aristotle's School*, Berkeley/Los Angeles/London 1972. In book v, where Romans are living in Athens and going to philosophy lectures, the Academy is deserted and Antiochus is teaching his new philosophy in a more recent building.

the theories which are current, working through the arguments for them and testing them by seeing how well they stand up to critical examination. The result, according to the Sceptical Academics, is that it turns out that none of the theories available warrants commitment to it. All have rational advantages – good arguments for them and against opponents – but they also all have rational flaws – arguments against them and internal weaknesses. A person interested in really searching inquiry thus has to withhold assent to any of them. This does not leave her with nothing; continued examination of the arguments for and against the theories produces in a fair-minded person the unavoidable impression that some of the theories are preferable to others, even though none of the preferable theories warrants whole-hearted assent. Thus Cicero clearly thinks that Epicureanism is a far weaker ethical theory than either Stoic ethics or a more Aristotelian theory; but the fact that he does not take Epicurus seriously as an option does not make it possible for him to decide firmly for or against Stoic ethics, and indeed Cicero appears to have gone back and forth on the arguments for and against the Stoic view all his life.

We can now see why *On Moral Ends* has the form it does; serious engagement with ethical theories involves learning not just what the positions are, but the arguments for and against adopting them. Only when the reader gets involved in thinking through the pros and cons of a position is she thinking for herself about it, and this is the crucial aspect of Plato's tradition of doing philosophy, according to the Academic Sceptics. It is not surprising that this mode of approaching philosophical issues should appeal to Cicero, who was famous for his argumentative talents in the law-courts. Someone notable for his success in both prosecuting and defending will naturally be aware of the distance between arguing for a case (and thus summoning up all the reasons for it and against the opponent) and being personally committed to it. They will also be open to the idea that the adversarial method of arguing for and against a claim, while open to rhetorical abuse, is a good method for finding the truth.

There is a complication, or rather there are two. As Plato's Academy came to its end, there were two developments, of which the second was important to Cicero, while he seems unaware of the first.

After many years of arguing against the Stoics in their own terms, the Sceptical Academy seems to have settled into a position of taking a Stoic framework for granted as the location of most of their arguments. One dissident member, Aenesidemus, grew to resent this narrowing of their argumentative horizons, and broke away to refound a more radically sceptical school, which he named after Pyrrho, a philosopher who had earlier argued for a sceptical way of living, but who wrote nothing and left no philosophical school. We know a lot about this new Pyrrhonian version of scepticism, because we possess extensive writings by a later Pyrrhonian sceptic, Sextus Empiricus. It is puzzling, though, that Cicero shows no awareness of this breakaway from the Academy.[6] When he refers to Pyrrho, it is only to the idea that he gives us no rational way of deciding everyday matters; Cicero regards this as an unserious position, and also as a basically ethical, rather than sceptical one. As a result, he does not associate philosophical scepticism with ideas which are familiar to us from later Pyrrhonism, such as that scepticism leads to tranquillity and is a way to happiness. For Cicero scepticism is simply the position of those who rigorously search for the truth.

Another dissident in the last days of the Academy was Antiochus of Ascalon, who made an equally radical move in the other direction, away from detached refusal to make a commitment. Antiochus reacted against a centuries-old tradition of adversarial argument and emphasis on differences between philosophical positions by looking instead for common ground and areas of agreement. Still seeing himself as being in the Platonic tradition, he claimed that Plato's true legacy was not endless inconclusive argument but rather certain prominent themes and ideas. Moreover, Antiochus claimed, these ideas were to be found not only in Plato's own work but in that of his immediate successors in the Academy, including Aristotle, and even, as we shall see, in that of the Stoics. Antiochus claimed to go back to what he called the 'Old Academy', rejecting the Sceptical, 'New' Academy as a development untrue to what is central to Plato, and thus as a false Platonic tradition. (This was a momentous move; from now on, anyone seeing himself or herself as being in Plato's tradition had to face the issue of whether the Academy had two traditions (sceptical and doctrinal) or only one, and, if one, which it was.)

In Antiochus' view, there was a single 'Old Academy' tradition, which we find explicated by Cicero in books IV (3–15) and V (9–14). Platonists and Aristotelians, he claims, agree on fundamentals and can be regarded as a single tradition. Moreover, this tradition includes one of the new schools of the Hellenistic period, the Stoics. Zeno of Citium had set up a new philosophical school around 300 in the Stoa Poikile or Painted Porch in Athens, a school which after some dispersal under Zeno's pupils had been reestablished by the powerful and productive Chrysippus. In many ways the Stoics introduce radically new ideas, and initially their position was strongly marked off from those of Plato and Aristotle. They are physicalists with no use for the Platonic or Aristotelian notions of form; they have a strikingly new system of logic; and in ethics they maintain a number of uncompromising theses: nothing is good except virtue, virtue is sufficient for happiness, emotions are always faulty, there are no gradations between virtue and vice.

---

[6] It is particularly puzzling because one of Aenesidemus' works was dedicated to Lucius Aelius Tubero 'from the Academy', an intimate friend of Cicero's. It has been denied that Aenesidemus was an Academic (which would solve this problem); see Fernanda Decleva Caizzi, 'Aenesidemus and the Academy', *Classical Quarterly* 42 (1992), 176–89; but this claim is effectively attacked by Jaap Mansfeld, 'Aenesidemus and the Academics', in L. Ayres (ed.), *The Passionate Intellect*, New Brunswick and London, 1995, Rutgers Studies in Classical Humanities VII, 235–48.

Antiochus, however, downplays the differences between his single Academy tradition and the upstart Stoics. All they are really doing, he claims, is to introduce new technical terms; the basic underlying ideas are the same. (This is an argument which is prominent in *On Moral Ends*.) On all important matters, Antiochus claims, the Platonists, Aristotelians and Stoics stand together. They stand united against the Epicureans, who disagree with all of them on most major points.

Antiochus' claim seems to modern eyes hopelessly unhistorical. It seems obvious to us, for example, that Aristotle diverges from Plato quite strongly at some points, and that the Stoics, who are physicalists, have metaphysical and epistemological positions which cannot be reconciled with anything in Plato. Awkward questions can easily be raised, such as, 'Where in this combined tradition are Plato's forms?' We should remember, however, that Antiochus was not a historian; he was a philosopher trying to find high-level similarities and to downplay the differences on which so much inconclusive argument had been lavished.[7] His emphases also reflect the interests of his day; the issue of Plato's forms, central to us, was uninteresting to contemporary debates. Further, for Antiochus, establishing the tradition of the 'Old Academy' was a matter of self-definition, not description of someone else's ideas, and so we should not judge him by historical standards. The result he aimed at is not an academic synthesis but a philosophy to live by.

From the passages in books IV and V we get some idea of Antiochus' hybrid theory as a whole; what matters for *On Moral Ends* was his attempt to put together a theory combining the advantages of Stoic and Aristotelian moral theory, while discarding their disadvantages. Modern histories of ethics have not been kind to Antiochus, either ignoring his theory or dismissing it, but the reader who persists with the arguments of books IV and V will get a better sense of what is at stake, in terms of both arguments and of motivation, in the ethical debate between Stoics and Aristotelians.

Cicero had studied with Antiochus at Athens in 79 (as is depicted in book V) and, although he casts himself as the theory's opponent in that book, was sympathetic to Antiochus' project, knew it thoroughly and was influenced by it. Some interpreters have seen in Antiochus a straightforward opponent to the influence of Philo and thus to Cicero's stance; after all, Antiochus and Philo represented conflicting views of Plato's philosophical tradition: Antiochus seeing it as doctrinal, Philo as sceptical. An Academic Sceptic, however, is committed to searching for the truth through inquiry and argument; nothing prevents him from seriously considering positive views, and we would expect him to be interested in promising new developments in philosophy. As long as he remains open-minded and detached from wholehearted commitment, there is no reason why he should not take on Antiochus' position, or any other, for

---

[7] Cf. Jonathan Barnes, 'Antiochus of Ascalon', in J. Barnes and M. Griffin (eds.), *Philosophia Togata I*, Oxford 1989, 51–96.

purposes of argument or developing that position.[8] Indeed, it is perfectly consistent for him to claim that this is the most convincing position to hold, as long as he continues to be open-minded about alternatives.

There is no need, therefore, to conclude that Cicero's philosophical perspective underwent radical changes on the ground that the philosophical works composed at the end of his life are written from an overtly Academic point of view, whereas works he wrote earlier (54–51) are not. These early works, which unfortunately we possess only in part, are his *On the State* (*De Re Publica*) and *On Laws* (*De Legibus*). As we can tell from the titles, they have Plato's *Republic* and *Laws* as literary models, and if read in isolation would not indicate that the author was an Academic. This is not a problem, however, if we take it that Cicero found these positions to be the most convincing on the subject; an Academic goes with the most convincing option available so far.[9] In these works he puts forward views about the state which he finds the most convincing. In the works written at the end of his life he has a different aim; he is introducing the reader to philosophical engagement with the major positions that philosophers debate. To do this he has to give a sense of the difficulties involved, and hence all three theories are presented as matters of debate, on which she has to make up her own mind, something which requires understanding and engaging with the arguments. Cicero does not pretend to be neutral himself, and he uses his rhetorical expertise to present the positions in appropriate ways. We see the same skills he deploys in his courtroom speeches, only put to a more worthwhile and intellectually serious end – for what could be more important to the reader than working out for herself which is the right way to live?

The most important function of the dialogue form is thus its epistemological one, the way it forces readers to think for themselves about the ideas being presented. There are other, more literary advantages. One is that the major speakers are characterized in ways that illuminate for the reader the ideas they present. Minor roles apart, there are four important characters in the work.

The spokesperson for Epicureanism is Lucius Manlius Torquatus, descendant of a famous and ancient noble family which, after a period of relative mediocrity, has become politically prominent again; Torquatus' father had been consul, the highest Roman elected office, in 65, and in 50, the dramatic

---

[8] This open-mindedness cannot extend to Antiochus' theory of knowledge, however, which adopts the Stoic view that we can have at least some 'apprehensions' or instances where we can not be wrong; despite the fragmentary nature of Cicero's works on epistemology (the *Academica*) it is clear that he is opposed to Antiochus on this front.

[9] John Glucker has argued that Cicero's attitude changes twice; see 'Cicero's Philosophical Affiliations', in J. M. Dillon and A. A. Long (eds.), *The Question of 'Eclecticism': Studies in Later Greek Philosophy*, Berkeley 1988, 34–69. This is countered by Woldemar Görler in 'Silencing the Troublemaker: *De Legibus* I.39 and the Continuity of Cicero's Scepticism', in J. G. F. Powell (ed.), *Cicero the Philosopher*, Oxford 1995, 85–113; see also the Introduction by J. G. F. Powell in the same volume, 1–35. It is not a problem, then, that Cicero can, when putting forward a position or set of arguments, criticize the Sceptical Academy itself (as *De Legibus* I 39 and *On Moral Ends* II (43).

date of the dialogue, Torquatus has been elected to the next-highest office of praetor and is looking forward to becoming consul himself. Cicero's readers know that this never happened; on the losing Pompeian side in the civil war, Torquatus was killed in 48 after military defeat.[10] As Cicero presents it, Epicureanism is an inappropriate and ridiculous philosophy for a successful politician to hold. Torquatus is depicted as having got hold of a few simple ideas, presenting them in a crude, bludgeoning way and unable to argue for them or meet criticisms; he is constantly deferential to Epicurus, reverently quoting or paraphrasing the Master's words. Cicero intends these touches to be not only critical of Epicureanism but an indication that it does not fit a Roman political and military life.

Marcus Porcius Cato ('Cato the Younger'), on the other hand, is an appropriate figure to present Stoic ethics. Cato's great-grandfather, 'Cato the Censor', was a figure of legendary severity, and Cato himself famous for being stubborn and unyielding on principle, a trait frequently frustrating to Cicero in his public career. Cato was attracted to Stoicism, and his death transformed him into a Stoic martyr; after defeat at the battle of Thapsus in 46, Cato refused Caesar's pardon and committed suicide rather than compromise with the destruction of the old Roman constitutional order. Writing soon after Cato's death, Cicero portrays him respectfully, as someone who thoroughly understands Stoic theory; the reader is expected to know that he died in accordance with its principles. His precision and pedantry in constantly referring to original Greek terms, together with his lack of tact at the beginning and his point-by-point rather than flowing presentation, similarly reflect an unwillingness to compromise or popularize his presentation.

Marcus Pupius Piso Frugi Calpurnianus defends Antiochus' theory in book v. Consul in 61, he had been born into the powerful Calpurnius Piso family, then adopted by Marcus Pupius. In his youth he was a promising orator, and also a friend of Cicero's. Later in life he gave up oratory (*Brutus* 236) and adopted political courses which brought him into conflict with Cicero. The positive portrayal of Piso, and his ample oratorical exposition of Antiochus' theory, hark back to happier and more co-operative days when he and Cicero studied together, and is also suited to Cicero's assessment of that theory as stronger on rhetorical appeal than on philosophical substance.

What of the fourth major figure? Although he is called Cicero, he is not to be straightforwardly identified with the author Marcus Tullius Cicero. 'Cicero' is the figure who shows us that the searcher for truth will take positions seriously, but always be open to the force of arguments against them. Here 'Cicero' serves the author's purpose in arguing against all the positive theories. In other works he can be found defending some of them. In his own

---

[10] See J. F. Mitchell, 'The Torquati', *Historia* 15 (1966), 23–31. In 62 Torquatus was the prosecutor when Cicero successfully defended Publius Cornelius Sulla on a charge of public violence. At *Brutus* 265–6 Torquatus is respectfully remembered, along with Triarius, as a good friend of both Cicero and Brutus.

dialogues Plato presents his teacher Socrates as doing both of these tasks. When Cicero, less modest than Plato, needs a Socrates figure he does not hesitate to cast himself in the role.

One final advantage of the dialogue form is that it allows Cicero, the author, to portray appealing settings which give the conversations contexts that would have significance for his readers. Here the settings of the first two dialogues, Roman country houses, are sketched only barely. The book v setting is more substantial; we are in Athens in 79, where Cicero and other Roman friends are going to philosophy lectures and, like modern tourists, visiting famous historical sites. Among these sites is the now-deserted Academy, where the philosophically inclined wax nostalgic. There is an obvious irony here; the Academy is evocatively empty because only a few years previously a Roman army had sacked Athens so thoroughly that all the philosophical schools had come to an end. Cicero probably means us to notice that Plato's Academy is now dead as a Greek institution, but lives on in the intellectual activity of Cicero and others like him, in the debates in this book and more generally in Cicero's attempt to get Romans to think philosophically in their own language.

Ethics and your final end

Why should moral theory be about our final or ultimate end, and what is this anyway?

Cicero writes in the mainstream of ancient ethical theory, which begins with Plato and Democritus, is formulated by Aristotle and provides the framework for ancient ethical theory thereafter. The assumption is that each of us has, implicitly, an ultimate or overarching end in terms of which we make sense of our everyday actions and our longer-term priorities. When I think of the actions I perform and the way my life is going, I can (and often do) think of this in a linear way – one thing after another. However, I can also think of the way that particular actions contribute to more general ends. I study, for example, in order to get a good job, practise in order to play tennis well, and so on. These more general ends, in turn, contribute to other ends specified at an increasingly general level. I play tennis, for example, in order to be healthy, get a good job in order to be self-supporting, and so on. Thinking about the way my actions contribute to my ends thus reveals what my most general goals and priorities are. It is an assumption of ancient ethical theory, first made explicit by Aristotle, that these more general ends – being healthy, having a career and so on – will also emerge in my thinking as contributing to my overall goal in life. Why should this be? I have, obviously, only one life, and thus the goals I have are bound to be ordered, whether explicitly or implicitly, towards the living of a single life to which they all contribute.

Thus my everyday actions and attitudes are, even before I reflect philosophically, implicitly oriented to my life as a whole, conceived as a unity. At some point most people make this thought explicit, and this serves as what I have called 'the entry-point for ethical reflection',[11] the start of reflections which get me to look at my life critically, ask whether my life currently embodies the right goals and priorities, and work out better ways of living. Ethical theory analyses, clarifies and refines my thoughts about my life as a whole and overall aims. Thus the person who embarks on ethical reflection will, in the ancient world, soon find himself confronted by a variety of theories offering different answers to the questions of how best to live and how properly to conceive of the overall, ultimate goal in living. By the time Cicero writes, there has been a long and sophisticated tradition of doing this.

Of course, then as now, there were irresponsible people who lived without ever reflecting on the overall shape of their lives; but in general the importance of doing this, and of exploring ethical theories as a result, was widely recognized. There was also one ethical school, that of the Cyrenaics, who rejected the idea that ethical thought should direct us to living a better life as a whole; they thought that we should aim at getting the most and most intense pleasure, meaning by that an experienced feeling. Thinking about your life as a whole will obviously dampen the pursuit of intense pleasant feelings. But the Cyrenaics were always seen as marginal, and the school was not influential, surviving in philosophical discussions as an example of an ethical theory that was obviously inadequate.[12]

In Plato (and possibly Democritus) we find the basic structure of ancient ethical thinking taken for granted, but not treated systematically. In some passages[13] we find it taken as an assumption of everyone's thought that we all seek a single final end in everything we do, that this must be 'complete' in including everything we need for the good life, and that this is what we all mean by seeking happiness, although people have radically different ideas as to what it takes to achieve happiness. Aristotle is the first to systematize and lay out these ideas: our final good, he says in the famous opening chapters of the *Nicomachean Ethics*, is 'complete' and 'self-sufficient' in including everything and omitting nothing that we need for living well. Moreover, everyone agrees on the common-sense level that in trying to achieve our overall good we are seeking happiness, though this settles nothing, since people disagree as to what happiness consists of.

Happiness in ancient Greek is *eudaimonia*, and because it is the central concept in Greek ethical thought the latter is often called eudaimonist. From the way it is introduced it is clear that it is defined formally, by the overarching role it plays in ethical thinking, and should not be identified with narrower modern concepts of having a good time, or pleasure. Indeed, ethical theory

---

[11] In *The Morality of Happiness*, Oxford 1993.
[12] The Cyrenaic school was founded by Aristippus of Cyrene (in North Africa), an associate of Socrates. It is uncertain whether he or his grandson, Aristippus the Younger, was the one to formulate the school's ideas. Some later Cyrenaics allowed that happiness, our final end, could play a role in our pursuit of pleasure, but clearly it is only an instrumental one: overall considerations may inhibit pursuit of pleasure, but only if greater pleasure will ensue eventually.
[13] *Euthydēmus* 278e–282a, *Symposium* 204c–205a, *Philebus* 20b–23a, 60a–61a.

develops as a series of attempts to specify what happiness is. Plato, the first to think systematically in these terms, holds very radically that living virtuously is sufficient for a happy life, recognizing that this overturns the views of most people, who identify happiness with a life in which you have things that are conventionally considered goods – money, good looks, success. Immediately, therefore, we find a focus on the other central concept in ancient ethics, virtue.

Like ancient happiness, ancient virtue is somewhat different from the modern notion.[14] Virtue is just the virtues, admirable traits of character like bravery and justice, united by the fact that they share good practical reasoning about what should be done. A virtue is a disposition, that is, a habit of acting which has been built up through practice, though it is never thought of as a mindless habit, since it is a disposition to deliberate and to make decisions. Virtue is built up by following role models (as Aristotle stresses) or rules and principles (as the Stoics stress) but the point of virtue is that the virtuous person learns to think for herself about ethical matters, so that all ancient theories depart radically from everyday thinking and are quite critical of it. (Aristotle is the least critical here.)

Virtue has two aspects, being both cognitive, a matter of deliberation and discernment, and also attitudinal, a matter of how you react to people and situations. The virtuous person will reason morally and discern what is the right thing to do (different schools laying weight on deliberation or insight). Modern theories of virtue tend to stay at this point, and discuss the different virtues, such as courage or wisdom, separately. Ancient theories, however, regard this as an unsatisfactory place to stop, since the virtues are then defined by the areas in which moral reasoning is applied, in a way which may depend upon social convention. Moreover, it is implausible that you could make correct judgements in only one area of your life, isolating considerations of bravery, say, from those of justice and issues of what is worth standing up for. Hence there is a tendency in all ancient schools to see the virtues as mutually dependent. Some emphasize this point to the extent of thinking of virtue just as being the achievement of excellent practical reasoning in all spheres. This implies that to the extent that we define virtues as different because of having different areas of application, we are merely tracing social convention, not marking off real distinctions in virtuous reasoning itself. The Stoics (following up indications in Plato) call virtue the skill or expertise of living; it is the disposition to make the right practical decisions, so that the virtuous person acts well in the way that the expert produces good results.

However, even schools which think of virtue as a skill also think of it as motivating; it is not like an expertise which you might choose to exercise or not, in a detached way. All the schools accept, in some version, Aristotle's

---

[14] If there is such a thing as a unified modern conception of virtue; the late twentieth century has seen a resurgence of virtue both in everyday discourse and in ethical theory, but it is not generally accepted that virtue is internally structured, and cognitively articulated, in the way that ancient virtue is uniformly supposed to be.

claim that there is a difference between the person he calls merely self-controlled, who reasons morally and does the right thing, but has to combat their inclinations to do so, and the virtuous person, who actually takes pleasure in being virtuous. Virtue is not merely a matter of having your practical reasoning in an excellent state; it is also a matter of having your emotional reactions and attitudes in conformity with your practical reasoning.

The comparison of virtue to a skill brings out the important point that it is never taken to be an inert disposition, but is rather to be thought of as a way of living. Similarly, happiness, our final goal, is not a state of the person that actions are to bring about; it is the happy *life*, a way of living. Ancient ethics is basically concerned with being a good person, but this is not cut off from concern with right action, since the virtuous person will be, precisely, the person who acts rightly. (A number of the arguments in book IV centre on this point.) Ancient ethical theories, however, do not aim to produce all-purpose answers to practical questions, answers available to anyone who reads the book. Rather, the point is to get the learner to understand the theory in such a way that they internalize it and are thus able to reason in accordance with it. What answers this will produce will, of course, depend on particular lives and their circumstances, something about which not much that is useful can be said on a general level. The theories Cicero presents take it that the most important thing in your life is to become a virtuous person and so to live and act in a morally worthy way; but you can only achieve this for yourself, by understanding the theory and using it to transform your life. No book can give you the answers in advance.

Aristotle denies Plato's claim that living virtuously is sufficient for happiness – that is, that the virtuous person has what matters for living the best life, even given the worst that life can throw at you. For Aristotle, common sense is correct in holding that to be happy you need some conventional goods; he regards it as ludicrous to hold that the virtuous person could be happy 'on the rack', in the depths of undeserved misfortune. This is the single most famous claim in Aristotle's ethical works, and the major debate in ancient ethics turned on the issue of whether he was right, as against Plato and the Stoics, who claimed that virtue, the way you live and deal with your circumstances, matters in a different way from those circumstances themselves, and has a radically different kind of value. In book III the Stoic arguments are put forward for thinking of virtue as valuable in a different kind of way from the material it is applied to, and for thinking that nothing but virtue can constitute the happy life. While it seems paradoxical at first, the idea is supported by surprisingly powerful arguments and worked out in a rigorous way.

Antiochus produced an ethical theory which restated Aristotle's ethics in the terms of contemporary debate, and so produced an updated version, recast in the form of a 'developmental' story made current by the Stoics.[15] The argu-

---

[15] See J. Annas, *The Morality of Happiness*, Oxford 1993, chs. 6, 12 and 20 for exposition and discussion of Antiochus' theory and another hybrid theory aiming to combine Stoic and Aristotelian positions, set out in Arius Didymus.

ments in book IV attack Stoic ethical theory from Antiochus' renewed Aristotelian point of view, one that now needs arguments against the Stoic position. Aristotle claimed on the basis of common sense that virtue could not be sufficient for happiness. However, once the Stoics have established a powerful theory claiming that virtue is sufficient for happiness, an opponent can no longer fall back on common sense, but must attack the Stoics. Whatever the force of Antiochus' own anti-Stoic arguments, however, his own position is somewhat exposed. He wants to recognize the force both of Aristotle's position and that of the Stoics. But virtue can hardly be sufficient *and* not sufficient for happiness. Antiochus solves the problem by distinguishing the happy life, for which virtue is sufficient, from the 'happiest' or 'truly happy' life, a life where the virtuous person enjoys conventional goods. This is a position which can be developed attractively, as it is in book V, with all the resources of Cicero's oratory. But it falls, he thinks, to a simple but powerful argument, delivered by Cicero himself: on this view it is the happiest life, not the happy life, which is complete, and so the spirit of the Stoic theory has not been retained at all. The contrast here between expansive, enjoyable oratory and short but deadly argument is meant to resonate with the reader, since understanding ethics philosophically requires having satisfactory arguments. The issue of whether happiness requires conventional goods, or merely a virtuous way of dealing with whatever your situation is, is one where it is easier to criticize the opposition than to find decisive arguments on your own side.

Cicero begins, not with disputes over the importance of virtue in happiness, but with a theory which identifies happiness with pleasure. (The next section suggests why he does this.) Epicurus claims that the happy life is simply the life of greatest pleasure; the most modern-sounding of the theories, it is in ancient terms problematic in its conception of both happiness and virtue. How can happiness, the happy life which is our complete end, amount to no more than pleasure? Epicurus tries to explicate pleasure in ways that meet eudaimonist criteria, but the arguments of book II show that this is an uphill task. Further, would we be interested in virtue if what we are aiming for is pleasure? Epicurus tries to show us that we would. In both cases, however, Epicurus runs into problems; eudaimonism, unlike some modern forms of ethical theory, is not hospitable to the idea that our final end is pleasure, even a form of pleasure of which Epicurus tries to show that it can meet eudaimonist demands on happiness and virtue.

Why these theories?

What the modern reader is initially likely to find most puzzling is the absence from this philosophical scene of the two philosophers most prominent in modern discussions of ancient ethics, Plato and Aristotle. Antiochus claimed that the schools of Plato and Aristotle together formed a single tradition, and it is the ethical part of this position which provides arguments against the

Stoics in book IV and is laid out in book V. But why prefer this later composite to the originals?

Cicero was well-read in both Plato and Aristotle, and greatly admired them.[16] He quotes from and refers to Plato frequently, often for ideas which are not to be found in Antiochus' amalgam of Platonic and other positions, and he clearly read Plato's dialogues closely for himself. He translated the *Timaeus* and *Protagoras* into Latin, as well as using the *Republic* and *Laws* as literary (though not philosophical) models. He admires Plato's literary brilliance and regrets the sharp divide Plato makes between philosophy and rhetoric, pursuits which he himself does not find incompatible.[17]

However, Cicero does not read Plato as a systematic thinker like the Stoics, for example, and does not try to fit him into the ethical debates of his own time; he sees him as a great philosopher of the past whose view does not correspond to any modern position in ethical debate.[18] The ethical discussions of Cicero's time assume that our ethical aims are limited to the fulfilment of our human nature; they are all naturalistic, in a common understanding of that term. Plato does not appear as a participant in these debates because his most striking claim is that the virtuous person should 'become like God', transcending human nature as much as he can.[19] This idea does not fit into Hellenistic ethical debate at all, though it was to have a great future in later antiquity.

Cicero also admires Aristotle, but likewise does not see him as a figure of contemporary relevance in ethical debate. He is familiar with the work we call the *Nicomachean Ethics* (book V, 12) – though he thinks of it as written by, rather than dedicated to, Aristotle's son Nicomachus – but grants it no special authority by comparison with the work of Aristotle's pupil Theophrastus. For him the main point of Aristotle's ethical theory is that it denies the sufficiency of virtue for happiness, maintaining that conventional goods are a part of happiness. This point is most familiar to him from Antiochus' version of it, and Antiochus' position, moreover, has the advantage of coming equipped with arguments against the Stoics. It is understandable that Cicero would think that Antiochus' hybrid theory contained the strongest and most up-to-date

---

[16] For instance, he called the two gymnasia at his favourite country house at Tusculum 'Academy' and 'Lyceum' after the gymnasia where Plato's and Aristotle's schools had started.

[17] For the material see T. B. DeGraff, 'Plato in Cicero', *Classical Philology* 35 (1940), 143–53. See A. A. Long, 'Cicero's Plato and Aristotle', in J. G. F. Powell (ed.), *Cicero the Philosopher*, Oxford 1995, 37–61, for a discussion of Cicero's attitude to Plato's contrast between philosophy and rhetoric.

[18] At *Tusculan Disputations* book 5, 34–6, he notes that Plato, as well as the Stoics, holds that virtue is sufficient for happiness, backing this up from two dialogues, the *Gorgias* 470e and the *Menexenus* 246d–248a (over-translating the latter passage to make a stronger claim than can strictly be found there). But he never sees Plato as having a systematic position in the debate on this topic which absorbs his interest in books III–V.

[19] This is most memorably put in the 'digression' at *Theaetetus* 171d – 177c. See J. Annas, *Platonic Ethics Old and New*, Ithaca, N.Y. 1999, ch. 3, for the idea and its prominence in later, systematic Platonism.

version of Aristotelian ethics. It is presented in developmental form and defends itself against a position of which Aristotle knew nothing. Hence, although he respects Aristotle's own ethical writings, Cicero does not put them to philosophical work.[20]

We may regret that the ethical debates of Cicero's time marginalize Plato and Aristotle, but it is important to note that this happens for several reasons. These philosophers were by this time classics from the past, and other theories were more current; Aristotle's own works were superseded by more recent versions of his ideas which presented them in more currently usable form. Further, ethical debate always takes place within an intellectual framework, and the positions and arguments that Cicero finds important make sense within the framework with which he is familiar. Central here is a division of available ethical options which, while put to work in the criticisms of book II (33–43) and book IV (49–50), is not fully stated until the discussion in book V, 16–22 (which takes place on the very spot where it was thought up, Plato's Academy).[21] This is Carneades' division of ethical theories – that is, theories that tell us how we should think of our final end.

Carneades begins from several assumptions; since Academic Sceptics argued only from premises shared with the opponents, these must have the status of assumptions taken for granted in ethical debate at the time. (Otherwise, Carneades would be importing into the debate substantial assumptions of his own, something which as an Academic Sceptic he cannot consistently do.) Firstly, what we are looking for is a way of achieving our overall goal which is a skill or expertise, something that can be taught and has intellectual content. From this it follows that the expertise we hope to learn must be directed at something other than itself, since no skill can coherently be directed only at itself. Secondly, ethics must appeal to some motivating factor already present in human nature. Carneades holds that in ethical debate we come down to three such motivating factors: pleasure, freedom from pain and natural goods of body and mind (beauty, intelligence and so on). Thirdly, an ethical theory must provide some criterion for choices, some actual help in our learning to do the right thing.

This already rules out quite a lot. The first assumption rules out theories that appeal to feelings rather than to reflection and reason to develop an ethical theory. In book II, 36–7 Cicero appeals to this to undermine the claims of Epicurus' theory, on the grounds that it appeals to the verdict of the senses

---

[20] Cicero was aware of the difference between Aristotle's popular works (now lost) and his 'notebooks' (cf. book III, 7), probably Aristotle's lecture and research notes, from which our Aristotelian corpus has come; he knew Tyrannion, the scholar who worked on them. There are puzzles, however; he regards his own work *Topics* as a version of Aristotle's work of the same name, but this cannot be our *Topics*. See A. A. Long (note 17) and J. Barnes, 'Roman Aristotle' in J.Barnes and M. Griffin (eds.), *Philosophia Togata II*, Oxford 1997, 1–69.

[21] It is briefly mentioned in book III, at 30–1, and also in *Lucullus* (the first version of the *Academica*) 130–2, and *Tusculan Disputations* book 5, 84–5. It is an argumentative framework which can be put to use in a variety of contexts.

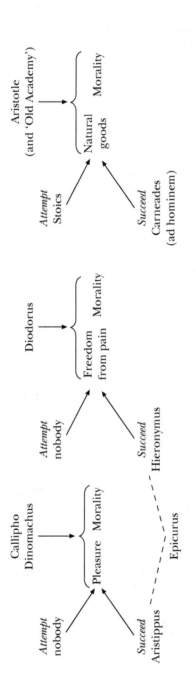

Figure 1 *Carneades' division of ethical theories by their ends. Ruled out as providing no practical guidance: Pyrrho, Aristo, Erillus.*

rather than that of reason and thinking. An empiricist like Epicurus would have to respond that his theory can, in fact, account for the production in humans of a structured understanding that has the complexity of a skill or expertise. At any rate, the thought behind the first assumption is that all parties to ethical debate agree that an ethical theory cannot merely appeal to feelings or to isolated reactions, but must present itself as having the intellectual complexity of an expertise, something with structured intellectual content that can be conveyed.

The second assumption is that an ethical theory must appeal to and start from a factor which is antecedently motivating to human nature, and construct its final end from this. This asssumption dominates Carneades' classification of theories, as we can see from Figure 1. Three motivating factors are posited: pleasure, freedom from pain and natural goods of body and mind (health, intelligence and so on). Theories are classified by reference to these motivating factors in two ways. One is that of whether they hold that our final end is to succeed in getting them, or merely to do our best to get them. Here we find that the classification is somewhat abstract, as some of the positions generated lack actual proponents. Aristippus, we are told, held that our end is to succeed in getting pleasure, and Hieronymus held that it is to succeed in getting freedom from pain, but nobody can be found to hold the theories that our final end is to *attempt* to get these things. With the natural goods it is the other way round. The Stoics, Carneades says, actually hold that our final end is to attempt to get these things, whether we succeed or not; but he cannot find anyone to defend the theory that our final end is actually to get them, and so he defends it himself for the sake of argument. (This option is sometimes referred to as 'Carneades' theory', but Cicero's readers would understand that the great sceptic defended no theory himself, so that any such theory would be defended only for purposes of argument.)

Theories are also classified according to whether they hold that our end should be limited to the original motivating factor, or should also include morality, in the form of virtue. Thus, while Aristippus is said to hold that our end is pleasure alone, the view that it is pleasure *and* virtue is ascribed to the otherwise completely unknown Callipho and Dinomachus. While Hieronymus is said to hold that freedom from pain alone is our final end, the obscure Diodorus is brought in to hold that it is freedom from pain *and* virtue. And, while the view that our final end is merely to get natural goods is defended only by Carneades for the sake of argument, the view that it is getting natural goods *and* virtue is ascribed to Aristotle and the 'Old Academy' tradition.

It is worth noting that this second assumption tacitly rules out theories which aspire to unworldly ends that transcend human nature, such as Plato's idea that virtue is 'becoming like God' and Aristotle's position in the work that we read as book 10 of the *Nicomachean Ethics*, that our final end is to contemplate abstract truths. In the period we are concerned with, such theories were not part of the mainstream discussion of ethics.

The third assumption rules out theories which give no general guidance about right action or hold that no general guidance can be given; Cicero accepts that this rules out the theories of Pyrrho the sceptic and the early Stoics Aristo and Erillus. Modern scholars accept that this is too swift a dismissal of Aristo and Erillus, and find the view taken of Pyrrho very puzzling.[22] In general, however, it is not too difficult to see the point of a demand that an ethical theory should offer some guidance as to how to go about living in one way rather than another. These theories are represented as presenting their basic principles but then refusing any actual guidance as to how these might be applied in a person's life in order to produce moral improvement. Their rejection can be seen as one aspect of the widespread ancient assumption that an ethical theory must be a theory to live by, an object of reflection which must produce some difference in the person's life. The modern assumption that we can divorce the truth of an ethical theory from its practicability is deeply alien to ancient ethical debate. For the ancients, if an ethical theory can provide no guidance as to how we can incorporate it into our ethical reflection, then it is not a serious ethical theory. Cicero's repeated verdict on these theories is that nobody bothers with them.

It is worth noting that many of the positions in Carneades' diagram (see Figure 1) are unoccupied, held solely for the sake of argument or held by utterly obscure people of whom we know little or nothing. Moreover, we can see that the theories of Epicurus and the Stoics are located in ways that make them appear odd. Epicurus' theory appears as a clumsy attempt to combine two different approaches, while the Stoics are introduced as thinkers interested in trying to get, rather than actually getting, natural goods.[23] These approaches dominate the arguments against Epicurus in book II and the Stoics in book IV.

The importance of Carneades' division for the arguments of Cicero's work may lead the reader to ask herself various questions. Are these assumptions all equally acceptable? Is the second, in particular, reasonable? Does it rule out in advance theories which hold that our final end is one that we can grasp only after a process of moral development, and so is distinct from any pre-moral motivation? Should the theories of Epicurus and the Stoics be introduced in this framework? We should recall, however, that Carneades is a sceptic. He is

---

[22] On Pyrrho see above, p. o and n. o. For Aristo see A.-M. Ioppolo, *Aristone di Chio e lo stoicismo antico*, Bibliopolis, Naples, *Elenchos* Collana XIX. For Erillus, see Ioppolo, 'Lo stoicismo di Erillo', *Phronesis* 30 (1985), 58–78.

[23] The Stoic theory in fact occupies an awkward position, since the way it is introduced does not advert to the role of virtue in the theory, although elsewhere the division introduces the Stoics as holding that our sole aim in trying to achieve happiness is virtue. Carneades may be assuming that his readers know that the Stoic theory can be introduced either way. It is possible that the awkwardness is due to Antiochus, or Cicero, applying the division in a way different from that originally intended. For a discussion of the complications in Carneades' arguments, and their indebtedness to earlier classifications by the Stoic Chrysippus, see K. Algra, 'Chrysippus, Carneades, Cicero: the Ethical *Divisiones* in Cicero's *Lucullus*', in B. Inwood and J. Mansfeld (eds.), *Assent and Argument*, Brill, Leiden 1997, 107–39.

not trying to capture the theories' self-conception or to emphasize their strong points – that is for others; his task is to produce effective arguments against them. His classification is well adapted to the use of it made in book v, 22, namely to simplify and structure the discussion. Theories that locate our final good in pleasure can be argued out of court, as Epicurus is; the only philosophically serious debate is between the Stoics and Aristotelians, and it hinges on whether we need conventional goods, as well as virtue, to be happy. It is important to get Epicurus out of the way, but energy is then devoted to the real issue: the role in happiness of virtue and of conventional goods.

Carneades produced this 'division' as a way of organizing arguments against all positive theories. It is interesting that later Antiochus found it useful in disposing of all theories – except his own. He took over, as suitable for his purposes, a scheme which rejects first the theory that our final end is pleasure, then the theory that our final end is virtue – but then, instead of arguing against all the options as Carneades did, he added on arguments for his own theory as the preferable option. It is a good example of the way that he tried to salvage something positive from the rubble of centuries of argument. It also suited the idea, which he puts to great use, that the Stoics were not really innovators, but took over ideas from the Old Academy (particularly, in ethics, from Aristotle) and cast them in new forms.

Cicero was influenced by both traditions stemming from Plato – the sceptical tradition of Carneades and Antiochus' attempt to build positively from differing views. In book v, however, he shows that in ethics at least he is unconvinced by Antiochus' own theory. By producing a powerful argument against it he shows that for him no theory is left standing as the clearly preferable one. Attractive as is a synthesis like that of Antiochus, we are, in Cicero's view, back where we always were: trying to think through for ourselves the arguments on each side and come to our own understanding of which is the best way to live. The Stoic and Aristotelian views are both powerful and attractive, but there are important objections to both of them, and we are not in a position to commit ourselves, with a good intellectual conscience, to either of them. We are left going through the arguments, still trying to find convincing ones. This message, rather than any positive doctrine, is what Cicero hopes to leave with his readers, and, whatever our historical interest in the theories he presents, it is a message that is still, and will always be, timely in ethical philosophy.

Chronology

Principal dates

BC	Life of Cicero	Theoretical works
106	Birth of Cicero, 3 January	
91–88	Serves under Pompey's father in Social War	
	Studying law with Q. Mucius Scaevola (Augur)	
88	Hears Philo of Larissa in Rome	
	Studying oratory	
87	Studying law with Q. Mucius Scaevola (Pontifex)	
86		*De Inventione* (*On Rhetorical Invention*) (written after 91)
80	Defends Sextus Roscius, his first public case	
79–8	Travels and studies in Greece and Asia: hears Antiochus of Ascalon, Posidonius, Zeno and Phaedrus (Epicureans)	
75–4	Quaestor at Lilybaeum in Sicily	
70	Prosecutes Verres for extortion in Sicily	
69	Aedile: gives games	
66	Praetor. Speaks for Pompey's command	
65	Birth of his son Marcus. His brother Quintus is aedile	
63	Consul with C. Antonius. Executes conspirators without trial	

BC	Life of Cicero	Theoretical works
62	Quintus Cicero praetor	
61	Testifies against P. Clodius on sacrilege charge Quintus Cicero governs Asia (61–58)	
58	Measures of P. Clodius send Cicero into exile in March	
57	Quintus Cicero serves under Pompey (57–6) Recalled from exile; returns to Rome in September	
56	Cicero warned and ceases to oppose them	*De Oratore (On Oratory)*
54	Quintus Cicero serves under Caesar in Gaul (54–52)	*De Re Publica (On the State)* begun
53	Elected augur in place of M. Crassus	
51	Goes to govern Cilicia, arriving 31 July. Quintus serves under him.	*De Re Publica (On the State)* published. *De Legibus (On Laws)* begun
50	Leaves Cilicia (30 July) and reaches Italy (24 November)	
49	Cicero continues peace efforts, though assigned a command by Pompey In June leaves Italy to join Pompey	
48	Cicero returns to Italy and waits for Caesar's pardon at Brundisium	
47	In July pardoned by Caesar along with Quintus and his nephew Quintus jr.	
46	Divorces Terentia Delivers *Pro Marcello*, thanking Caesar for his clemency, in the Senate Marries Publilia	*Eulogy of Cato Brutus (Brutus) Paradoxa Stoicorum (Stoic Paradoxes) Orator (The Orator)*
45	In January Tullia gives birth to a son but dies in February In April young Marcus begins his studies in Athens	*Consolation to himself *Hortensius*: Exhortation to Philosophy Academica (Academic Scepticism)*

BC	Life of Cicero	Theoretical works
45 (*cont.*)		*De Finibus* (*On Moral Ends*) *Tusculan Disputations* and *De Natura Deorum* (*On the Nature of Gods*) begun
44		*Cato Maior de senectute* (*Cato the Elder: On Old Age*
	In April–June visiting his country villas in Italy	*De Divinatione* (*On Divination*) finished
	On 17 July leaves for Greece but quickly returns	*De Fato* (*On Fate*)
		*De Gloria (*On Reputations*)
	On 31 August returns to Rome	*Topica* (*Kinds of Argument*)
	On 2 September delivers First Philippic Oration against Antony	*Laelius de amicitia* (*Laelius on Friendship*)
	In October–December visiting his villas in Italy; writing Second Philippic	*De Officiis* (*On Duties*)
43	Delivers Fifth-Fourteenth Phlippic On 9 December Cicero killed	

Notes:
* = lost
Some minor undateable works have been omitted.
N.B. Some of the dates are approximate.
Source: From Cicero *On Duties*, ed. M. T. Griffiths and E. M. Atkins, Cambridge Texts in the History of Political Thought, Cambridge, 1991.

Figure 2 — Cicero's philosophical background

	Pythagoreans	Other 'Presocratics'	Pyrrhonists	Platonists	Aristotelians	Stoics	Epicureans	Cyrenaics	Other (school unknown)
500 BC	Pythagoras	Heraclitus							
400 BC	Archytas Arion Echecrates Timaeus	Gorgias Democritus		Socrates Plato Speusippus Xenocrates Polemo	Aristotle Theophrastus Dicaearchus Aristoxenus	Socrates Zeno of Citium Aristo of Chios Erillus Cleanthes Dionysius of Heraclea	Epicurus Metrodorus Hermarchus Polyaenus Themista Charmides	Socrates Aristippus Aristippus the Younger	
300 BC			Pyrrho	Arcesilaus	Strato Demetrius of Phaleron Lyco Hieronymus				Callipho Dinomachus
200 BC				Carneades	Aristo of Ceos Critolaus Diodorus	Chrysippus Diogenes of Babylon Antipater Panaetius Mnesarchus Posidonius			
100 BC			(Aenesidemus)	(Philo of Larisa) — Antiochus Aristus	Staseas	Posidonius	Phaedrus Zeno of Sidon Siro Philodemus		

Figure 2 *Cicero's philosophical background (all names are mentioned in* On Moral Ends *except for those in brackets).*

Further reading

The text used is *M. Tulli Ciceronis De Finibus Bonorum et Malorum Libri Quinque*, ed. L. D. Reynolds, Oxford 1998 (Oxford Classical Texts). Also consulted are the text, translation and notes in *Cicéron: des termes extrêmes des biens et des maux*, ed. J. Martha, 2 vols., Paris 1967 (Budé edition) and the text and notes in *Cicero: De Finibus bonorum et malorum libri V*, ed. N. Madvig, Copenhagen 1876, reprinted Olms, Hildesheim, 1965. There is a text and translation in *Cicero, De Finibus*, trans. by H. Rackham, Cambridge, Mass. 1931, reprinted 1971 (Loeb library). *Cicero On Stoic Good and Evil*, by M. R. Wright, is a text with translation and notes of book III with the *Paradoxa Stoicorum* (Aris and Phillips, Warminster, 1991).

For Cicero's life see A. E. Douglas, *Cicero, Greece and Rome*, New Surveys in the Classics, Oxford 1968; D. L. Stockton, *Cicero: a Political Biography*, Oxford 1971; and E. D. Rawson, *Cicero, A Portrait*, London 1975, reprinted Bristol 1983. Cicero's other philosophical works are all available in the Loeb library series, with Latin and facing English. There is a recent translation of *On Duties*, with introduction and notes, by E. M. Atkins and M. Griffin, Cambridge 1991 (Cambridge Texts in the History of Political Thought).

For Cicero's philosophical background see two books edited by Miriam Griffin and Jonathan Barnes: *Philosophia Togata* I: *Essays on Philosophy and Roman Society* Oxford 1989 and *Philosophia Togata* II: *Plato and Aristotle at Rome*, Oxford, 1997. There is an excellent selection of essays in J. G. F. Powell, *Cicero the Philosopher*, Oxford 1995. See also Günther Patzig, 'Cicero as Philosoph, am Beispiel der Schrift "De Finibus"', 251–72 in Patzig, *Gesammelte Schriften* III, Wallstein, Göttingen, 1996. For Cicero's Academic background see *Assent and Argument: Studies in Cicero's Academic Books* (Proceedings of the 7th Symposium Hellenisticum, Utrecht, 21–5 August 1995), Brill, Leiden/New York/Köln, 1997. See also Carlos Lévy, *Cicero Academicus: Recherches sur les Academiques et sur la Philosophie Cicéronienne*. Collection de l'école française de Rome 162. Rome, Ecole française de Rome 1992.

The main sources for Epicurean and Stoic ethics are to be found in B. Inwood and L. Gerson, *Hellenistic Philosophy*, second edition, Hackett,

Indianapolis, 1997, and also in A. A. Long and D. Sedley, *The Hellenistic Philosophers*, Cambridge 1987 (vol. 1 with translations and comments on Latin and Greek texts collected in vol. 2). Long and Sedley provide more annotation but chop the texts up more than Inwood and Gerson. The two major passages on early Stoic ethics other than Cicero, from Diogenes Laertius and Arius Didymus, are translated in full in Inwood and Gerson. There is also a text and translation of the Arius in A. J. Pomeroy, *Arius Didymus: Epitome of Stoic Ethics*, Society of Biblical Literature, Atlanta, Ga., 1999. The Epicurean material is also collected in B. Inwood and L. Gerson, *The Epicurus Reader*, Hackett, Indianapolis 1994. For Antiochus there is no collection of primary material in translation. See the chapter on Antiochus in J. Dillon, *The Middle Platonists*, Ithaca 1977; J. Glucker, *Antiochus and the Late Academy*, Vandenhoeck and Ruprecht, Göttingen 1978, Hypomnemata 56; and J. Barnes, 'Antiochus of Ascalon' in *Philosophia Togata* I (above), 51–96.

On ethics in the Hellenistic period see R. Sharples, *Stoics, Epicureans, Sceptics*, London 1997, chs. 5 and 6. J. Annas, *The Morality of Happiness*, Oxford 1993, gives a picture and discussion of Greek ethics from Aristotle through Epicurus and the Stoics to the later hybrid theories like that of Antiochus. On Epicurus see P. Mitsis, *Epicurus' Ethical Theory*, Ithaca 1988; on the Stoics see B. Inwood, *Ethics and Human Action in Early Stoic Ethics*, Oxford 1985. Valuable articles on all the major figures and schools can be found in K. Algra and others (eds.), *The Cambridge History of Hellenistic Philosophy*, Cambridge 1999. The *Encyclopaedia of Classical Philosophy*, ed. D. Zeyl, Westport, CT, 1997, is valuable on both schools and individual philosophers.

Note on the text

Greek and Roman names

Greeks of this period had a single personal name ('Chrysippus', 'Epicurus'), and could be further identified by a patronymic ('son or daughter of') and city of origin ('of Soli', 'of Athens'). Cicero refers to familiar people and uses the personal name alone. In the note on a person's first appearance I have added the city of origin and dates (often very vague).

There were three elements to a Roman name of this period. The *praenomen*, the first element, served many of the functions of our forename, except that women did not have a public *praenomen*, and those of men were taken from a very small list: Gaius, Lucius, Marcus, Publius, and so on (eighteen in all). The main element, the *nomen*, was an inherited family or clan name, for example Tullius, Porcius, Sulpicius, Cornelius. The *cognomen* was an addition originally used to mark out individuals, often by achievement or distinguishing characteristic. This could become hereditary, and was useful in marking out different branches of the same family. Additional such names could be tacked on, indicating further branches of the family. The function of our surname was fulfilled by the *nomen* alone or by *nomen* plus *cognomen*. Thus we have Gaius Marius (*nomen* alone), Titus Manlius Torquatus (*nomen* plus *cognomen*), Publius Cornelius Scipio Africanus (*nomen* plus two *cognomina*). Prominent Roman families who lacked an heir would often adopt a son from another family, and a name ending in -anus indicates this. Thus the name of the main speaker in book v, Marcus Pupius Piso Frugi Calpurnianus, shows that he was born into the Piso Frugi branch of the Calpurnius family and adopted into the Pupius family.

In the text, Cicero usually refers to people by a *cognomen* if they have one, or by this together with the *praenomen*. Thus Marcus Porcius Cato is addressed and referred to as Cato, or Marcus Cato. I give a person's full name in the note on the first occurrence.

Indexing Roman names is problematic. The logical procedure, followed by the *Oxford Classical Dictionary* and other reference works, is to index under the family name (*nomen*). However, a modern reader of this book is unlikely to look up Cato under Porcius, or Cicero under Tullius. I have therefore indexed Romans under the name used in Cicero's text, which is anyway most likely to be familiar to a modern reader, although this means that some people are indexed under the *nomen* (Pompeius, Marius) and others under a *cognomen* (Cicero, Cato).

Roman offices

By the end of the Republic, when Cicero was writing, the Roman constitution had become complex and unwieldy; only a few points are mentioned here.

The Senate was a body of originally 300, though the numbers had greatly increased as a result of late Republican reforms. It was composed of ex-magistrates; the holder of even the lowest elected office became a senator for life. Its function was technically advisory, but as the only permanent government body it had gained a large *de facto* control of much government business, especially foreign policy.

Magistrates, the executive branch, were elected by a system of voting assemblies, which tended to favour better-off citizens. Candidates could stand for senior offices only after first having held the more junior ones. These were: a financial post (quaestor), a post covering city administration (aedile), and tribune of the plebs, a post open only to plebeians. These were not an underclass but families other than the patricians, a historically distinct group of settlers. By the end of the Republic plebeians were often rich and prominent. Tribunes protected the interests of the plebeians, and could veto legislation. In the late Republic the office of tribune provided opportunities for populist-minded politicians.

The two senior offices were praetor and consul. Every year eight praetors (at this date) and two consuls were elected. Praetors had judicial duties, mainly serving as judges in a number of courts involving both Romans and foreigners. The consulship was the highest office, aimed at by all ambitious politicians. Since there were only two a year, competition was intense, and after the elections, which were often marked by bribery and violence, prosecutions for electoral malpractice were common. Consuls were the chief executives, summoning voting assemblies and with veto power; they presided over the Senate and were commanders-in-chief of the army. They gave their name to their year of office, and had the regalia and a few of the religious functions of the original Roman kings. As the first of his family to reach the consulship (in 63) Cicero is understandably keen to stress his tenure of the office. Every five years two censors were selected from ex-consuls. They were in charge of the census of citizens and the register of senators, as well as the leasing of public lands and contracts for public buildings and collecting taxes.

In times of crisis the Senate authorized the appointment of an extraordinary short-term executive, called a Dictator or Master of the People, who could make decisions not subject to veto. This was originally a short-term emergency appointment to perform a specific task, typically in times of military crisis, but by the end of the Republic Sulla and then Caesar used the office to institute long-term constitutional changes.

Translator's note

Cicero is by common consent a great prose stylist, but *On Moral Ends* (in Latin *De Finibus*) is one of his most technical works, dealing at times with some fairly abstruse philosophical ideas. Moreover he is drawing heavily on Greek sources (most of which are now lost to us) for much of its content. He sets out these ideas, as he tells us himself (I, 6), in his own arrangement and not uncritically; but the technical and relatively derivative nature of the work imposes some constraint on stylistic fluency by comparison with, say, his forensic oratory. None the less, *On Moral Ends* still scores remarkably well stylistically. Cicero's Latin is intricately constructed and highly polished throughout.

Given the high quality of Cicero's prose, the translator of *On Moral Ends* has a duty to render the text in as clear and fluent a manner as possible, and this has been my main aim. Such a remark usually comes with the codicil 'without a sacrifice of accuracy'; while fully endorsing the codicil, I perhaps naively believe that clarity and accuracy tend to go hand-in-hand. In translating the text I have rarely felt these demands pull in opposite directions. Others will have to judge how happy a congruence has actually been achieved.

One important difference worth mentioning between Cicero's Latin and contemporary English is that the former makes much use of long sentences, and in particular sentences containing multiple subordinate clauses. To attempt to render this feature directly into English would result on most occasions in something approaching gobbledegook. The translation has therefore been ruthless (at least in intent) in breaking down Cicero's grand periods into smaller and more manageable units. This process also sometimes required some fairly drastic changes in clause order. Literalness in these respects would, I think, distort rather than preserve Cicero's meaning in a modern English idiom.

A word about the issue of gender. I have endeavoured to keep the translation as gender-neutral as possible. A case against such a policy might be offered on grounds of either anachronism or inaccuracy, but neither point tells with respect to *On Moral Ends*. The philosophical schools that Cicero discusses, in particular the Stoics and Epicureans, hold that it is neither easy nor impossible for members of either sex to become wise and good; and the Latin term that Cicero uses for the morally paradigmatic 'wise person', namely *sapiens*, can be either masculine or feminine. The Latin word *vir*, however, which refers specifically to the male of the human species, is translated on occasions as 'man'.

The Latin text translated is the Oxford Classical Text (OCT) of *De Finibus* edited by L. D. Reynolds. Places where I have varied from the OCT, or where the text seems corrupt or incomplete, are indicated in lettered footnotes (the editor's footnotes are numbered).

I would like to offer my heartfelt thanks to Julia Annas and Desmond Clarke for a host of helpful comments and suggestions on earlier drafts of the translation, and generally for keeping a benevolent eye on my neophytic efforts. I have not made a great deal of use of other translations of *De Finibus*, but I have profited from consulting that of Rackham in the Loeb edition.

Below I give a brief glossary of a few important Latin words or phrases in the text:

De Finibus/ De Finibus Bonorum Et Malorum

The first of these phrases is the common abbreviation of the full Latin title of the work; the second phrase is the full title. For the title of this volume, *De Finibus* – literally 'On Ends' – has been translated as 'On Moral Ends', indicating that Cicero is discussing the ends or goals to which a person's ethical life should be directed. The full title means literally, 'On Ends Of Goods And Evils', which is fairly nonsensical in English. Here 'ends (of)' functions in effect as an adjective qualifying 'goods and evils', and the core phrase is translated as 'highest goods and evils' where it appears in the main body of the text. Cicero also talks in the singular of the supreme/highest/ultimate good or (as the case may be) evil, using (in no particular order) the Latin adjectives **summum/extremum/ultimum** with the noun for 'good', **bonum**, or 'evil', **malum**.

Honestum

Translated in most contexts as 'moral' or 'morality', though in some less technical contexts as the more literal 'honourable'. In a technical context the word is used by Cicero for the Greek *kalon*, to capture the idea of moral goodness, in particular as relating to qualities or actions that are praiseworthy in their own right.

Officium

Translated as 'appropriate action' in technical contexts, in particular those relating to Stoic ethical theory. The word is Cicero's translation of the Stoic Greek term *kathêkon*, literally 'appropriate (thing)', and is used to describe any action which may be rationally justified. In such contexts the common translation of this word as 'duty' is misleading, since 'duty' has strong deontological connotations lacking in the Stoic usage. In some contexts, however, Cicero's usage does have a flavour of 'duty' and the term is occasionally so translated.

RAPHAEL WOOLF

On Moral Ends

Book I

(1) In this work I am putting into Latin themes which philosophers of the highest talent and most refined learning have dealt with in Greek, and I am well aware, Brutus[1], that this will incur criticism of various kinds. Some people, by no means uneducated, altogether disapprove of philosophizing. Others do not criticize it so long as it is done in an easygoing manner, but consider that one should not devote so much of one's enthusiasm and attention to it. There will also be people, learned in Greek and contemptuous of Latin, who say that they would rather spend their time reading Greek. Finally, I suspect that there will be some who will call on me to follow other literary pursuits, claiming that this kind of writing, however elegantly done, is none the less not worthy of my character and position. (2) Against all of these critics I think that some brief reply ought to be made.

To those who pour scorn on philosophy I made an adequate response in the book in which I defend and laud philosophy against the accusations and attacks of Hortensius.[2] This book appeared to please you and all those whom I consider competent to judge, and so I undertook to write more, fearing that otherwise I might be perceived as exciting people's enthusiasm but unable to sustain it.

As for those who take great pleasure in philosophy, but want it to be practised only to a moderate extent – they are demanding a restraint that is hard to exercise. Philosophy is a pursuit which, once entered upon, cannot be limited or held back. In consequence, I regard as almost more just those who would altogether turn me away from philosophy, than those who would set

---

[1] Marcus Junius Brutus, c. 85–42, famous as one of the leaders in the assassination of Julius Caesar in 44. He is a suitable dedicatee for this book, since he had considerable philosophical interests (see below, para. 8 and book III, 6). Though he is sometimes considered a Stoic, the evidence is that he identified himself as a follower of Plato, belonging to the hybrid 'Old Academy' school of Antiochus (cf. book V, 8). See David Sedley, 'The Ethics of Brutus and Cassius', *Journal of Roman Studies* (1997), 41–53.

[2] Quintus Hortensius Hortalus (114–49), a famous orator, introduced by Cicero as a partner in discussion in his lost work *Hortensius* (written in the same year as *On Moral Ends*) in which Hortensius argued against the study of philosophy, and Cicero gave the other speaker, Catulus, arguments in its defence.

bounds on the infinite and desire moderation when the greater the study, the greater the reward. (3) If wisdom can be attained, one should not just acquire it but enjoy it to the full. And if its attainment is hard, there is none the less no end to the search for truth except its discovery. To tire of the search is disgraceful given that its object is so beautiful. And if writing philosophy delights, who would be so churlish as to turn one away from it? Even if it is an effort, who is to set a limit on another's industriousness? Terence's Chremes was civil in not wishing his new neighbour 'to dig or plough or bear any burden at all', for he was discouraging him not from industriousness but from menial labour.[3] But those who take offence at a pursuit, such as mine, which gives me nothing but joy, are simply prying.

(4) It is more difficult to satisfy those who claim to despise anything written in Latin. What amazes me above all about these people is that their native tongue gives them no pleasure when it deals with matters of the highest import, and yet they willingly read mere plays in Latin translated word-for-word from Greek. After all, who is so inimical almost to the word 'Roman' itself as to spurn and reject Ennius' *Medea* or Pacuvius' *Antiope* on the grounds that one loves the same plays by Euripides but hates Latin literature? Surely, it may be asked, one does not read Caecilius' *Sunephoboi* or Terence's *Woman of Andros* rather than either of these titles by Menander? (5) I disagree so much with this view that, however wonderfully written Sophocles' *Electra* may be, I none the less think that I should read Atilius' bad translation. Licinus described Atilius as 'a wooden writer, but still, I hold, a writer, and so worthy of being read'. For to be completely unversed in our poets is a sign either of extreme indolence or extreme fastidiousness.

In my view no one is well educated who is ignorant of our literature. So do we read Ennius' 'Would that not, in a glade . . .' no less than its Greek original, but disapprove of Plato's discussions of the good and happy life being set out in Latin?[4] (6) What of it, if I do not perform the task of a trans-

---

[3] Line 69 from Terence's play *The Self-Tormentor* (see next note).

[4] Sophocles (*c.* 495–406) and Euripides (*c.* 480–407/6) are fifth-century authors of tragic dramas in Greek, which became 'classics' and continued to be performed throughout antiquity. Cicero refers to translations and adaptations of their works into Latin by Quintus Ennius (239–169), who also translated Homer into Latin, and Marcus Pacuvius (*c.* 220–130). The quotation from Ennius is from the opening lines of Euripides' *Medea*. Porcius Licinus is a poet and critic probably of the end of the second century. Menander (*c.* 344/3–292/1) is the most famous Greek author of 'New Comedy', of which we have many Latin adaptations by Titus Maccius Plautus (active 205–184) and Publius Terentius Afer (Terence), active in the 160s. We have only fragments of Caecilius Statius (active 179–168), the title of whose play here remains in Greek (the *sunepheboi* are 'young companions'). The Atilius mentioned here as a translator of Sophoclean tragedy may be the same as a writer of comedies earlier than Caecilius.

Cicero is referring to Greek classics in Latin translations which by his day were already part of the Roman literary tradition in their own right.

Perhaps Cicero picks Plato (427–347; see Introduction pp. x–xii, xxi–xxii) as the philosopher most famous for his literary style in Greek. Plato's ideas about the good life are conspicuously absent from the *De Finibus*, except as taken up into Antiochus' hybrid theory (see Introduction, pp. xiii–xiv).

lator, but preserve the views of those whom I consider sound while contributing my own judgement and order of composition? What reason does anyone have for preferring Greek to that which is written with brilliance and is not a translation from Greek?[5] If one were to say that these topics have already been covered by the Greeks, then there is no reason to read even as many of the Greek authors themselves as one is supposed to read. For what, in the case of the Stoics, has been left out by Chrysippus?[6] Yet we read Diogenes, Antipater, Mnesarchus, Panaetius and many others, not least our friend Posidonius.[7] Does Theophrastus give us only moderate pleasure when he deals with topics already covered by Aristotle?[8] Do the Epicureans desist from writing in their own fashion on topics which Epicurus and the ancients had already written about?[9] If Greeks are read by Greeks, on the same subjects covered in a different way, why should not our Romans be read by Romans?

(7) Even if I were to translate Plato or Aristotle literally, as our poets did with the Greek plays, I hardly think I would deserve ill of my fellow-citizens for bringing those sublime geniuses to their attention. Though I have not thus far adopted this method, I do not consider that I am disbarred from doing so. If I think fit, I will translate certain passages, particularly from those authors I just mentioned, when it happens to be appropriate, as Ennius often does with Homer or Afranius with Menander.[10] Nor, unlike Lucilius,[11] will I forbid

---

[5] Cicero lacks modesty but makes a good point; his own excellent philosophical training puts him in a position to make synoptic and creative use of his sources without excessive dependency on any one of them.

[6] Chrysippus of Soli (280/76–208/4), third head of the Stoa after its founder Zeno of Citium (c. 334/3–262/1) and Cleanthes of Assos (c. 331/0–230/29) was regarded in the ancient world as the second founder of Stoicism; at a time when Zeno's ideas were subject to divergent interpretations and the influence of the school was becoming dispersed, Chrysippus wrote voluminously (we have 705 book titles) on all aspects of Stoicism in a way that developed and defended Zeno's ideas with rigour, acumen and force, establishing the basic tradition of Stoic teachings.

[7] Diogenes of Babylon (c. 228–140), Antipater of Tarsus (c. 200–c. 130) were heads of the Stoic school, Mnesarchus of Athens (c. 170–88) a leading figure in it. Panaetius of Rhodes (c. 185–109) and Posidonius of Apamea (c. 135–51) were more cosmopolitan Stoics who associated with leading Romans, introducing them to Stoic thought.
  Cicero is not just showing off his learning here; in *On Duties*, for example, he further develops a work of Panaetius and contributes to a debate between the positions of Diogenes and Antipater. However, the intended audience for the present work is not expected to be knowledgeable in such detail.

[8] Theophrastus of Eresus (372/1–288/7) was the pupil and successor of Aristotle of Stageira (384–322). Little of Theophrastus' voluminous work survives; in the ancient world it was popular and well regarded for its style. Cicero is aware that Aristotle's more serious philosophical works were different from his more popular works (see Introduction, pp. xxii and n. 20).

[9] Epicurus of Athens (341–270) encouraged his followers to study and memorize his own words, and the school did not value originality, but there is a large Epicurean philosophical literature.

[10] Lucius Afranius (second half of the second century) was a dramatist who made adaptations from Menander (see note 4 above).

[11] Gaius Lucilius (c. 180–102/1) was a Roman author best known for cutting satires and invectives, a friend of Scipio Aemilianus (see next note).

anyone from reading my work. How I wish that a Persius were alive today! Still more a Scipio or Rutilius.[12] Lucilius, fearing the criticism of such people, said that he wrote for the ordinary folk of Tarentum, Consentia and Sicily. Here as elsewhere he writes with panache: but really in his day there were no critics learned enough to make him struggle to meet their favourable judgement, and his writings have a lightness of touch which reveals a consummate elegance but only moderate learning.

(8) Besides, which reader should I fear, given that I have been bold enough to dedicate my book to you, Brutus, a man who yields not even to the Greeks as a philosopher? Indeed it was you who roused me to the task by dedicating to me your wonderful book *On Virtue*. However, I believe that the reason why some people are averse to Latin literature is that they have tended to come across certain rough and unpolished works which have been translated from bad Greek into worse Latin. I sympathize with these people, provided only that they consider that the Greek versions too are not worth reading. On the other hand, if a Latin book has a worthy subject and is written with dignity and style, who would not read it? The only exception would be one who wanted to be called a Greek pure and simple, as in the case of Albucius when he was greeted by Scaevola who was praetor in Athens. (9) Lucilius again narrates the occasion with great charm and perfect wit, and has Scaevola say brilliantly:

'Albucius, rather than a Roman or Sabine, a fellow-citizen of those distinguished centurions Pontius and Tritanius, who held the standard in the front line, you preferred to be called a Greek. And so when I was praetor in Athens, and you came to pay your respects, I greeted you in the way that you preferred. "*Chaire*, Titus!" I cried, and "*Chaire*, Titus!" cried my lictors, my whole cavalry and my infantry. Hence your hostility to me, Albucius, hence your enmity.'[13]

(10) Scaevola was right. I for my part never cease to wonder where this excessive distaste for home-grown products comes from. This is certainly not the place for a lecture on the subject, but my view is, as I have often argued, that, far from lacking in resources, the Latin language is even richer than the

[12] Lucilius wrote that he did not wish his works to be read either by the ignorant or by the very learned, using a certain Persius as an example of the latter (see Cicero's *On the Orator* II, 25). Here Cicero wishes for a learned and sympathetic audience such as was available to the earlier writer.

Publius Cornelius Scipio Aemilianus Africanus (185/4–129), prominent Roman statesman and general, in 146 captured and destroyed Carthage. He was friendly with various intellectuals, and interested in Greek culture, and has been seen as the centre of a 'Scipionic circle' of aristocrats with intellectual interests. Cicero presents an idealized picture of him in his earlier work *On the State*.

Publius Rutilius Rufus (*c.* 160–*c.* 80) a friend of Scipio's, but less successful, went into exile in 92 after a conviction for corruption; he thereupon wrote an influential history of his times.

[13] *Chaire* is a Greek greeting. By having his official Roman entourage greet the Roman Albucius in Greek, the poem's Scaevola implies that Albucius' love of all things Greek has made him lose his pride in his Roman identity. This kind of anxiety and chauvinism about Greek culture was not uncommon among Romans.

Greek.[14] When, after all, have we, or rather our good orators and poets, lacked the wherewithal to create either a full or a spare style in their work, at least since they have had models to imitate? As for me, as far as my public duties are concerned, and their attendant struggles and dangers, I consider myself never to have deserted the post at which the Roman people placed me. Surely, then, I ought to strive as hard as I can to put my energy, enthusiasm and effort into improving the learning of my fellow-citizens as well? There is no need to waste time picking a fight with those who prefer to read Greek texts, provided only that they do read them, and do not just pretend to. My task is to serve those who either wish to enjoy writings in both languages, or, if they have available to them works in their native tongue, do not feel any need of works in Greek.

(11) On the other hand, those who would rather I wrote on a different topic should be equable about it, given the many topics on which I have written, more indeed than any other Roman. Perhaps I shall live to write still more. In any case, no one who has habitually and carefully read my philosophical works will judge that any is more worth reading than this one. For nothing in life is more worth investigating than philosophy in general, and the question raised in this work in particular: what is the end, what is the ultimate and final goal, to which all our deliberations on living well and acting rightly should be directed? What does nature pursue as the highest good to be sought, what does she shun as the greatest evil?

Given that there is violent disagreement on these matters among the most learned philosophers, who could think that it is beneath whatever dignity one may care to bestow on me to inquire into the question of what is best and truest in every area of life? (12) We have our leading citizens debate the question of whether the offspring of a female slave is to be regarded as *in fructu*, with Publius Scaevola and Manius Manilius on one side, and Marcus Brutus dissenting.[15] To be sure, this kind of question is an acute one, and far from irrelevant for the conduct of civil society – I am happy to read such writings and others of the same sort, and shall go on doing so. But shall questions that relate to life in its entirety then be neglected? Legal discussions might have better sales, but philosophical discussions are certainly richer. However, this is a point which one may leave the reader to decide. For my part, I consider that this work gives a more or less comprehensive discussion of the question

---

[14] Cicero defends the capacity of Latin to translate Greek philosophy, given the relative paucity in Latin of developed abstract vocabulary and lack of the syntactical devices (such as the definite article) which are heavily used in philosophical Greek. For Cicero as a philosophical translator, see J. G. F. Powell, 'Cicero's translations from Greek' in J. G. F. Powell (ed.), *Cicero the Philosopher*, Oxford 1995, 273–300.

[15] A legal dispute: if a female slave is hired by B from her owner A, does a child born to her during this period belong to A or to B? Publius Mucius Scaevola, consul in 133, Manius Manilius, consul in 149 (who appears as a character in Cicero's *On the State*) and Marcus Junius Brutus (active in the early first century, a distant relative of Marcus Junius Brutus the assassin of Caesar) were all famous jurists and legal theorists of the past.

of the highest goods and evils. In it I have investigated not only the views with which I agree, but those of each of the philosophical schools individually.

(13) To start from what is easiest, let us first review Epicurus' system, which most people know best. You will discover that the exposition given by me is no less accurate than that given by the school's own proponents. For we wish to find the truth, not refute anyone adversarially.

An elaborate defence of Epicurus' theory of pleasure was once given by Lucius Torquatus, a man learned in every philosophical system. I gave the response, and Gaius Triarius, a young man of exceptional seriousness and learning, was present at the discussion.[16] (14) They had each come to call on me in my house at Cumae, and after a short discussion on literature, of which they were both keen students, Torquatus said: 'Since we have for once found you at leisure, I am determined to hear what it is about my master Epicurus which I shall not say you hate, as those who disagree with him generally do, but which at any rate you do not approve of. I myself regard him as the one person to have seen the truth, and to have freed people's minds from the greatest errors, and handed down everything which could pertain to a good and happy life. I feel that you, like our friend Triarius, dislike him because he neglected the stylistic flourish of a Plato, Aristotle or Theophrastus. For I can hardly believe that his views do not seem to you to be true.'

(15) 'You are quite mistaken, Torquatus', I replied. 'It is not the style of that philosopher which offends: his words express his meaning, and he writes in a direct way that I can comprehend. I do not reject a philosopher who has eloquence to offer, but I do not demand it from one who does not. It is in his subject-matter that Epicurus fails to satisfy, and in several areas at that. Still, since there are "as many views as people", perhaps I am wrong.' 'Why is it that he does not satisfy you?' asked Torquatus. 'For I consider you a fair judge, provided you have a good knowledge of what Epicurus says.' (16) 'All of Epicurus' views are well-enough known to me', I replied, 'assuming that you do not think that Phaedrus or Zeno, both of whom I have heard speak,[17] were misleading me – though they persuaded me of absolutely nothing except their earnestness. Indeed I frequently went to hear these men with Atticus, who was an admirer of both, and who even loved Phaedrus dearly. Atticus and I would discuss each day what we had heard, and there was never any dispute over my understanding, though plenty over what I could agree with.'[18]

---

[16] The dialogue is set in 50 at Cicero's country house at Cumae, on the coast north of Naples. On Torquatus and Triarius see Introduction, pp. xv–xvi and n. 10.

[17] Phaedrus (probably of Athens, 138–70), whom Cicero heard in Rome; see Introduction p. xi. Cicero admired his character and his elegant style, unusual for an Epicurean. Zeno of Sidon (c. 150–after 79/8) was head of the Epicurean school in Athens, and Cicero heard him lecture there in 79–78. Cicero dislikes his abusive style; for example he called Socrates 'the clown from Athens'. Zeno's works have all been lost, but the content of some of his lectures and classes survives in the work of Philodemus of Gadara, one of his pupils, especially his work *On Signs*.

[18] Titus Pomponius Atticus (111–32), a lifelong friend of Cicero's and recipient of many of his letters. His sympathy for Epicureanism, though Cicero dislikes it, made him a safely neutral

(**17**) 'Then tell me about it', said Torquatus, 'I very much want to hear what you take issue with.' 'Firstly', I replied, 'his physics, which is his proudest boast, is totally derivative. He repeats Democritus' views,[19] changes almost nothing, and what he does try to improve, he seems to me only to distort. Democritus believes that what he calls "atoms" – that is, bodies which are indivisible on account of their density – move in an infinite void, in which there is no top, bottom or middle, no innermost or outermost point. They move in such a way as to coalesce as a result of collision, and this creates each and every object that we see. This atomic motion is not conceived to arise from any starting-point, but to be eternal.

(**18**) 'Now Epicurus does not go greatly astray in those areas where he follows Democritus. But there is much in both that I do not agree with, and especially the following: in natural science, there are two questions to be asked, firstly what is the matter out of which each thing is made, and secondly what is the power which brings a thing into being. Epicurus and Democritus discuss matter, but neglect the power or efficient cause. This is a defect common to both men.

'I turn to the failings peculiar to Epicurus. He believes that those same solid and indivisible bodies move downwards in a straight line under their own weight and that this is the natural motion of all bodies. (**19**) At the same time our brilliant man now encounters the problem that if everything moves downwards in perpendicular fashion – in a straight line, as I said – then it will never be the case that one atom can come into contact with another. His solution is a novel one. He claims that the atom swerves ever so slightly, to the absolutely smallest extent possible. This is how it comes about that the atoms combine and couple and adhere to one another. As a result, the world and all its parts and the objects within it are created.

'Now this is all a childish fiction, but not only that – it does not even produce the results he wants. The swerve itself is an arbitrary invention – he says that the atom swerves without a cause, when the most unprincipled move that any physicist can make is to adduce effects without causes. Then he groundlessly deprives atoms of the motion which he himself posited as natural to all objects that have weight, namely travel in a straight line in a downwards direction. And yet he fails to secure the outcome that motivated these inventions. (**20**) For if all the atoms swerve, none will ever come together; while if some swerve and others follow their natural tendency to fall in a straight line, then, firstly, this will be equivalent to placing the atoms in two separate classes, those that move in a straight line and those that move

political figure on whom Cicero could rely. He acquired his nickname of Atticus through his love of Attica – that is, Athens and its culture (this is referred to in v, 4).

[19] Cicero frequently accuses Epicurus of taking much of his philosophy from Democritus of Abdera (*c.* 460–*c.* 350), the major defender of atomism. The charge is repeated at book II, 102 and book IV, 13. (In book v Democritus figures as an ethical philosopher; see v, 23 and 87.) Atomism may not have been as basic to Epicurus as Cicero suggests; he took it over as being the best science of his day, but gave it his own philosophical role.

off-line; and secondly, the disorderly clash of atoms which he posits – and this is a problem for Democritus too – could never bring about our ordered universe.[20]

'Then again it is highly unscientific to believe that there is an indivisible magnitude. Epicurus would surely never have held that view had he chosen to learn geometry from his friend Polyaenus rather than make Polyaenus himself unlearn it.[21] Democritus thought the sun was of great size, as befits a man of education, well-trained in geometry. Epicurus thought that it was maybe a foot across. He took the view that it was more or less as big as it looked.[22]

(21) 'Thus when he changes Democritus he makes things worse; when he follows Democritus there is nothing original, as is the case with the atoms, the void, and the images (which they term *eidôla*)[23] whose impact is the cause of both vision and thought. The notion of infinity (what they call *apeiria*) is wholly Democritus', as is the notion of innumerable worlds being created and destroyed on a daily basis. Even if I have no agreement with these doctrines myself, I would still rather Epicurus had not vilified Democritus, whom others praise, while taking him as his sole guide.

(22) 'Take next the second main area of philosophy, the study of inquiry and argument known as logic.[24] As far as I can gather, your master is quite defenceless and destitute here. He abolishes definition, and teaches nothing about division and classification. He hands down no system for conducting and concluding arguments; he gives no method for dealing with sophisms, or for disentangling ambiguities; he locates judgements about reality in the senses, so that once the senses take something false to be true, he considers that all means of judging truth and falsehood have been removed.[a]

(23) 'Pride of place he gives to what he claims nature herself ordains and approves, namely pleasure and pain. For him these explain our every act of pursuit and avoidance. This view is held by Aristippus, and the Cyrenaics[25] defend it in a better and franker way than Epicurus does; but I judge it to be

---

[20] Cicero is prejudicial in his presentation of the 'atomic swerve', whose nature and role are extremely controversial; for survey and discussion see W. Englert, *Epicurus on the Swerve and Voluntary Action*, Atlanta, Ga. 1987.

[21] Polyaenus of Lampsacus (*c.* 340–278/7) was an early convert to Epicureanism and became one of the four major founding figures of the school. Originally a prominent mathematician, he abandoned this when Epicurus, according to Cicero (*Varro* 106) convinced him that geometry was all false, since atomism precludes infinite divisibility.

[22] Cicero is again being unsympathetic; the Epicurean view is more complex. See J. Barnes, 'The size of the sun in antiquity', *Acta Classica Universitatis Scientiarum Debreceniensis* 15, (1989), 29–41.

[23] *Eidôla* are thin films of atoms which constantly stream from the surfaces of things and whose impact on our sense organs accounts for the ways we represent things in perception and thought.

[24] Epicurus 'abolishes' definition in rejecting traditional philosophical arguments about things' nature as futile, relying instead on direct evidence from the senses; this issue comes up below at 29 (and see note 31) and book II, 4 (and see note 6).   [25] See Introduction p. xviii.

[a] It is likely, given the abruptness of the transition to the next paragraph, that some text has been lost at this point.

the sort of position that seems utterly unworthy of a human being. Nature has created and shaped us for better things, or so it seems to me. I could be wrong, of course. But I am quite certain that the man who first won the name of "Torquatus" did not tear that famous chain from his enemy's neck with the aim of experiencing bodily pleasure. Nor did he fight against the Latins at Veseris in his third consulship for the sake of pleasure. Indeed, in having his son beheaded, he even appears to have deprived himself of many pleasures. For he placed the authority of the state and of his rank above nature herself and a father's love.[26]

(24) 'Take next Titus Torquatus, who was consul with Gnaeus Octavius. Consider the severity with which he treated the son whom he gave up for adoption to Decius Silanus. This son was accused by a deputation from Macedonia of having taken bribes while praetor in that province. Torquatus summoned him into his presence to answer the charge, and having heard both sides of the case, determined that his son had not held office in a manner worthy of his forebears, and banished him from his sight.[27] Do you think he acted thus with his own pleasure in mind?

'I need not even mention the dangers, the efforts, and, yes, the pain that the very best people endure for the sake of their country and family. Far from courting pleasure, such people renounce it entirely, preferring in the end to bear any kind of pain rather than neglect any part of their duty.

'Let us turn to cases that are no less significant, even if they appear more trivial. (25) Is it pleasure that literature affords you, Torquatus, or you, Triarius? What of history, science, the reading of poetry, the committing to memory of acres of verse? Do not reply that you find these activities pleasurable in themselves, or that your forebears, Torquatus, found theirs so. Neither Epicurus nor Metrodorus[28] ever offered that sort of defence, and nor would anyone who has any sense or is acquainted with Epicurus' teachings.

'As to the question why so many people are followers of Epicurus, well, there are many reasons, but what is most alluring to the masses is their per-ception that Epicurus said that happiness – that is, pleasure – consists in per-forming right and moral actions for their own sake. These good people fail to realize that if this were so then the whole theory is undermined. For once it is conceded that such activities are immediately pleasant in themselves,

---

[26] Titus Manlius Imperiosus Torquatus, a fourth century Roman, consul three times, legendary for strict and harsh rule-following, exemplified in various stories. Though abusively treated by his father, he loyally saved him from prosecution for it. He acquired the name Torquatus from the torque he took from a Gaul he killed in single combat in 361. Later, when his own son, serving under him, disobeyed orders to fight a similar duel, Torquatus had him executed on the spot.

[27] This happened in 141. The son thereupon committed suicide; his father refused to attend the funeral.

[28] Metrodorus of Lampsacus (331–278), one of Epicurus' original associates, regarded as a co-founding figure of the school.

without reference to the body, then virtue and knowledge will turn out to be desirable in themselves, and that is something which Epicurus would utterly reject.

(26) 'These are the aspects of Epicurus' position with which I take issue', I concluded. 'For the rest, I wish that Epicurus had been better equipped intellectually (you must surely agree that he lacks sophistication in those areas which go to make a person well educated), or that he had not at any rate deterred others from study – though I see that at least he has not deterred you.'[29]

I had made these remarks more to draw out Torquatus than to deliver a speech of my own, but Triarius then said with a gentle smile: 'You have pretty much expelled Epicurus in his entirety from the choir of philosophers. What have you left for him except that, however he may have expressed himself, you understand what he is saying? His physics is derivative, and in any case you dispute it. Whatever he tried to improve, he made worse. He had no method of argument. When he called pleasure the highest good, this firstly showed a lack of insight in itself, and secondly was also derivative. Aristippus had said it before, and better. Finally, you threw in his lack of learning.'

(27) 'Triarius', I replied, 'when one disagrees with someone, one must state the areas of disagreement. Nothing would prevent me from being an Epicurean if I agreed with what Epicurus said – especially as it is child's play to master his doctrines. Mutual criticism is therefore not to be faulted; though abuse, insult, ill-tempered dispute and wilful controversy seem to me to be unworthy of philosophers.'

(28) 'I utterly agree', interjected Torquatus. 'One cannot have debate without criticism; but one should not have debate involving bad temper and wilfulness. But I should like to say something in reply to your criticisms, if you do not mind.' 'Do you think', I replied, 'that I would have made them had I not wanted to hear your response?' 'Would you like me to run through all of Epicurus' teaching, or just to discuss the single issue of pleasure, on which our whole debate is centred?' 'That is entirely up to you', I said.

'Then here is what I shall do', he replied. 'I shall expound one question, the most important one. Physics I shall return to on another occasion, and prove to you both the notorious swerve of the atoms and the size of the sun, as well as the full extent of the criticisms and corrections that Epicurus made to Democritus' errors. But for now I shall discuss pleasure. It will certainly not be an original contribution. But I feel sure that even you will agree with it.' 'Rest assured', I said, 'that I will not be wilful. If you persuade me of your claims, I shall gladly assent.' (29) 'I shall persuade you', he replied, 'provided you are as fair as you are presenting yourself to be. But I prefer to speak con-

---

[29] Probably Cicero means us to think of a notorious saying of Epicurus' to his young follower Pythocles: 'Spread your sails, fortunate one, and flee all culture' (Diogenes Laertius 10.6).

tinuously rather than proceed by question and answer.' 'As you wish', I said, whereupon he began his discourse.[30]

'I shall begin', he said, 'in the way that the author of this teaching himself recommended. I shall establish what it is, and what sort of thing it is, that we are investigating. This is not because I think you do not know it, but in order that my exposition should proceed systematically and methodically.[31] We are investigating, then, what is the final and ultimate good. This, in the opinion of every philosopher, is such that everything else is a means to it, while it is not itself a means to anything.[32] Epicurus locates this quality in pleasure, which he maintains is the highest good, with pain as the highest evil. Here is how he sets about demonstrating the thesis.

(30) 'Every animal as soon as it is born seeks pleasure and rejoices in it, while shunning pain as the highest evil and avoiding it as much as possible. This is behaviour that has not yet been corrupted, when nature's judgement is pure and whole.[33] Hence he denies that there is any need for justification or debate as to why pleasure should be sought, and pain shunned. He thinks that this truth is perceived by the senses, as fire is perceived to be hot, snow white, and honey sweet. In none of these examples is there any call for proof by sophisticated reasoning; it is enough simply to point them out. He maintains that there is a difference between reasoned argumentative proof and mere noticing or pointing out; the former is for the discovery of abstruse and complex truths, the latter for judging what is clear and straightforward.

'Now since nothing remains if a person is stripped of sense-perception, nature herself must judge what is in accordance with, or against, nature. What does she perceive and judge as the basis for pursuing or avoiding anything, except pleasure and pain? (31) Some Epicureans wish to refine this doctrine: they say that it is not enough to judge what is good and bad by the senses. Rather they claim that intellect and reason can also grasp that pleasure is to be sought for its own sake, and likewise pain to be avoided. Hence they say

---

[30] From 29 to 42 Torquatus defends Epicurus' conception of our final end, pleasure, against misunderstandings; 42–54 outline the virtues; 55–65 defend Epicurus' end against the Stoics; 65–70 give accounts of friendship; 71–2 concludes.

[31] Torquatus begins, as a good Epicurean, by examining our *prolēpsis* or concept of pleasure. This is the idea we build up, as we learn the use of a word by reference to our experiences; it can be articulated as a belief and thought of as a mental image. A *prolēpsis* is clear and reliable as long as it is drawn from experience and not contaminated by our other beliefs. Thus our idea of pleasure is clear and accurate as long as we stick to experience, one reason for beginning here with infants, who have no beliefs to confuse their ideas of pleasure and pain. Belief and argument are, however, required to clear away misconceptions (para. 31). Torquatus conspicuously does not mention the Epicurean distinction between static and kinetic pleasure which will play a large role later.

[32] Epicurus here and in 42 clearly accepts that ethical theory is about a correct specification of our final end; see Introduction, pp. xvii–xix.

[33] This is what Antiochus at V, 55 refers to as 'visiting the cradle'; young children and animals, since they have no beliefs, are not influenced by false beliefs in their behaviour, which therefore reveals what our natural aim is. Both Stoics (in III, 16–17) and Aristotelians (in V, 30–1) reject the Epicurean claim here that this is in fact pleasure.

that there is as it were a natural and innate conception in our minds by which we are aware that the one is to be sought, the other shunned. Still others, with whom I agree myself, observing the mass of arguments from a multitude of philosophers as to why pleasure is not to be counted a good, nor pain an evil, conclude that we ought not to be over-confident of our case, and should therefore employ argument, rigorous debate and sophisticated reasoning in discussing pleasure and pain.

(32) 'To help you see precisely how the mistaken attacks on pleasure and defences of pain arose, I shall make the whole subject clear and expound the very doctrines of that discoverer of truth, that builder of the happy life. People who shun or loathe or avoid pleasure do not do so because it is pleasure, but because for those who do not know how to seek pleasure rationally great pains ensue. Nor again is there anyone who loves pain or pursues it or seeks to attain it because it is pain; rather, there are some occasions when effort and pain are the means to some great pleasure. To take a slight example, which of us would ever do hard bodily exercise except to obtain some agreeable state as a result? On the other hand, who could find fault with anyone who wished to enjoy a pleasure that had no harmful consequences – or indeed to avoid a pain that would not result in any pleasure?

(33) 'Then again we criticize and consider wholly deserving of our odium those who are so seduced and corrupted by the blandishments of immediate pleasure that they fail to foresee in their blind passion the pain and harm to come. Equally blameworthy are those who abandon their duties through mental weakness – that is, through the avoidance of effort and pain. It is quite simple and straightforward to distinguish such cases. In our free time, when our choice is unconstrained and there is nothing to prevent us doing what most pleases us, every pleasure is to be tasted, every pain shunned. But in certain circumstances it will often happen that either the call of duty or some sort of crisis dictates that pleasures are to be repudiated and inconveniences accepted. And so the wise person will uphold the following method of selecting pleasures and pains: pleasures are rejected when this results in other greater pleasures; pains are selected when this avoids worse pains.[34]

(34) 'This is my view, and I have no fear that I will be unable to accommodate within it your examples of my forebears. You recalled them accurately just now, and in a way which showed considerable amity and goodwill towards me. But your praise of my ancestors has not compromised me or made me any less keen to respond. In what way, I ask, are you interpreting their deeds? Are you imagining that they took up arms against the enemy and treated their sons, their own blood, with such harshness, with no consideration for utility or their own advantage? Not even wild animals behave in such a disorderly and turbulent fashion that we can discern no purpose in their movements and

---

[34] Torquatus is echoing Epicurus' *Letter to Menoeceus* 129: 'Sometimes we pass over many pleasures, when more discomfort follows for us from them, and we consider many pains superior to pleasures, whenever greater pleasure follows for us when we stand the pains for a long time'.

impulses. So do you really think that such distinguished men would have acted without a reason? (35) 'What their reason was I shall consider later. Meanwhile, I maintain that if they performed those undoubtedly illustrious deeds for a reason, their reason was not virtue for its own sake. "He dragged the chain from the enemy's neck." Indeed, and so protected himself from death. "But he incurred great danger." Indeed, but in full view of his army. "What did he gain from it?" Glory and esteem, which are the firmest safeguards of a secure life. "He sentenced his son to death." If he did so without a reason, I would not wish to be descended from someone so harsh and cruel; but if he was bringing pain upon himself as a consequence of the need to preserve the authority of his military command, and to maintain army discipline at a critical time of war by spreading fear of punishment, then he was providing for the security of his fellow-citizens, and thereby – as he was well aware – for his own.

(36) 'Now this principle has wide application. The kind of oratory you practise, and especially your own particular brand, with its keen interest in the past, makes great play of recalling brave and distinguished men and praising their actions for being motivated not by gain but by the simple glory of honourable behaviour. But this notion is completely undermined once that method of choice that I just mentioned is established, namely that pleasures are foregone when this means obtaining still greater pleasures, and pains endured to avoid still greater pains.

(37) 'But enough has been said here about distinguished people and their illustrious and glorious deeds. There will be room later on to discuss the tendency of all virtues to result in pleasure. For now I shall explain the nature and character of pleasure itself, with the aim of removing the misconceptions of the ignorant, and providing an understanding of how serious, sober and severe is Epicurean philosophy, notwithstanding the view that it is sensual, spoilt and soft.

'We do not simply pursue the sort of pleasure which stirs our nature with its sweetness and produces agreeable sensations in us: rather, the pleasure we deem greatest is that which is felt when all pain is removed. For when we are freed from pain, we take delight in that very liberation and release from all that is distressing. Now everything in which one takes delight is a pleasure (just as everything that distresses one is a pain). And so every release from pain is rightly termed a pleasure. When food and drink rid us of hunger and thirst, that very removal of the distress brings with it pleasure in consequence. In every other case too, removal of pain causes a resultant pleasure. (38) Thus Epicurus did not hold that there was some halfway state between pain and pleasure. Rather, that very state which some deem halfway, namely the absence of all pain, he held to be not only true pleasure, but the highest pleasure.[35]

---

[35] Torquatus is making use of, without having formally introduced, the Epicurean distinction between 'kinetic' pleasure and 'static' pleasure, the latter consisting in tranquillity and freedom from pain and disturbance. It is the latter which is our final end.

'Now whoever is to any degree conscious of how he is feeling must to that extent be either in pleasure or pain. But Epicurus thinks that the absence of all pain constitutes the upper limit of pleasure. Beyond that limit pleasure can vary and be of different kinds, but it cannot be increased or expanded. (39) My father used to mock the Stoics with wit and elegance by telling me how, in the Ceramicus at Athens, there is a statue of Chrysippus sitting with an outstretched hand, that hand symbolizing the delight Chrysippus took in the following little piece of argument: "Does your hand, in its present condition, want anything?" "Not at all." "But if pleasure were a good, it would be wanting it." "I suppose so." "Therefore pleasure is not a good."

'My father remarked that not even a statue would produce such an argument, if it could speak. Though the reasoning has some force against a Cyrenaic position, it has none whatsoever against Epicurus. If pleasure were simply the kind of thing which, so to speak, titillated the senses and flooded them with a stream of sweetness, then neither the hand nor any other part of the body could be satisfied with mere absence of pain and no delightful surge of pleasure. But if, as Epicurus maintains, the highest pleasure is to feel no pain, well then, Chrysippus, the initial concession, that the hand in its present condition wants nothing, was correct; but the subsequent one, that if pleasure were a good the hand would have wanted it, is not. For the reason that it did not want it was that to have no pain is precisely to be in a state of pleasure.

(40) 'That pleasure is the highest good can be seen most readily from the following example: let us imagine someone enjoying a large and continuous variety of pleasures, of both mind and body, with no pain present or imminent. What more excellent and desirable state could one name but this one? To be in such a state one must have a strength of mind which fears neither death nor pain, since in death there is no sensation, and pain is generally long-lasting but slight, or serious but brief. Thus intense pain is moderated by its short duration, and chronic pain by its lesser force. (41) Add to this an absence of terror at divine power, and a retention of past pleasures which continual recollection allows one to enjoy, and what could be added to make things any better?[36]

'Imagine on the other hand someone worn down by the greatest mental and physical pain that can befall a person, with no hope that the burden might one

---

[36] Torquatus is paraphrasing the first four of Epicurus' *Principal Doctrines:* '(1) What is blessed and indestructible neither has troubles itself nor produces them for anything else, so that it is affected by feelings neither of anger nor of gratitude. For everything of that kind is due to weakness. (2) Death is nothing to us; for what has been dissolved has no sensation, and what has no sensation is nothing to us. (3) The limit of magnitude of pleasures is the removal of everything that pains. Wherever there is pleasure, as long as it is there, there is nothing that pains or distresses or both. (4) What pains does not last continuously in the flesh. The extreme kind lasts the shortest time, while what merely exceeds pleasure in the flesh does not last many days. Ailments which last a long while contain pleasure in the flesh which exceeds what pains.' These were sometimes simplified down to the 'Fourfold Remedy': 'God provides no fears; death no worries; the good is easy to get; the dreadful is easy to endure.'

day be lifted, and with no present or prospective pleasure either. What condition can one say or imagine to be more miserable than that? But if a life filled with pain is to be above all avoided, then clearly the greatest evil is to live in pain. And from this thesis it follows that the highest good is a life of pleasure. Our mind has no other state where it reaches, so to speak, the final point. Every fear and every sorrow can be traced back to pain, and there is nothing other than pain that by its own nature has the power to trouble and distress us.

(42) 'Furthermore, the impulse to seek and to avoid and to act in general derives either from pleasure or from pain. This being so, it is evident that a thing is rendered right and praiseworthy just to the extent that it is conducive to a life of pleasure. Now since the highest or greatest or ultimate good – what the Greeks call the *telos* – is that which is a means to no other end, but rather is itself the end of all other things, then it must be admitted that the highest good is to live pleasantly.

'Those who locate the highest good in virtue alone, beguiled by the splendour of a name, fail to understand nature's requirements. Such people would be freed from egregious error if they listened to Epicurus. Those exquisitely beautiful virtues of yours – who would deem them praiseworthy or desirable if they did not result in pleasure? We value medical science not as an art in itself but because it brings us good health; navigation too we praise for providing the techniques for steering a ship – for its utility, not as an art in its own right. In the same way wisdom, which should be considered the art of living, would not be sought if it had no practical effect. As things are, it is sought because it has, so to speak, mastered the art of locating and obtaining pleasure. (43) (What I mean by "pleasure" you will have grasped by now, so my speech will not suffer from a pejorative reading of the term.)

'The root cause of life's troubles is ignorance of what is good and bad. The mistakes that result often rob one of the greatest pleasures and lead to the harshest pains of mental torment. This is when wisdom must be brought to bear. It rids us of terror and desire and represents our surest guide to the goal of pleasure. For it is wisdom alone which drives misery from our hearts; wisdom alone which stops us trembling with fear. Under her tutelage one can live in peace, the flame of all our desires extinguished. Desire is insatiable: it destroys not only individuals but whole families; often it can even bring an entire nation to its knees. (44) It is from desire that enmity, discord, dissension, sedition and war is born. Desire not only swaggers around on the outside and hurls itself blindly at others: even when desires are shut up inside the heart they quarrel and fight amongst themselves. A life of great bitterness is the inevitable result. So it is only the wise person, by pruning back all foolishness and error, who can live without misery and fear, happy with nature's own limits.

(45) 'There is no more useful or suitable guide for good living than Epicurus' own classification of desires. One kind of desire he laid down as

both natural and necessary; a second kind as natural but not necessary; and a third as neither natural nor necessary. The basis for this classification is that necessary desires are satisfied without much effort or cost. Natural desires do not require a great deal either, since the riches with which nature herself is content are readily available and finite. But there is no measure or limit to be found in the other, empty desires.[37]

(46) 'So we see that life becomes completely disordered when we err through lack of knowledge, and that wisdom alone will free us from the onrush of appetite and the chill of fear. Wisdom teaches us to bear the slings of fortune lightly, and shows us all the paths that lead to tranquillity and peace. Why then should we hesitate to declare that wisdom is to be sought for the sake of pleasure and ignorance to be avoided on account of distress?

(47) 'By the same token we should say that not even temperance itself is to be sought for its own sake, but rather because it brings our hearts peace and soothes and softens them with a kind of harmony. Temperance is what bids us follow reason in the things we seek and avoid. But it is not enough simply to decide what must or must not be done; we have also to adhere to what we have decided. Very many people, unable to hold fast to their own decisions, become defeated and debilitated by whatever spectre of pleasure comes their way. So they put themselves at the mercy of their appetites, and fail to foresee the consequences; and thus for the sake of some slight and non-necessary pleasure – which might have been obtained in a different way, or even neglected altogether without any ensuing pain – they incur serious illness, financial loss, a broken reputation, and often even legal and judicial punishment.

(48) 'On the other hand, those who are minded to enjoy pleasures which do not bring pain in their wake, and who are resolute in their decision not to be seduced by pleasure and act in ways in which they feel they ought not to, obtain the greatest pleasure by foregoing pleasure. They will also often endure pain, where not doing so would result in greater pain. This makes it clear that intemperance is not to be avoided for its own sake, and temperance is to be sought not because it banishes pleasures but because it brings about still greater ones.

(49) 'The same rationale applies in the case of courage. Neither hard effort nor the endurance of pain is enticing in its own right; nor is patience, persistence, watchfulness, nor – for all that people praise it – determination; not even courage. We seek these virtues because they enable us to live without trouble or fear, and to free our mind and body as much as possible from distress. Fear of death can shake to the roots an otherwise tranquil life; and succumbing to pain, bearing it with a frail and feeble spirit, is pitiable. Such

---

[37] A paraphrase of Epicurus' *Principal Doctrine* 29: 'Of desires, some are natural and necessary, others natural and not necessary, and others neither natural nor necessary but come about dependent on empty belief.' These desires are themselves called 'empty' at *Letter to Menoeceus* 127.

weak-mindedness has led many to betray their parents, their friends, in some cases even their country; and in most cases, deep down, their own selves. On the other hand, a strong and soaring spirit frees one from trouble and concern. It disparages death, in which one is simply in the same state as before one was born; it faces pain with the thought that the most severe pain ends in death, slight pain has long intervals of respite, and moderate pain is under our governance. Thus if the pain is tolerable, we can endure it, and if not, if life no longer pleases us, we can leave the stage with equanimity. Hence it is clear that cowardice and faint-heartedness are not condemned in their own right, nor courage and endurance praised. We reject the former because they lead to pain; we choose the latter because they lead to pleasure.

(50) 'Only justice remains, and then we will have discussed all the virtues. But here too there are pretty similar things to be said. I have demonstrated that wisdom, temperance and courage are so closely connected with pleasure that they cannot be severed or detached from it at all. The same judgement is to be made in the case of justice. Not only does justice never harm anyone, but on the contrary it also brings some benefit. Through its own power and nature it calms the spirits; and it also offers hope that none of the resources which an uncorrupted nature requires will be lacking. Foolhardiness, lust and cowardice unfailingly agitate and disturb the spirits and cause trouble. In the same way, when dishonesty takes root in one's heart, its very presence is disturbing. And once it is activated, however secret the deed, there is never a guarantee that it will remain secret. Usually with dishonest acts there first arises suspicion, then gossip and rumour, then comes the accuser, and then the judge. Many wrongdoers even indict themselves, as happened during your consulship.[38]

(51) 'But even those who appear to be well enough fortified and defended against discovery by their fellow humans still live in fear of the gods, and believe that the worry which eats away at their heart day and night has been sent by the immortal gods to punish them. Any contribution that wicked deeds can make to lessening the discomforts of life is outweighed by the bad conscience, the legal penalties, and the hatred of one's fellow-citizens that looms as a result. Yet some people put no limit on their greed, their love of honour or power, their lust, their gluttony, or any of their other desires. It is not as if ill-gotten gain diminishes these desires – rather it inflames them. They must be choked off, not reformed. (52) That is why true reason calls those of sound mind to justice, fairness and integrity. Wrongdoing is of no avail to one who lacks eloquence or resources, since one cannot then easily get what one is after, or keep hold of it even if one does get it. For those, on the other hand, who are well-endowed materially or intellectually, generosity is more appropriate. Those who are generous earn themselves the goodwill of

---

[38] Cicero seldom resists the chance to make a favourable reference to his consulship in 63, during which he uncovered an attempted coup by the disaffected aristocrat Lucius Sergius Catilina.

others and also their affection, which is the greatest guarantor of a life of peace.

'Above all there is never any reason to do wrong. (53) Desires which arise from nature are easily satisfied without resort to wrongdoing, while the other, empty desires are not to be indulged since they aim at nothing which is truly desirable. The loss inherent in any act of wrongdoing is greater than any profit which wrongdoing brings. Thus the right view is that not even justice is worthy of choice in its own right, but only in so far as it affords the greatest abundance of pleasure. To be valued and esteemed is agreeable just because one's life is thereby more secure and full of pleasure. Hence we consider that dishonesty is to be avoided not simply because of the troublesome turn of events which it leads to, but much rather because its presence in one's heart prevents one ever breathing freely or finding peace.

(54) 'So if not even the virtues themselves, which other philosophers praise above all else, have a purpose unless directed towards pleasure, but it is pleasure above all which calls us and attracts us by its very own nature, then there can be no doubt that pleasure is the highest and greatest of all goods, and that to live happily consists entirely in living pleasantly.[39]

(55) 'Now that this thesis has been firmly and securely established, I shall briefly expound some corollaries. There is no possibility of mistake as far as the highest goods and evils themselves – namely pleasure and pain – are concerned. Rather, error occurs when people are ignorant of the ways in which these are brought about. Pleasures and pains of the mind, we say, originate in bodily pleasures and pains – and so I concede your earlier point that any Epicurean who says otherwise cannot be defended. I am aware that there are many of this sort, albeit ignorant. In any event, although mental pleasure does bring one joy and mental pain distress, it remains the case that each of these originates in the body and is based upon the body.

'But this is no reason for denying that mental pleasure and pain may be much greater than physical pleasure and pain. For in the case of the body, all we can feel is what is actually now present. With the mind, both the past and future can affect us. To be sure, when we feel physical pain we still feel pain; but the pain can be hugely increased if we believe there is some eternal and infinite evil awaiting us. The same point applies to pleasure: it is all the greater if we fear no such evil. (56) It is already evident, then, that great mental pleasure or pain has more influence on whether our life is happy or miserable than does physical pleasure or pain of equal duration. But we do not hold that when pleasure is removed distress immediately follows, unless it is a pain that happens to take its place. Rather, we take delight in the removal of pain even

---

[39] Notice that Torquatus' account of all four standard virtues has revised ordinary views about them in a way favourable to the idea that they are practised for the sake of pleasure. Courage, for example, has been removed from the context of the need for self-defence and restricted to that of withstanding internal motives such as fear of death. These virtues make most sense in the unthreatening and co-operative context of an Epicurean community.

if this is not followed by the kind of pleasure that arouses the senses. One can see from this the extent to which pleasure consists in the absence of pain.

(57) 'Still, we are cheered by the prospect of future goods, and we enjoy the memory of past ones. But only fools are troubled by recollected evils; the wise are pleased to welcome back past goods with renewed remembrance. We have within us the capacity to bury past misfortune in a kind of permanent oblivion, no less than to maintain sweet and pleasant memories of our successes. But when we contemplate our whole past with a keen and attentive eye, the bad times will cause us distress, though the good ones happiness.

'What a splendid path to the happy life this is – so open, simple and direct! There can certainly be nothing better for a person than to be free of all pain and distress, and to enjoy the greatest pleasures of body and mind. Do you see, then, how this philosophy leaves out nothing which could more readily assist us in attaining what has been set down as life's greatest good? Epicurus, the man whom you accuse of being excessively devoted to pleasure, in fact proclaims that one cannot live pleasantly unless one lives wisely, honourably and justly; and that one cannot live wisely, honourably and justly without living pleasantly.[40] (58) For a state cannot be happy if it is engaged in civil strife, nor a household where there is disagreement over who should be its head. Still less can a mind at odds and at war with itself taste any part of freely flowing pleasure. One who constantly entertains plans and projects that compete amongst themselves and pull in different directions can know nothing of peace or tranquillity. (59) Yet if life's pleasure is diminished by serious illness, how much more must it be diminished by a sickness of the mind! And sickness of mind is the excessive and hollow desire for wealth, glory, power and even sensual pleasure. Additionally it is the discomfort, distress and sadness that arises to eat up and wear out with worry the hearts of those who fail to understand that there need be no mental pain except that which is connected to present or future physical pain.

'Yet there is no foolish person who does not suffer from one of these sicknesses; there is none therefore who is not miserable. (60) Consider also death, which hangs over such people like Tantalus' rock.[41] Then there is superstition – no one steeped in it can ever be at peace. Moreover foolish people are forgetful of past successes, and fail to enjoy present ones. They simply await success in the future, but because that is necessarily uncertain, they are consumed with anxiety and fear. They are especially tormented when they realize, too late, that they pursued wealth or power or possessions or honour to no avail, and have failed to obtain any of the pleasures whose prospect drove them to endure a variety of great suffering.

(61) 'Look at them! Some are petty and narrow-minded, or in constant

---

[40] A close rendering of *Principal Doctrine* 5.
[41] A Greek myth: Tantalus, for offending the gods (there are a number of different stories) was punished in the Underworld by being offered food and drink but either never being able to reach them or, as here, by being under constant threat of being crushed by a huge boulder.

despair; others are spiteful or envious, surly or secretive, foul-mouthed or moody. There are still others who are dedicated to the frivolity of romances; there are the reckless, the wanton, the headstrong, lacking at the same time both self-control and courage, constantly changing their mind. That is why there is never any respite from trouble for such people. So no fool is happy, and no one wise is unhappy. We support this maxim in a much better and truer way than do the Stoics. For they deny that there is any good except for some sort of shadowy thing which they call "morality", a term of more splendour than substance.[42] They also deny that virtue, which rests upon this morality, has any need of pleasure. Rather, it is sufficient unto itself as far as a happy life is concerned.

(62) 'But there is a way in which this theory can be stated which we would not only not repudiate but actually approve. Epicurus represents the wise person who is always happy as one who sets desire within limits; is heedless of death; has knowledge of the truth about the immortal gods, and fears nothing; and will not hesitate to leave life behind if that is best. Equipped with these principles, the wise are in a constant state of pleasure, since there is no time in which they do not have more pleasure than pain. They recall the past with affection; are in full possession of the present moment and appreciate how great are its delights; have hopes for the future, but do not rely on it – they are enjoying the present. They are entirely lacking in the faults of character that I just listed above. A comparison of their life with that of the foolish affords them great pleasure. If the wise suffer any pain, the pain will never have sufficient force to prevent them having more pleasure than distress. (63) Epicurus made the excellent remark that "Chance hardly affects the wise; the really important and serious things are under the control of their own deliberation and reason. No more pleasure could be derived from a life of infinite span than from the life which we know to be finite."[43]

'Epicurus considered that the logic of your Stoics provides no way of improving the quality either of one's life or one's thought. But he deemed physics to be of the very highest importance.[44] It is through physics that the meaning of terms, the nature of speech, and the rules of inference and contradiction can be understood. By knowing the nature of all things we are freed from superstition and liberated from the fear of death. We are not thrown into confusion by ignorance and by the chilling fear that often results from ignorance alone. Finally, we will even have a better character once we have learned what nature requires.

---

[42] Epicureans take a reductive, debunking view of the conception of virtue and morality which the Stoics and other philosophers defend.

[43] A paraphrase of two *Principal Doctrines*, 16 and 19.

[44] Perhaps maliciously, Cicero gives Torquatus a muddled account of the relation of the parts of philosophy, ascribing to physics both its own role and that of logic. The criterion 'sent from heaven' is an (absurdly deferential) reference to Epicurus' *Kanôn* or work on the basis of knowledge.

'Moreover, if we possess solid scientific knowledge, and hold to that criterion which has as it were been sent from heaven to enable us to understand all things, and to which we refer all our judgements, then we will never allow anyone's rhetoric to sway us from our views. (64) But if we do not clearly grasp the nature of the universe, then there is no way in which we will be able to defend the judgements of our senses. And everything that comes before our mind has its origin in sense-perception. If all sense-perceptions are true, as Epicurus' system teaches,[45] then knowledge and understanding are in the end possible. Those who do away with sense-perception and deny that anything can be known, are unable, once sense-perception is removed from the scene, even to articulate their own argument. Besides, once knowledge and science have disappeared, with them go any rational method for conducting one's life and one's activities.

'Thus physics gives us the courage to face down fear of death, and the strength of purpose to combat religious terror. It provides peace of mind, by lifting the veil of ignorance from the secrets of the universe; and self-control, by explaining the nature and varieties of desire. Finally, as I just showed, it hands down a criterion of knowledge, and, with judgement thereby given a foundation, a method of distinguishing truth from falsity.

(65) 'There remains a topic that is absolutely essential to this discussion, and that is friendship. Your view is that if pleasure is the highest good then there is no room for friendship. But Epicurus' view is that of all the things which wisdom procures to enable us to live happily, there is none greater, richer or sweeter than friendship. This doctrine he confirmed not simply by the persuasiveness of his words but much more so by his life, his actions and his character. The mythical stories of old tell how great a thing is friendship. Yet, for all the quantity and range of these stories, from earliest antiquity onwards, you will scarcely find three pairs of friends among them, starting with Theseus and ending with Orestes. Epicurus, however, in a single household, and one of slender means at that, maintained a whole host of friends, united by a wonderful bond of affection.[46] And this is still a feature of present-day Epicureanism.

'But to return to our theme, since there is no need to speak of individual cases: (66) I understand that friendship has been discussed by Epicureans in three ways. Some deny that the pleasures which our friends experience are to be valued in their own right as highly as those we experience ourselves. This

---

[45] Epicurus' claim that all perceptions are true (64) is a particular butt of Cicero's scorn, though the theory is less naive than is apparent here. See S. Everson, 'Epicurus on the truth of the senses', in S. Everson (ed.), *Epistemology*, Cambridge 1990, 161–83.

[46] Epicurean communities were famous for their closeness and mutual support, but it is probably malicious of Cicero to make Torquatus compare these to famous friendships like that of Theseus, mythical king of Athens and Pirithous his companion, and that of Orestes, son of Agamemnon and his friend Pylades, since these are examples of close and intense bonds between particular individuals, something Epicureans have reason to deplore, as being a source of anxiety and of laying oneself open to fortune.

position has been thought to threaten the whole basis of friendship. But its proponents defend it, and acquit themselves comfortably, so it seems to me. As in the case of the virtues, which I discussed above, so too with friendship, they deny that it can be separated from pleasure. Solitude, and a life without friends, is filled with fear and danger; so reason herself bids us to acquire friends. Having friends strengthens the spirit, and inevitably brings with it the hope of obtaining pleasure. (67) And just as hatred, jealousy and contempt are the enemies of pleasure, so too is friendship not only its most faithful sponsor, but also the author of pleasures as much for our friends as for ourselves. Friends not only enjoy the pleasures of the moment, but are cheered with hope for the near and distant future. We cannot maintain a stable and lasting enjoyment of life without friendship; nor can we maintain friendship itself unless we love our friends no less than we do ourselves. Thus it is within friendship that this attitude is created, while at the same time friendship is connected to pleasure. We delight in our friends' happiness, and suffer at their sorrow, as much as we do our own.

(68) 'Hence the wise will feel the same way about their friends as they do about themselves. They would undertake the same effort to secure their friends' pleasure as to secure their own. And what has been said about the inextricable link between the virtues and pleasure is equally applicable to friendship and pleasure. Epicurus famously put it in pretty much the following words: "The same doctrine that gave our hearts the strength to have no fear of ever-lasting or long-lasting evil, also identified friendship as our firmest protector in the short span of our life."[47]

(69) 'Now there are certain Epicureans who react a little more timidly to your strictures, though still with some intelligence. They fear that if we hold that friendship is to be sought for the sake of our own pleasure, then the whole notion of friendship will look utterly lame. And so these people hold that the early rounds of meeting and socializing, and the initial inclination to establish some closeness, are to be accounted for by reference to our own pleasure, but that when the frequency of association has led to real intimacy, and produced a flowering of affection, then at this point friends love each other for their own sake, regardless of any utility to be derived from the friendship. After all, familiarity can make us fall in love with particular locations, temples and cities; gymnasia and playing-fields; horses and dogs; and displays of fighting and hunting. How much more readily and rightly, then, could familiarity with our fellow human beings have the same effect?

(70) 'A third group of Epicureans holds that, among the wise, there exists a kind of pact to love one's friends as much as oneself. We certainly recognize that this can happen, and often even observe it happening. It is evident that nothing more conducive to a life of pleasure could be found than such an association.

---

[47] A translation of *Principal Doctrine* 28.

'All of this goes to show not only that the theory of friendship is not threatened by the identification of the highest good with pleasure, but it even demonstrates that the whole institution of friendship has no basis without it.

(71) 'So if the philosophy I have been describing is clearer and more brilliant than the sun; if it is all drawn from the fount of nature; if my whole speech gains credibility by being based on the uncorrupted and untainted testimony of the senses; if inarticulate children and even dumb beasts can, under the direction and guidance of nature, almost find the words to declare that there is nothing favourable but pleasure, and nothing unfavourable but pain – their judgement about such matters being neither perverted nor corrupted; if all this is so, then what a debt of thanks we owe to the man who, as it were, heard nature's own voice and comprehended it with such power and depth that he has managed to lead all those of sound mind along the path to a life of peace, calm, tranquillity and happiness.[48]

'He seems to you to lack education: the reason is that he thought all education worthless which did not foster our learning to live happily. (72) Should he have spent his time reading poetry, as you urge me and Triarius to do, in which there is nothing of real use to be found but only childish amusement? Should he, like Plato, have wasted his days studying music, geometry, arithmetic and astronomy? Those subjects start from false premises and so cannot be true. And even if they were true, they have no bearing on whether we live more pleasantly – that is, better. Should he really have pursued those arts, and neglected the greatest and most difficult, and thereby the most fruitful art of all, the art of life? It is not Epicurus who is uneducated, but those who think that topics fit for a child to have learned should be studied until old age.'

Torquatus then concluded: 'I have set out my own view, with the intention of hearing your opinion of it. I have never before now been given this latter opportunity, at least to my own satisfaction.'

---

[48] Torquatus ends with exaggerated personal deference to Epicurus, rather than further rational defence of his ideas.

Book II

(1) At this point they both looked at me and signalled that they were ready to hear me. I began by saying, 'Let me first of all beg you not to expect me to expound a formal lecture to you like a philosopher. Indeed this is a procedure I have never greatly approved of even in the case of philosophers. After all, when did Socrates, who may justly be called the father of philosophy, ever do such a thing? It was, rather, the method of those known at the time as sophists. Gorgias of Leontini was the first of their number bold enough, at a public meeting, to "invite questions", that is, to ask anyone to name a topic for him to speak on.[1] A daring venture – I would have called it impudent, had this procedure not been adopted later by our own philosophers.

(2) 'But we know from Plato that Gorgias and the other sophists were mocked by Socrates. Socrates' own technique was to investigate his interlocutors by questioning them.[2] Once he had elicited their opinions in this way, he would then respond to them if he had any view of his own. This method was abandoned by his successors, but Arcesilaus revived it and laid it down that anyone who wanted to hear him speak should not ask him questions but rather state their own opinion. Only then would he reply.[3] Now Arcesilaus' audiences would defend their position as best they could. But the practice with other philosophers is that a member of the audience states a view, and then is silent. This in fact is what currently happens even in the Academy.[4]

---

[1] Gorgias of Leontini (c. 485 to early fourth century) was one of the most famous 'sophists' or intellectuals who in the fifth century travelled round cities offering instruction in oratory and argument. Gorgias was renowned for elaborate set speeches, of which two survive, and also for the procedure described here, mentioned at Plato's *Gorgias* 447 c–d.

[2] Cicero, who sees himself as an Academic follower of Plato, contrasts Gorgias' procedure of holding forth about his own position with that of Plato's Socrates, who searches for the truth by investigating the claims of others, and arguing on the basis of what they accept.

[3] Arcesilaus of Pitane (316/15–241/40) as head of Plato's Academy turned it from positive doctrine to the sceptical practice of arguing only against the views of others, thus beginning the Sceptical Academic tradition, which Cicero sees as his intellectual tradition, and which is here presented as a preferable alternative to positive dogmatizing. See Introduction, pp. x–xii.

[4] The Academy had been defunct as an institution for some time at the dramatic date of this dialogue. Cicero may be thinking of Antiochus, who had set his school up as a non-sceptical successor to the Academy (see Introduction pp. xiii–xiv). Or he may have in mind his own procedure, as a follower of the Academy, in the *De Finibus*, where, despite his respect for the

One who wants to hear the philosopher's view says perhaps: "In my opinion pleasure is the highest good." The philosopher then puts the contrary position in a continuous discourse. Evidently, then, the one who had declared that such-and-such was their view did not really hold that opinion but simply wanted to hear the opposing arguments.

(3) 'Our procedure, though, is a better one. Torquatus stated not only what he thought, but why he thought it. I believe, however, much as I enjoyed hearing him speak uninterrupted, that it is none the less more manageable if one stops after each individual point and ascertains what each of the listeners is happy to concede, and what they would reject. One can then draw the inferences one wishes from the points conceded and reach one's conclusion. When, on the other hand, the speech races on like a torrent, carrying with it all manner of material, then there is nothing the listener can grasp at or get hold of. There is no way to check the raging flood.

'In philosophical inquiry, every discourse which is to proceed methodically and systematically must begin with a preface, like those we find in certain legal formulae: "The matter at hand is as follows." This enables the parties to the debate to agree on what the subject for debate actually is. (4) Plato set out this procedure in the *Phaedrus*,[5] and Epicurus approved of it and felt that it ought to be followed in any discussion.[6] But he failed to see the most obvious consequence. He says that he is not interested in defining his terms; but without this it can often be impossible for the disputants to reach agreement on what it is they are discussing. Consider the very topic that we are debating now. We are enquiring into the highest good. But can we really understand what sort of thing this is unless we have sounded each other out on what we mean by "highest" and what indeed we mean by the term "good" itself when we speak of the highest good?

(5) This bringing to the surface of what may be hidden, each item being clearly revealed, is definition. Even you occasionally resorted to definition without realizing it. You defined the highest, greatest and ultimate good as that to which all right actions are a means, while it is not itself a means to anything else. Excellent. If the need had arisen, perhaps you would have defined the good itself as that which is attractive by nature, or as what is beneficial, or helpful, or just pleasing. So if it is not too much trouble, and seeing that you do not altogether reject definition and indeed practise it when you want to, I

Socratic method of arguing, we do in fact have continuous speeches for and against the philosophical theories.
[5] *Phaedrus* 237b.
[6] Epicurus stresses that before discussing a topic, we must be clear about the concept or *prolêpsis* which we build up from experience as we learn the use of words (*Letter to Herodotus* 37–38; see book I note 31). However, he dismisses the kind of 'definition' of terms which other philosophers establish by argument, as being trivial and merely about language, not things. Cicero treats Epicurus' empiricism here as a rejection of proper philosophical method (cf. book I para. 22); the exchanges at 5ff. show that for Cicero Epicureans use the word 'pleasure' without having achieved reflective understanding of it.

should like you now to define pleasure, since that is the whole topic of our investigation.'

(6) 'Are you telling me', exclaimed Torquatus, 'that there is anyone who does not know what pleasure is, and who needs some definition to understand it better?' 'I would cite myself as an example', I replied, 'if I did not think that I understood pleasure well, and that I had a pretty firm conception and grasp of it. As things are, I would claim that Epicurus himself does not know what pleasure is. He vacillates, and despite repeatedly saying that we must take care to articulate the underlying meaning of our terms, he sometimes fails to understand what this term "pleasure" signifies, and what the substance is that underlies the word.'

Torquatus laughed and said, 'That really is a good one – the man who said that pleasure is the highest of all desirable things, the greatest and ultimate good, is ignorant of the nature and character of pleasure!' 'Well', I replied, 'either Epicurus does not know what pleasure is or the rest of the human race does not know.' 'How so?' he asked. 'Because everyone believes that pleasure is something that arouses the senses when experienced and floods them with a delightful feeling.' (7) 'So what?' he replied. 'Are you saying that Epicurus overlooks that kind of pleasure?' 'Not always', I said. 'Indeed sometimes he recognizes it all too well. I am thinking of his statement to the effect that he cannot even understand what is good or where it might be found except for the good obtained by eating, drinking, hearing sweet sounds and indulging in the more indecent pleasures.[7] Do you deny that he said this?' 'As if I am ashamed of it', he replied, 'and could not explain the exact force of his words.' 'I have no doubt', I said, 'that you could easily do that, and there is nothing to be ashamed of in agreeing with a wise person. Epicurus alone, as far as I know, dared to proclaim himself wise. I do not think Metrodorus did, though I believe that when Epicurus named him wise he did not refuse the honour. The seven wise men of old, by contrast, received their title not by their own vote but by that of all peoples.[8]

(8) 'In any event, for the time being I assume that in his statement Epicurus understood the term "pleasure" in the same sense as everyone else does. Everyone agrees that the Greek word *hêdonê* and the Latin word *voluptas* refer to an agreeable stimulus that gladdens the senses.' 'Then what more do you want?' he asked. 'I will tell you', I replied, 'and I am asking in order to learn rather than because I wish to criticize you or Epicurus.' 'I too', he said, 'would rather learn anything you have to contribute than criticize you.' 'Then do you recall', I asked, 'what Hieronymus of Rhodes says the supreme good is, by ref-

---

[7] In a notorious passage from *On our Final End* Epicurus says that he does not know how to conceive of the good if he leaves out the pleasures of taste, sex, sound and vision (fragment 67 Usener).

[8] Cicero ridicules what he sees as Epicurus' arrogance in thinking that he (and some other founding figures) had actually become a *sophos* or ideally wise and virtuous person. Epicurus did in many ways set himself up as an ideal for his school.

erence to which all other things ought to be judged?' 'I do', he replied. 'He says that one's ultimate aim is to be free from pain.'[9] 'Well then', I said, 'what was that same philosopher's view of pleasure?' (9) 'He held that it should not be sought for its own sake.' 'So his view is that pleasure is one thing, freedom from pain quite another.' 'Yes', he replied, 'and he is grievously mistaken. As I showed a little while ago, the upper limit of pleasure is the removal of all pain.'

'I shall consider the meaning of "freedom from pain" later', I said. 'But unless you are going to be utterly stubborn about it, you must surely concede that "pleasure" has a different meaning from "not being in pain".' 'Well, on this matter you will find me stubborn', he replied. 'For my position could not be more true to the facts.' 'Then tell me', I said, 'in the case of one who is thirsty, is drinking a pleasure?' 'Who could deny it?' 'Is it the same pleasure as having a quenched thirst?' 'No, it is quite a different kind. A quenched thirst is a "static" pleasure, whereas the pleasure of having one's thirst quenched is "kinetic".' 'Then why', I asked, 'do you use the same word for such dissimilar things?'[10]

(10) 'Do you not remember', he replied, 'what I said a little while ago,[11] that once all pain is removed, pleasure can vary in kind but not be increased?' 'I do indeed', I said, 'but though your language was well formed, its meaning was obscure. "Variation" is certainly a word in our language, and in its strict sense is applied to differences in colour, though it may be used derivatively for many kinds of difference. There may be variation in a poem or a speech, in one's behaviour or fortune, and pleasure too is often said to involve variation in the sense that quite different things may produce quite different pleasures. If that is the variation you were speaking of, I would understand it – I understand it even though you are not speaking of it. The variation you are speaking of is rather unclear: you say that the height of pleasure is to be free from pain, and that when we taste those pleasures which give the senses a sweet sensation, then we experience "kinetic" pleasure. It is this sort of pleasure, you claim, which brings variation, but fails to add to the pleasure of being free from pain, though why you call the latter pleasure at all is a mystery to me.'

(11) 'Can anything be more pleasant than being in no pain?' he asked. 'Let it be granted', I replied, 'that nothing is better (I will not query the point for the time being). Surely that does not show that a state of no pain, if I may call it that, is the same thing as pleasure?' 'Absolutely the same thing', he said, 'indeed the greatest pleasure, the very greatest possible.' 'Then if', I said, 'this

---

[9] Hieronymus of Rhodes (mid third century), a follower of Aristotle. Only a few fragments survive, and we have little background to his account of our final end as freedom from pain, a view which appears odd for an Aristotelian (cf. book v, 14).

[10] There is little on this important distinction in extant Epicurean texts, and it is much disputed. 'Static' pleasure is the pleasure of being in a state of having had one's desires satisfied and thus being untroubled and tranquil, which is the Epicurean final end. This passage suggests that 'kinetic' pleasure is the pleasure of having a desire fulfilled; other texts are more puzzling.

[11] Book I, para. 38.

is how you define the supreme good, as wholly constituted by freedom from pain, why is it that you are equivocal about maintaining, upholding and defending this? (12) Why do you need to drag pleasure into the company of the virtues, like a common harlot in a gathering of well-bred ladies? The very name arouses ill-feeling, notoriety and suspicion. That is why you Epicureans resort so often to saying that the rest of us do not understand what Epicurus meant by pleasure. This is a claim that tends to make my hackles rise whenever it is made (and it is not infrequently made), however good-natured I may be in debate. It is as if I did not know what *hêdonê* is in Greek, or *voluptas* in Latin. Which language is it that I do not understand? And how come that I do not understand it, whereas anyone you like who has chosen to be an Epicurean does?

'Your school indeed has the quite wonderful argument that there is no need for a would-be philosopher to be well read. Our ancestors famously brought Cincinnatus in from his plough to be dictator.[12] Now you are scouring every little village to gather in your collection of worthy but hardly erudite supporters. (13) Is it that they understand what Epicurus means and I do not? Let me show you that I do. Firstly, what I mean by *voluptas* is exactly what he means by *hêdonê*. We often have to search for a Latin equivalent to a Greek word with the same sense. No search is called for in this case. No Latin word can be found which captures a Greek word more exactly than *voluptas* does. Everyone in the world who knows Latin takes this word to convey two notions: elation in the mind, and a delightfully sweet arousal in the body.

'This elation is described by one character in Trabea as "excessive mental pleasure" and by another in Caecilius when he tells us he is "glad with every gladness".[13] But there is the following difference: the term "pleasure" is applicable to the body as well as the mind (in the latter case it is an example of vice according to the Stoics,[14] who define it as "the irrational exulting of a mind that takes itself to be enjoying some great good"), whereas elation and joy are not applicable to the body. (14) Every Latin speaker takes pleasure to consist in the perception by the senses of some delightful stimulation. The term "delight" may, if you wish, also be applied to the mind, since "to delight" can be used in either case, as can "delightful", which is derived from it. It must, however, be understood, that someone might say, "I am so elated that everything is in a whirl", and someone else might say, "Truly my mind

[12] In 458 Lucius Quinctius Cincinnatus, according to tradition, was called from the plough and appointed military dictator to defeat the invading Aequi; having completed the task in fifteen days he returned to the ploughing. Cicero uses the story to sneer at the Epicureans' alleged low intellectual level.

[13] Caecilius: see book I note 4. Trabea is a slightly earlier comedy-writer. Caecilius is the source of the second quotation in paragraph 14; the source of the first is unknown.

[14] An aside: the Stoics consider pleasure to be bad because it involves the false belief that something other than virtue is good. 'Joy' is what they call the affective state of the virtuous person who has the right belief that only virtue is good, while other things have a different kind of value.

is now in torment". The former is wildly delighted, the latter racked with pain, but there is room in the middle for neither joy nor anguish. Likewise, in the case of the body, between the enjoyment of the most sought after pleasures and the agony of the most intense pains there is the condition that is free of either.

(15) 'So have I demonstrated a sufficient grasp of the meaning of the terms, or am I still in need of instruction in either Greek or Latin? Suppose, however, I do not understand what Epicurus is saying. I do, I think, have a pretty good knowledge of Greek. So perhaps it is Epicurus' fault for using language in a way that is hard to understand. There are two circumstances in which this might be excusable: first, if it is done deliberately, as in the case of Heraclitus, "to whom the nickname 'the Obscure' attaches for his all too obscure narration on nature".[15] Second, if the difficulty is caused by the obscurity of the subject-matter rather than the words used, as with Plato's *Timaeus*. Now Epicurus, in my view, does not set out to avoid speaking plainly and directly. Nor is his subject difficult, like the physicist's, or technical, like the mathematician's. Rather it is a clear and straightforward topic, widely familiar to the public. Your claim is that people like me fail to grasp not what pleasure is, but what Epicurus means. This shows that it is not we who lack understanding of the meaning of the word "pleasure", but Epicurus, who uses language in his own way and has nothing to do with our standard usage.

(16) 'If he means the same as Hieronymus, who considers that the supreme good is a life without any trouble, why is his preference to talk of pleasure rather than freedom from pain, as Hieronymus does? Hieronymus at least understands his own meaning. If, on the other hand, he thinks that kinetic pleasure ought to be included (he calls the sweet sensation "kinetic" pleasure; the freedom from pain "static" pleasure), what direction is he going in? He cannot make those who have self-knowledge – that is, who have clearly perceived their own nature and senses – believe that freedom from pain is the same as pleasure. That, Torquatus, is to do violence to the senses, and to rip from people's minds an understanding of terms that is deeply ingrained. Everyone realizes that there are three natural states: first, to feel pleasure; second, to be in pain; and the third, in which I am currently, and I take it you are as well, is to be in neither state. One feels pleasure when dining well, pain when on the rack. Surely between these two extremes you observe a great multitude of people who are feeling neither pleasure nor pain?

(17) 'Absolutely not', he replied. 'All who are free from pain have pleasure, and I claim that this is the summit of pleasure.' 'So do you claim that in mixing a drink for another when one is not thirsty oneself one feels the same pleasure as the thirsty person who drinks it?' At this Torquatus said, 'An end to questioning, if you please. I told you my own preference right from the

---

[15] Heraclitus of Ephesus (late sixth to fifth century), philosopher of cosmic and human nature, who wrote in aphorisms in an evocative style, later notorious as an example of deliberate obscurity.

beginning, precisely because I foresaw this kind of dialectical quibbling.'[16] 'So you prefer to debate in the rhetorical rather than dialectical style?' I asked. 'As if', he replied, 'continuous discourse is only for orators and not for philosophers!' 'Zeno the Stoic shared your view', I said. 'He declared, following Aristotle, that the art of speaking is divided into two categories. Rhetoric is like an open palm, because orators speak in an expansive style; dialectic is like a closed fist, since the dialectical style is more compressed. I bow, then, to your wishes, and will use, if I can, the rhetorical style, but it shall be the rhetoric of philosophers rather than lawyers.[17] The latter is designed for a popular audience, and so is sometimes of necessity a little lacking in subtlety.

(18) 'You know, Torquatus, Epicurus despised dialectic. Yet it comprises in a single art a complete method for discerning the essence of each thing; for identifying its properties; and for conducting arguments rationally and systematically. In consequence, his manner of exposition is his downfall. He lacks all skill and care in making the points he wants to put across. Take the very topic we have just been discussing. You claim that pleasure is the supreme good. So one should start by explaining what pleasure is. Otherwise the subject of the investigation must remain unclear. If Epicurus had been clear about it, he would not have got into such difficulty. He would either have defended Aristippus' view, that pleasure is the sweet and gratifying arousal of the senses – even animals would call this pleasure if they could speak. Or if he preferred to use his own idiom rather than that of "All the Danaans and the Myceneans, sons of Attica",[18] and all the other Greeks whom this stanza cites, then he would have called freedom from pain alone by the name of pleasure, and thereby have disparaged Aristippus' position. Alternatively, if he were advocating both positions, as he in fact is, then he should have combined freedom from pain with pleasure and presented two ultimate goods.

(19) 'Many fine philosophers have in fact made similar conjunctions of ultimate goods: Aristotle combined the practice of virtue with prosperity over a complete lifetime. Callipho combined morality with pleasure, Diodorus combined it with freedom from pain.[19] Epicurus would have achieved an analogous result had he combined Hieronymus' position with Aristippus' venerable view. These two disagree with one another, and so each employs his

---

[16] Cicero presents Epicureans as unused to, and inept at, philosophical argument; this conveniently allows him to proceed with a continuous speech (see note 4 above).

[17] Cicero has no problem in putting rhetoric to philosophical use, though some philosophers, such as Plato in the *Gorgias,* had claimed that rhetoric and philosophy have sharply divergent aims. Here he claims the Stoics as allies. Stoic rhetoric, however, was notoriously remote from actual oratory, and in book IV, 7 Cicero has harsh words for it.

[18] From an unknown Roman tragic drama.

[19] These three 'combined final ends' come from the structure of Carneades' division; see Introduction, pp. xxiii–xxvii. Aristotle held the well-known position that virtue and external goods are both necessary for happiness, but we have very little information about the other theories, which are known to us mainly for the positions they occupy in Carneades' division. Callipho was probably second century; we have no indication which philosophical school he belonged to. Diodorus was a Peripatetic, but we know little else (cf. Book V, 14).

own individual highest good. Since they use Greek perfectly correctly, Aristippus does not count freedom from pain as pleasure when he makes pleasure his supreme good; and Hieronymus never uses the term "pleasure" to mean "not being in pain" when he lays down that his supreme good is freedom from pain. Indeed he does not regard pleasure as desirable at all.

(20) 'These are two distinct states as well, in case you think that the difference is merely verbal. One is that of lacking pain; the other, of having pleasure. You Epicureans attempt to create not just a single term on the basis of radically different states (something I might more readily tolerate) but a single state out of the two, and that is quite impossible. Since Epicurus espouses both, he ought to have put both to use – and in fact he does, while failing to mark them as distinct by his terminology. Thus he very often praises precisely the kind of pleasure that we all agree on calling pleasure, and is bold enough to claim that he cannot imagine any good unconnected with Aristippean pleasure. That is what he says in his treatise entirely devoted to the supreme good. Indeed in another work, containing concise distillations of his major views, a revelation, so it is said, of oracular wisdom, he writes the following words – they are, of course, well-known to you, Torquatus, since every Epicurean has learned the great man's *kuriai doxai*, these pithy sayings being considered of the utmost importance for a happy life. Consider carefully, then, whether I am translating this particular saying correctly: (21) "If those things in which the indulgent find pleasure freed them from fear of the gods, and from death and pain, and taught them the limits of desire, then we would have nothing to reproach them for. They would have their fill of pleasures in every way, with no element of pain or distress, that is, of evil."'[20]

At this point Triarius could contain himself no longer, and cried, 'Torquatus, I ask you, did Epicurus really say that?' (I think he knew full well, but just wanted to hear Torquatus admit it.) Torquatus, though, was undaunted, and replied with complete assurance, 'In those very words, though you fail to understand his meaning.' 'If he means one thing but says another', I exclaimed, 'I shall never understand his meaning. But what he understands he states plainly enough. If he is saying that the indulgent should not be reproached so long as they are wise, then his statement is ridiculous. It is as if he were saying that murderers should not be reproached so long as they are not avaricious and have no fear of the gods and of death and pain. Even so, what is the point of granting the indulgent this saving grace? It involves inventing a group of people who, despite their indulgent lives, would escape reproach from our philosopher supreme so long as they avoided the other flaws.

(22) 'But Epicurus, why are you not reproaching the indulgent for the very reason that their lives are aimed at attaining pleasures of any and every kind?

---

[20] A translation of number 10 of Epicurus' forty *kuriai doxai* or *Principal Doctrines*, which Epicureans learned by heart.

After all, according to you, the greatest pleasure is precisely to feel no pain. In fact, we shall find sybarites who are so lacking in respect for the gods that they will "eat from the votive dish" and so unafraid of death that the verse from the *Hymnis* is always on their lips: "Six months of life enough for me; in the seventh I pledge myself to Hell."[21] As for pain, they will take a draught of the well-known Epicurean remedy, "Short if it is severe; light if it is long." There is just one thing I cannot grasp, and that is how the indulgent can ever set a limit on their desires.

(23) 'What, then, is the point of saying, "I would have nothing to reproach them for if they set limits on their desires?" This amounts to saying, "I would not reproach sybarites if they were not sybarites." He might as well say that he would not reproach the wicked if they were good. Here, then, is our strict moralist, expressing the view that sensual indulgence is not in itself blameworthy. If pleasure really is the supreme good, then damn it all, Torquatus, his view is perfectly correct. For my part, I would resist your habit of imagining the kind of sybarite who vomits at the table and then has to be carried home from the party, only to return still queasy to the trough the following day. Such a person, as the saying goes, has seen the sun neither set nor rise, and ends up destitute, with their inheritance squandered.

'None of us thinks that that type lives a pleasant life. But think of those with taste and refinement, who use the best chefs and pastry-cooks, the finest fish, fowl and game. Such people avoid indigestion; "their wine is poured golden from a fresh bottle", as Lucilius puts it, "all rough edges mellowed by the wine-strainer".[22] A recital accompanies their meal, as do all the prerequisites without which Epicurus proclaimed that he did not know what goodness was. Let them have handsome boys too, to wait on them. Give them drapery, silver, Corinthian bronzes, all matching perfectly the room's ambience. Imagine sybarites of this kind, and I would still deny that they live well or happily.

(24) 'The upshot is, not that pleasure is not pleasure, but that it is not the supreme good. The renowned Laelius, a pupil of Diogenes the Stoic in his youth and later of Panaetius, was called wise not because he did not know what the finest flavours were (a wise heart does not mean a foolish palate), but because he considered it of little importance:[23]

> Sorrel, they dismiss you and know not who you are
> Yet Laelius the Wise used to sing your praises
> And rebuke our gluttons one by one

---

[21] *Hymnis* is a play adapted from Menander by Caecilius (see book I note 4).
[22] This and the following quotations are from Lucilius (see book I note 11). Publius Gallonius is a contemporary gourmand.
[23] Gaius Laelius (*c*. 190–after 129), Roman politician, praetor in 145 and consul in 140. He was a close friend of Scipio Aemilianus (see book I note 12), and shared his philosphical and intellectual tastes, acquiring the nickname *Sapiens* ('wise person' or 'sage'). Cicero makes him a character in his *On the State* (cf. below, para. 59) and he is the central character in *On Friendship*. On Diogenes of Babylon and Panaetius see book I note 7.

Well done, Laelius, wise indeed. The following lines also have it right:

> "Publius Gallonius," he cried, "With your bottomless craw
> What a wretch you are
> You have never dined well in your life
> Though you spend everything on lobster
> And sturgeon of immense size."

'The speaker here puts no value on pleasure, while affirming that one who makes pleasure the be all and end all cannot dine well. He is not, however, denying that Gallonius ever dined pleasantly – that would be false – but that he dined well. His separation of pleasant from good is that strict and severe. This leads one to conclude that all who dine well dine pleasantly, but that those who dine pleasantly do not necessarily dine well. Laelius always dined well. (25) What does "well" mean? Lucilius will tell us:

> Food well-cooked and seasoned
> But now for the main course:
> Honest conversation
> The result – if you ask – a pleasant meal

'And this because he came to dinner to satisfy nature's needs with a tranquil mind. So Laelius is right to deny that Gallonius ever dined well, right to call him wretched, even though all his energies were directed at the dinner table. Yet he does not deny that Gallonius dined pleasantly. Then why not well? Because "well" means uprightly, modestly and honourably, whereas Gallonius, by contrast, dined corruptly, disreputably and dishonourably. He did not therefore dine well. Not that Laelius ranked the flavour of sorrel higher than that of Gallonius' sturgeon. Rather, he was indifferent to fine flavour altogether. And this could hardly have been the case had he regarded pleasure as the supreme good.

'Pleasure must therefore be removed from the equation altogether, not just in the pursuit of right conduct but also to ensure that your language is suitably modest. (26) At any rate, we can hardly call pleasure the supreme good in a life when it is evidently not even the supreme good in a meal. But what does our philosopher say? "There are three kinds of desire: natural and necessary, natural but not necessary, and neither natural nor necessary."[24] First of all, this is a clumsy division. What were really two classes he has made into three. This is not dividing but splintering. Those who have learned the skills of analysis that Epicurus despised tend to put things thus: "There are two kinds of desires, natural and empty; the natural desires are further divided into necessary and unnecessary." That would have been the proper procedure, since it is a mistake to count a species as a genus when making a division.

---

[24] Cf. Book I para. 45, with note 34. Cicero's criticism of the division is not warranted by Epicurus' statements.

(27) 'Of course we should not press the point. Epicurus has no time for the niceties of argument, and his exposition lacks order. But we must tolerate his ways, so long as his views are correct. However, I can hardly commend, but barely endure, a philosopher who talks of setting limits on desire. Is it possible for desire to be limited? It needs rather to be rooted out and destroyed, or else desire of every kind might be legitimate. So we would allow greed within limits, adultery within bounds, licentiousness likewise. What sort of philosophy is it that offers not to expunge wickedness but to rest content with a moderate degree of vice? As far as the division itself is concerned, I do concede its substance, though I wish it had been drawn with more care. Let him talk of natural needs rather than desires. The latter term he should reserve for another occasion, to be put on trial for its life when greed, intemperance and all the major vices are discussed.

(28) 'The division is something he talks about frequently and expansively. I find no fault with him on that score. It is, after all, the mark of a great and famous philosopher to defend his doctrines boldly. However, he often seems to embrace pleasure in the everyday sense of the term rather too warmly. This sometimes lands him in grave difficulty, committing him to the view that no deed is foul enough to consider refraining from so long as it is done for the sake of pleasure and no one is watching. Should this make him blush (the power of nature is always decisive) he takes refuge in the claim that nothing can be added to the pleasure of one who feels no pain. But that static condition of not being in pain is simply not called pleasure. "I am not concerned with names." But the thing itself is totally different. "I can find many people, countless of them in fact, less inquisitive and troublesome than you are, who can easily be persuaded of anything I should wish." In that case, is there any reason to doubt that the greatest pain consists in feeling no pleasure, if the greatest pleasure consists in feeling no pain? Why is this not so? "Because the opposite of pain is not pleasure, but absence of pain."

(29) 'Here he fails to see that this provides the strongest possible argument against that type of pleasure in whose absence he claims not to understand what goodness is. This is spelled out as the enjoyments of flavours and sounds, and of various other activities whose names would need to be prefaced with an apology. This category, which our strict, austere philosopher recognizes as the only good, turns out to be not even worth seeking, since according to this selfsame thinker we have no need of it so long as we are free from pain! What a contradictory position! (30) If he had ever learned definition and division, if he had learned how to express himself properly or even to use words in their customary way, then he would never have fallen into such a hole. You can now see what is happening. He calls by the name of pleasure what had never been so called; and he turns two separate things into one. The "kinetic" sort of pleasure (this he terms those pleasures that produce, as it were, a sweet sensation) he will sometimes disparage to such an extent that

you would think it were Manius Curius speaking.[25] Yet on other occasions he will praise it so lavishly that he claims to be able to imagine no other good beside it. This is the kind of talk that should be dealt with not by a philosopher but by a censor. It represents a fault not simply in his language but in his morals too. He fails to condemn indulgence so long as it is free of unrestricted desire and fear. In so doing he seems to be on the lookout for recruits. Do you want to indulge? Become a philosopher first!

(31) 'I believe he traces the source of the supreme good back to the very birth of each living thing.[26] As soon as a living creature is born, it delights in pleasure and seeks it as a good, while shunning pain as an evil. He says moreover that the question of what is good and evil is best decided by reference to living things whose age has not yet corrupted them. This is the view that you expound yourself, and it is the language of the school that you support. But what a nest of fallacies! Which sort of pleasure, static or kinetic (to use the terminology we have learned from Epicurus, heaven help us), will the bawling infant use to determine the supreme good and evil? If static, then clearly its natural instinct is for self-preservation, which I accept. If kinetic, as you in fact claim, then there will be no pleasure too foul to be experienced. Moreover, our new-born creature will not be starting from the highest pleasure, which you regard as the absence of pain.

(32) 'Indeed Epicurus could hardly have obtained proof of this equation from looking at young children or even at animals, though he regards them as mirrors of nature. He could hardly have claimed that natural instinct leads them to seek the pleasure of feeling no pain. This is not the sort of thing that can arouse appetitive desire. The static condition of freedom from pain produces no motive force to impel the mind to act (on this point Hieronymus is also mistaken). Only the caress of sensual pleasure has this effect. So it is the fact that kinetic pleasure is attractive to young children and animals that Epicurus relies on to demonstrate that pleasure is what we naturally seek. He makes no appeal to static pleasure, which consists simply in the absence of pain. Surely, then, it is inconsistent to say that nature proceeds from one kind of pleasure, but the supreme good from another?

(33) 'In truth I have no faith in the judgement of animals. Their instincts can be corrupt without being corrupted. One stick may deliberately be bent and distorted, another grow that way. So too an animal's nature may not have been corrupted by bad upbringing but of its own nature be corrupt. In fact the young are not moved by nature to seek pleasure but simply to love

---

[25] Manius Curius Dentatus, consul in 290, died 260, successful Roman general and politician legendary for frugality and incorruptibility.

[26] After criticizing Epicurus' concept of pleasure, Cicero turns to his claim about infant behaviour; see book I para. 30 and note 30. Cicero here rejects Epicurus on the grounds, shared by the Stoics (book III, 16–17) and Antiochus (book V, 24–33) that the infant is motivated by self-love, having a conception of the kind of being it is; he goes beyond the Stoics in rejecting the evidence of animal behaviour.

themselves and to wish to keep themselves safe and sound. Every living creature, as soon as it is born, loves both itself and all its parts. It cherishes above
all its two major components, namely mind and body, and then the parts of
each. Both mind and body possess certain excellences. At first these are dimly
perceived, then incipiently distinguished, with the result that nature's
primary attributes are sought and their contraries rejected. (34) Whether the
former category includes pleasure or not is a difficult question. But it seems
to me the height of folly to think that it consists of nothing except pleasure,
with no room for the limbs or senses, for mental activity, bodily soundness or
good health.

'This must provide the basis for any theory of goods and evils.[27] Polemo,
and before him Aristotle, held that the primary attributes are those I just mentioned.[28] Hence the view of the Old Academy and the Peripatetics arose, to
the effect that the highest good is to live in accordance with nature, namely to
enjoy with the accompaniment of virtue the primary natural attributes.
Callipho added nothing to virtue except pleasure, Diodorus nothing but
freedom from pain.[a] The highest goods of all these thinkers I have mentioned
can then be deduced: for Aristippus it is pleasure pure and simple; for the
Stoics harmony with nature, by which they mean a life based on virtue, that
is, a moral life. This is further explained as a life that understands what it is
that happens by nature, and selects those things that are in accordance with
nature, their contraries being rejected.

(35) 'Thus there are three theories of the highest good which make no reference to morality: the first that of Aristippus or Epicurus, the second that of
Hieronymus, and the third that of Carneades.[29] There are three others – those
of Polemo, Callipho and Diodorus respectively – in which morality is combined with some other thing. Then there is one theory, whose author is Zeno,
which is non-complex and based entirely on decency, that is, morality. (As for

---

[27] Cicero here (34–44) classifies theories according to Carneades' division (see Introduction, pp.
xxiii–xxvii). This assumes that a moral theory must be established by reason; hence Cicero
criticizes Epicurus at 36–7 for his empiricism. Secondly, such a theory must appeal to an exist-
ing motivation of pleasure, freedom from pain or natural bodily and mental goods to establish
our final end. At 35 Epicurus is said to appeal to kinetic pleasure as our original motivation in
order to establish static pleasure as our final end. Thirdly, ethical theory should guide and
improve our lives. At 38 Cicero shows that in his view Epicurus' position will be eliminated;
the only serious debate is between the Stoics and the Aristotelians, over the issue of whether
happiness requires only virtue, or external goods as well. This view is reflected in the structure of *On Moral Ends* as a whole.

[28] Polemo (born *c.* 350, head of Plato's Academy 315/4–266/5) was head of the Academy
when its interests moved from metaphysics to ethics; Polemo seems to have made nature
the basis for ethics, and was later seen as the teacher of Zeno the Stoic. Here we see the influence of Antiochus' view that the Old Academy was in agreement with the Aristotelians in
ethics.

[29] Carneades as a sceptic held no theories of his own; this is one he put forward for the sake of
argument (cf. below, 42) to make his classification complete.

[a] There is apparently a lacuna in the text here, in which Cicero will have mentioned (at least)
Aristippus and the Stoics, in the light of the sentence that follows.

Pyrrho, Aristo and Erillus, their theories have long been dismissed.[30]) All these thinkers except Epicurus were self-consistent, their ultimate goods coinciding with their first principles. Thus pleasure was the ultimate good for Aristippus, for Hieronymus it was freedom from pain, and for Carneades it was the enjoyment of the primary natural objects. Now Epicurus said that pleasure was the primary object of attraction. If he meant by pleasure what Aristippus did, then he ought to have upheld the same ultimate good as Aristippus. But if the pleasure he made his ultimate good was that of Hieronymus, then he should have treated that same type of pleasure as the primary object of attraction.

(36) 'By claiming that the senses alone decide that pleasure is good and pain evil, Epicurus grants more authority to the senses than the law allows us when we sit in judgement on law-suits. We can only judge what falls within our jurisdiction. Judges tend when announcing their verdict to add the phrase, "if it is within my jurisdiction" – an empty phrase, since cases that are outside their jurisdiction are not brought within it by this utterance. What are the senses competent to judge? Sweetness and bitterness, smoothness and rough-ness, proximity and distance, rest and motion, squareness and roundness. (37) Hence a fair verdict can only be delivered by reason, assisted in the first place by knowledge of things human and divine, which is rightly called wisdom, and in the second place by the virtues, which reason puts in charge of every domain, whereas you want them to be a servant ministering to pleasure. After consulting these advisors, reason shall deliver its first decision: there is no place for pleasure either to claim sole occupancy of the throne of the supreme good that we are investigating, or even to sit side by side with morality. (38) The same verdict will be delivered on freedom from pain. Carneades too will be rejected, and no theory of the supreme good will be approved if it gives either pleasure or freedom from pain a role, or gives no role to morality.

'This leaves just two views. After thorough consideration of each, reason may determine that only what is moral is good, and only what is immoral is evil, all else being of no importance or of so little importance that it should be neither sought nor avoided, but merely selected or rejected. Or else reason might prefer

---

[30] These theories are ruled out, given Carneades' classification, because they provide no guid-ance in life; they are listed together on this ground also at 43, book IV, 43, 49, 60, and book V, 23. This is artificial. Pyrrho of Elis (*c.* 360–c. 270) was the founding figure for Pyrrhonian scepticism. He held that when an enquirer comes to see that considerations on either side of a claim are equally balanced, he experiences what was later called suspension of judgement; he can commit himself to neither. A criticism (which later Pyrrhonists countered) was that this left the person with no guidance in acting. Cicero puts this with the positions of the early Stoics Aristo and Erillus, mid third-century students of Zeno, who both denied that system-atic rules could be given for moral conduct and progress. Erillus probably stressed the intel-lectual side of the Stoic doctrine of virtue rather than independently setting up mere knowledge as our final end. Both Aristo and Erillus, rather than denying that they cared about anything other than virtue (as Cicero suggests) thought that correct choices could be made only in a non-rule-governed way by someone with complete and correct understanding of Stoic principles. Their theories faded after Chrysippus established what became Stoic ortho-doxy (see book I note 6).

the theory which is seen to include not just morality in all its splendour, but also the riches of nature's primary objects and of a perfectly rounded life. The verdict will be all the clearer if it has first been established whether the difference between these two theories is substantive or merely verbal.

(39) 'I shall now undertake the same task, using reason as my guide. I shall narrow down the competition as much as I can by assuming that all non-complex positions that leave no room for virtue are to be eliminated from philosophy altogether. That accounts for Aristippus and all the Cyrenaics, who did not shrink from regarding pleasure as the supreme good – I mean the kind of pleasure that arouses the senses with an intense sweetness. They had no time for that freedom from pain of yours. (40) These thinkers failed to realize that just as horses are born to run, oxen to plough and hounds to hunt, so humans are born to do two things, as Aristotle says: think and act, like a kind of mortal god. Their idea, by contrast, was that this divine creature was created to be a slow and lazy sheep, fit for grazing and the pleasures of procreation. What could be more absurd?

(41) 'So much by way of reply to Aristippus, who held that pleasure in the sense generally understood is not just the supreme but the only kind of pleasure. Your school takes a different view. But Aristippus, as I said, was wrong. The shape of the human body and the amazing powers of reasoning of the human intellect hardly indicate that human beings were born to do nothing but enjoy pleasures.

'Hieronymus must not be given a hearing either. He posited the same supreme good – namely freedom from pain – that you do sometimes, or in fact too often. Even if pain is an evil, being without is not sufficient for a good life. Ennius may say if he likes, "He who has no evil has more than enough good."[31] Let us none the less judge a life as happy not by the evils it avoids but by the goods it enjoys. Let us not seek this life in a surrender either to pleasure, as Aristippus does, or to freedom from pain. Let us seek it in action or in reflection.

(42) 'These same points serve to refute the supreme good of Carneades, though he proposed it less as a theory he espoused than as a weapon in his battle with the Stoics. It is, however, the sort of thing that, when added to virtue, may be thought to have some importance and to bring to absolute perfection the happy life, which is the whole object of our inquiry. Those, on the other hand, who combine with virtue either pleasure, which virtue values least of all, or freedom from pain, which even if devoid of evil is still not the supreme good, are proposing an unlikely combination. Moreover, I fail to understand why they proceed in such a mean and niggardly way. They act as if what they are adding to virtue has to be bought. So first they select the cheapest additions, then they distribute just one each, instead of combining with morality everything which nature would have deemed primary.

---

[31] From the tragedy *Hecuba* by Ennius (see book I note 4).

(43) 'Aristo and Pyrrho considered all such items valueless, resulting in their claiming that there was absolutely no difference between being in excellent health and being gravely ill. People long ago stopped bothering to argue against this position, and rightly so. It seeks to make virtue the only thing that matters, to such an extent that it is stripped of its power of choice and is given nowhere to start from or to rest upon. In consequence that very virtue they would cherish is destroyed. Erillus, in reducing everything to knowledge, saw one particular thing as good, but it was neither the best thing, nor could it be used to guide one's life. So Erillus too has long been discarded. Since Chrysippus, no one has so much as picked a quarrel with him.

'There remains your position. A contest with the Academics has little purpose, since they affirm nothing and as if despairing of certain knowledge propose to follow whatever is plausible.[32] (44) Epicurus is trickier, however. Firstly, he is a mixture of two different kinds of pleasure. Secondly, in addition to himself, his friends and the many subsequent defenders of his views, he has also somehow won over the group that possesses the lowest authority but the greatest power, namely the general public. Unless we succeed in refuting these opponents, all virtue, all decency and all genuine merit must be forsaken. Now that we have removed all the other contestants, the unfinished battle is not between Torquatus and me, but between pleasure and virtue. A philosopher as insightful and observant as Chrysippus did not take this battle lightly. Indeed he thought that the whole decision about the supreme good turned on a comparison between these two combatants. In my view, if I can show that there is a morality worth seeking for its own essence and its own sake, then your whole system collapses. So I shall begin by defining morality with such brevity as the occasion demands. I shall, then, Torquatus, so long as memory does not fail me, deal with each of your points.

(45) 'By "moral", then, I mean that which can justly be esteemed on its own account, independently of any utility, and of any reward or profit that may accrue.[33] Its nature can be grasped not so much by the formal definition I have just given, though that makes some contribution. Observe, rather, the common verdict of people in general, and the aims and actions of the finest individuals, who do a great many things not because they see any advantage ensuing, but for no other reason than that it is the decent, right and honourable thing to do. Humans differ from animals in a host of ways, but the greatest difference is this: they are endowed by nature with reason and with a sharp and vigorous intellect that is capable of performing a large number of operations simultaneously at high speed. This intellect is, as it were, keen-sighted

---

[32] Cicero emphasizes that as an Academic he is attacking Epicurus not from a position of his own, but from premises shared in any reasonable ethical debate. See, however, the Introduction, p. xii.

[33] From 45 to 77 Cicero criticizes Torquatus' account of the virtues in book I, 42–54; 78–84 criticize the account of friendship in book I 65–70; 84 to the end criticizes Epicurus' account of happiness, defended in book I 55–65 and 71–2.

in its ability to grasp the causes and effects of things, to compare similarities, to combine different items together, and to connect the future with the present, comprehending the whole course of a subsequent life. The same power of reason makes people want each other's company and has produced a natural congruence of language and behaviour. Beginning with the bonds of affection between family and friends, we are prompted to move gradually further out and associate ourselves firstly with our fellow citizens and then with every person on earth. As Plato wrote to Archytas, we bear in mind that we are born not just for ourselves but for our country and our people, so much so that only a small fraction of us remains for ourselves.[34]

(46) 'This same nature has also implanted in us a desire to know the truth, a desire most readily manifested in our hours of leisure, when we are eager to discover even what goes on in the celestial sphere. From the early stages of this desire we are led on to love truth in general, namely everything that is trustworthy, open and consistent; and likewise to hate what is deceptive, false and misleading, such as fraud, perjury, malice and injustice. Our own reason has an element within itself that is lofty and noble, better suited to giving orders than to taking them. It regards all human misfortune as not just endurable but trivial. Reason takes wing and soars, fearing nothing, yielding to no one, ever invincible.

(47) 'These three kinds of moral quality aside, a fourth one follows on from them, possessing the same beauty: the quality of order and restraint. We see its likeness in the grace and integrity of outward forms, and then apply it to all that is honourable in word or deed. The three noble qualities that I initially mentioned each makes its contribution to the fourth, which dreads thoughtlessness; shrinks from harming anyone with an insolent word or act; and is anxious not to do or say anything which may appear lacking in courage.

(48) 'Here, then, Torquatus, is a picture of morality that is rounded and complete, a whole constituted by these four virtues, which even you mentioned yourself. Yet your wonderful Epicurus says that he has no idea what nature or character is claimed for morality by those who judge the supreme good with reference to it. If their sole standard is morality, and pleasure is excluded, then according to Epicurus they are making empty noises (these are the actual words he uses[35]) and he cannot see or grasp that there is any meaning to be attached to the noise: in everyday language, "moral" means no more than what wins renown in the popular esteem. "And such renown", he says, "although sweeter than many pleasures, is still sought for pleasure's sake."

(49) 'At this point the gulf between our views becomes apparent. A famous philosopher, influential not just in Greece and Italy but all over the world,

---

[34] Pseudo-Platonic letter 9, 358a.
[35] Epicurus does often claim that discourse about virtue which fails to relate it to pleasure is 'empty' or meaningless (e.g. Usener 423, where people who do this are said to walk around babbling emptily about the good), since pleasure is our final end, that for the sake of which everything else is sought; cf. book I, 61 and note 38.

declares that he has no idea what morality consists in if not pleasure, unless perhaps it is whatever wins the acclaim of the crowd. In my judgement, though, what wins this acclaim is often actually immoral. On those occasions when it is not, what makes it such is the fact that the praise of the crowd is directed at something correct and praiseworthy in its own right. Even here the reason for calling it moral is not its praise by the crowd but its possession of a character that renders it praiseworthy in virtue of its own beauty and form, regardless of whether anyone knows it or acclaims it. That is why the same philosopher, overcome by the irresistible power of nature, says elsewhere what you said yourself a little while ago,[36] namely that one cannot live pleasantly unless one lives morally.

(50) 'What, then, does he mean now by "morally"? The same as "pleasantly"? So he means that one cannot live morally unless one lives morally? Or does he mean "with popular acclaim"? So is he then denying that he can live pleasantly without such acclaim? Is there anything more disgraceful than that the life of the wise should be dependent on the views of the foolish? What, then, does he understand by "moral" here? He can only mean what is praiseworthy for its own sake . To explain morality as a means to pleasure is to give it no more than a market value. When Epicurus makes morality so important that he denies it is possible to live pleasantly without it, he is not treating "moral" as a synonym for "popular" and stating that one cannot live pleasantly without popular acclaim. His notion of moral is nothing other than what is upright and praiseworthy in itself, by its own essence and nature, and on its own account.

(51) 'And so, Torquatus, when you mentioned how Epicurus cries out that no life can be pleasant unless it is honourable, wise and just, it seemed to me that you were taking a good deal of pride in this yourself. The very words possess a power drawn from the dignity of the things they signify. They had you standing tall, making the occasional dramatic pause, fixing us with your gaze by way of bearing witness to the fact that Epicurus occasionally praises morality. You were certainly well suited to using such words. And if philosophers did not use them, then we would have altogether no use for philosophy! It is through their love of these words, words like wisdom, courage, justice and temperance, which Epicurus so seldom utters, that those of the very highest ability have devoted themselves to the study of philosophy. (52) As Plato says: "The eyes are our keenest sense, but we cannot see wisdom with them. What blazing passion wisdom would have aroused for herself if we could!"[37] Why is this so? Surely not because wisdom has the shrewdness required to best procure pleasures? Why is justice praised? What, in other words, is the origin of the venerable saying, "someone you would trust even in the dark"? This specific proverb indicates the general rule that how we act should be unaffected by whether we are witnessed.

---

[36] Book I, 57, and see note 37.   [37] *Phaedrus* 250d.

(53) 'The deterrents to wickedness that you mentioned are really weak and feeble: the torments of a guilty conscience, the fear of the punishment that wrongdoers either incur or dread incurring in the future. We should not take as our model of wickedness trembling ninnies who torture themselves and fear every shadow whenever they do anything wrong. Picture instead a shrewd calculator of advantage, sharp-witted, wily, a sly old fox, practised at devising methods for cheating covertly – no witnesses, no accomplices. (54) So do not imagine that I am thinking of Lucius Tubulus. While praetor, he openly took bribes offered to influence his verdict when presiding over murder trials – so openly that the following year Publius Scaevola, the tribune of the people, brought the matter before the public assembly, where it was decided to launch an inquiry. Acting on the plebiscite, the Senate appointed the consul Gnaeus Caepio to conduct the inquiry. Tubulus, however, fled the country forthwith, without daring to defend himself – it was an open and shut case.[38]

'What we are investigating, then, is not wickedness *per se*, but a cunning wickedness, as exemplified by Quintus Pompeius when he repudiated the treaty he had made with the Numantians.[39] Nor are we concerned with the timid sort, but with the kind of person above all who pays no heed to conscience – not that conscience is something particularly difficult to stifle – a person who is stealthy and elusive, so far from self-incrimination as to give every appearance of regret at the wrongdoing of others. I did say that we were dealing with a sly old fox!

(55) 'I remember on one occasion I was with Publius Sextilius Rufus, who was discussing the following matter among friends.[40] He was the heir of Quintus Fadius Gallus. Fadius' will contained a statement to the effect that Fadius had asked Sextilius to pass on the whole inheritance to Fadius' daughter. Sextilius denied the arrangement, which he could do with impunity since there was no one to gainsay him. None of us believed Sextilius. It was more likely that he was lying than that Fadius was. Sextilius stood to gain from a lie, whereas Fadius had merely confirmed in writing that he had made a request that he was bound to make.

---

[38] This inquiry was lauched in 141 by Publius Mucius Scaevola; Lucius Hostilius Tubulus went into exile rather than face investigation.

[39] Quintus Pompeius, consul in 141 (reportedly through sharp practice). In 140 he had to negotiate a treaty in his unsuccessful attack on Numantia, a city in Spain, but on the arrival of another general repudiated it, and managed to get the Senate to approve this action.

[40] This case and the one in 58 depend on the fact that the Voconian law (169), a law restricting inheritances, had as its most notorious provision a clause preventing women from inheriting estates in the highest property bracket. The obvious unfairness to only daughters is criticized elsewhere by Cicero (*Against Verres* 2, 1, 107–14 and *On the State* 3, 17). Fadius had left his estate to Sextilius to evade the law; the will contained Sextilius' solemn promise (*fideicommissum*) to hand the estate over to Fadia, but at this date a *fideicommissum* was not legally enforceable. Sextilius shamelessly denies having made the promise, and refuses to hand the estate over, saying that as a magistrate he has sworn to uphold the laws, including the Voconian law. Sextilius has (at this date) the law on his side, and can even get approval from (carefully chosen) friends. See Suzanne Dixon, 'Breaking the Law to Do the Right Thing: the Gradual Erosion of the Voconian Law in Ancient Rome', *Adelaide Law Review* 9 (1985), 519–34.

'Sextilius added that he had actually sworn to uphold the Voconian law and did not dare act in breach of it, unless his friends thought otherwise. I was only a young man at the time, but many of those present were of great eminence, and not one of them thought that Fadia should get more than she was entitled to under the Voconian law. So Sextilius obtained a huge inheritance, not a penny of which would have come his way had he followed the opinion of people who placed morality and uprightness above any consideration of profit or advantage.

'Do you imagine that afterwards Sextilius was racked with guilt and remorse? Not a bit of it. On the contrary, the inheritance had made him rich and that pleased him no end. He reckoned that he had come into a fortune not just without breaking the law but actually in accordance with the law. In fact, if one is an Epicurean, one should look to make money even if there is some risk, since money brings many pleasures in its wake.

(56) 'Those who think that uprightness and morality are to be sought for their own sake must often take risks in order to uphold morality and decency. In the same way you Epicureans, who measure everything in terms of pleasure, ought to take risks in the interest of procuring great pleasure. Say that a large amount of money or a fat inheritance is at stake. Money of course procures countless pleasures. In view of this, your dear Epicurus ought to act in exactly the same way as Scipio did, if he wishes to attain his own highest good. Glory awaited Scipio if he could draw Hannibal back into Africa. In consequence, think of the danger he incurred![41] After all, the aim of his whole enterprise was honour rather than pleasure. So the wise Epicurean, when motivated by the prospect of large monetary gain, will fight just as hard if need be, and with good reason. (57) If the dastardly deed goes undetected, fine. And if it is discovered, any punishment will be treated with contempt, since Epicurean training teaches disparagement of death, of exile, even of pain itself. True, you Epicureans treat pain as unbearable when you are fixing some punishment for the wicked. But when you require the wise person to have more goods than evils, it becomes quite tolerable.

'You must imagine that our wrongdoer possesses not just cunning, but the immense power of a Marcus Crassus, though Crassus in fact generally deferred to his own sense of decency,[42] as our friend Pompey does

---

[41] Publius Cornelius Scipio Africanus (236–184), consul 205, famous Roman general in the war against Hannibal. He succeeded, against opposition, in carrying the war into Africa; in 204 he landed, winning battles against the Carthaginians and eventually defeating Hannibal there at Zama in 202.

[42] The reference here may be to Marcus Licinius Crassus, consul 70, third member of a political alliance (the first triumvirate) with Pompey and Caesar, which dominated Roman politics at the end of the Republic, who died in battle 55. It is, however, odd to find such a complimentary reference, given the very negative way this Crassus figures in book III, 75, where he is characterized by his two most notorious features, the great wealth he amassed (at a time of civil upheaval) and the ambition which led to his death in an unwinnable war. A better subject for the present reference would be the triumvir's father, but his name was Publius. At book V, 92, a Marcus Crassus is referred to who has been identified as the triumvir's grandfather, but

---

today.[43] We should all be thankful for Pompey's upright conduct, since he has the power to commit any injustice he likes with impunity. But there are innumerable injustices that anyone might commit without being caught. (58) Say a dying friend of yours asked you to pass on his estate to his daughter and failed (unlike Fadius) to put this in writing or even to tell anyone: what would you do? I am sure that you would pass the estate on. Perhaps Epicurus would have done the same, as Sextus Peducaeus did. Sextus was a scholar, and a thoroughly good and just man. In his son he has left with us an image of his own refinement and probity. Now the distinguished Roman knight Gaius Plotius of Nursia had made such a request of Sextus without anyone else knowing. Of his own accord Sextus went to Plotius' widow and explained, to her surprise, the instructions her husband had given him. He then handed over the estate.

'Now the question I am asking you is this: since you would certainly have done the same thing, surely you must realize that the power of nature is all the more affirmed? Even you Epicureans act in ways that make it evident that you are pursuing not pleasure but duty, and that an uncorrupted nature carries more weight than a corrupted reason. This is despite your claim that your only basis for action is your own pleasure and profit. (59) As Carneades says, imagine you know that a viper is lurking somewhere, and that someone whose death would benefit you is about to sit down on it unawares. You would be doing wrong if you failed to warn this person not to sit down. Yet you could do so with impunity. Who could prove that you knew? But I am labouring a point. It is obvious that if fairness, honesty and justice do not originate in nature, and all merely serve utility, then there is nobody good to be found. This issue is more than adequately discussed by Laelius in my work *On the State*.

(60) 'Apply the same principle to moderation or temperance, which means the curbing of one's desires in obedience to reason. If someone yields to an appetite in secret, does this mean that decency is preserved? Or rather, are there things that are shameful in themselves even if no loss of reputation ensues? And again, do brave soldiers go into battle to spill blood for their country only when a hedonistic calculation is in its favour, or is it rather a passionate spirit that drives them on? Well, Torquatus, consider which of our speeches about your great ancestor Torquatus, "the Imperious", the man himself would have preferred.[44] Mine, which stated that he acted entirely for his country's sake and never for his own, or yours, which, on the contrary, put everything down to his own self-interest? Suppose you had wanted to make

footnote 42 (*cont.*)
    again notable members of the Licinius Crassus family of the period tend to be called Publius rather than Marcus. (The triumvir's father and elder brother were called Publius, as was his own eldest son.) This and the book V reference are thus puzzling.
[43] At the dramatic date, Gnaeus Pompeius Magnus (106–48) is represented by Cicero as the powerful but constitutionally scrupulous leader of the Roman Republic; his readers would be aware of Pompeius' defeat by Caesar in the civil war and Caesar's assumption of unconstitutional power.   [44] Book I, 23, 34–6.

things even clearer and had stated more explicitly that he acted entirely for the sake of pleasure, how do you think he would have reacted to that?

(**61**) 'But I grant your view, if you like. Say that Torquatus acted for his own advantage (I prefer to talk of advantage rather than pleasure, especially with regard to such a great man). What, though, of his colleague Publius Decius, the first in his family to become consul?[45] When he charged at the massed Latin ranks, entrusting himself to death and setting his horse at a gallop, did he have any thought of his own pleasure? Where and when would he enjoy it? He knew he was to die at any moment, and he sought death with a greater passion than Epicurus would have us seek pleasure. Had his action not been worthy of the praise it garnered, his son would not have imitated it in his fourth consulship, nor his son in turn when waging war as consul against Pyrrhus. He too fell in battle, a third generation in succession to have made the supreme sacrifice for their country.

(**62**) 'Enough of examples. The Greeks provide few – Leonidas, Epaminondas, some three or four.[46] But if I were even to start counting our own heroes, I think I could ensure that pleasure handed herself over as virtue's prisoner, except that the sun would long since have set. Aulus Varius, who was regarded as a pretty severe judge, used to say to his colleagues on the bench, when yet more witnesses were being called to supplement those who had already appeared: "If we do not have sufficient evidence by now, then I do not know what sufficient is." You have certainly heard sufficient evidence from me. But take your own case – and you are more than worthy of your ancestors. Was it pleasure that led you, as a mere youth, to remove Publius Sulla from the consulship, and leave it open for your father? A man of the utmost courage, your father, a great consul and a great citizen before and after his consulship. It was his support that enabled me to carry through my own piece of business that put the common interest ahead of mine.[47]

(**63**) 'You thought you had made a fine case, when you put in one corner someone who had an abundance of the greatest pleasures and no pain present

---

[45] Publius Decius Mus, consul 340; in that year he ritually 'devoted' himself and the enemy Latins to death in battle at Veseris, charging the enemy to his certain death to bring about a Roman victory. His son of the same name, consul several times, performed the same ritual act in 295 at Sentinum, again with the result of victory for the Romans. His son, also of the same name, was killed in battle, also as consul, in 279, at Ausculum Satrianum fighting the Greek King Pyrrhus. It is less certain that he had devoted himself to death, and this time the Romans were defeated.

[46] Leonidas, king of Sparta, and three hundred Spartans, fought to their deaths against the invading Persians at the pass of Thermopylae in 480. Epaminondas, a Theban general, was the leader in breaking Spartan power in Greece; he was killed in the moment of victory at the battle of Mantinea in 362. Both are further described below at 97. Cicero clearly displays the Roman belief that Greeks are generally less patriotic and civic-minded than Romans. Cf. 67–68 (where, however, more patriotic Greek heroes are mentioned).

[47] A reference to Cicero's consulship in 63. Torquatus successfully prosecuted Publius Cornelius Sulla, a relative of Sulla the dictator, for electoral fraud in 65 after he was elected consul; Torquatus' father was thereupon elected consul. See also the reference to the elder Torquatus at 72 below.

or in prospect, while in the other corner was someone whose whole body was racked with the most severe pain, with no pleasure or hope of pleasure to mitigate it. Who, you asked, was more miserable than the latter or happier than the former? You then arrived at the conclusion that pain is the supreme evil, and pleasure the supreme good.

'Well, once there lived Lucius Thorius Balbus of Lanuvium, whom you would not remember. His rule in life was to have a plentiful supply of all the choicest pleasures that could be found. He had a great appetite for pleasure and a boundless ingenuity in procuring it. He was devoid of superstition, so much so that he would belittle the many shrines and sacrifices that his native region was famous for. And he had no fear of death, given that he died fighting for his country. **(64)** He paid no heed to Epicurus' classification of desires. His only limit was his own repletion. But he looked after his health. He took sufficient exercise to ensure that he came hungry and thirsty to the table. He ate food that was easily digested as well as beautifully flavoured. He drank enough wine for pleasure but not enough for damage. And he was a devotee of all the other pleasures without which Epicurus claims not to understand what goodness is. Pain was absent from his life, though had he encountered it he would have borne it with fortitude, albeit with the assistance of a doctor rather than a philosopher. He had a bloom in his cheeks and a sound constitution. He was extremely popular. In short his life was packed with every sort of pleasure.

(65) 'You would call Thorius happy. Your theory compels it. Yet I would rank above him – I dare not say. Virtue herself will speak on my behalf and will not hesitate to rank Marcus Regulus above that happy creature of yours.[48] Regulus left his homeland and returned to Carthage of his own free will, under no other compulsion than the keeping of a promise he had made to an enemy. Virtue proclaims him happier than Thorius even when he suffers the agonies of starvation and sleep deprivation while Thorius sips wine on his rose-strewn couch. Regulus had fought great wars, served twice as consul and celebrated a triumph. Yet he regarded those earlier achievements as less noble and illustrious than this final catastrophe, which he had embraced to maintain his honesty and integrity. To us listeners it seems like a miserable end, but it was full of pleasure for the one enduring it. It is not frolicking and merry-making that makes people happy, nor laughter and jokes, frivolity's playmates. People are happy often even when sad, if they are steadfast and true.

(66) 'When Lucretia was raped by the king's son, she proclaimed the wrong done to her before her fellow citizens, then took her own life. The indignation that her fate aroused in the Roman people led to the nation's liberation under

---

[48] Marcus Atilius Regulus, consul in 267 and 256, was captured fighting the Carthaginians in 255. Cicero makes much of the story, which may not be historical, that Regulus was sent to Rome to negotiate an exchange of prisoners, but opposed the exchange as not being in the Romans' interest, though he knew that on returning to Carthage he would be tortured to death (which he was). Regulus recurs in book v, 82 and 88, as an example of the unjustly suffering virtuous person, and his story features prominently in the third book of Cicero's *On Duties*.

the leadership and guidance of Brutus. Her husband and her father became the Republic's first consuls in her memory. Sixty years after our freedom had been won, Lucius Verginius, a poor and humble man, killed with his own hand his virgin daughter, rather than allow Appius Claudius, who at the time held the highest office of state, to have his lustful way with her.[49]

(67) 'Either you must denigrate their actions, Torquatus, or you must give up your advocacy of pleasure. What kind of advocacy is it, what sort of case does pleasure have, if no witness or supporter can be found among those of greatest renown? On my side the historical record brings forth people who spent their whole life striving for glory and were deaf to the call of pleasure. In your argument, history is silent. I have never heard Lycurgus mentioned in Epicurus' school, or Solon, Miltiades, Themistocles or Epaminondas, all of whom receive due acknowledgement from other philosophers.[50] Now that we Romans have begun to philosophize as well, our friend Atticus can supply us with a vast quantity of heroic names from his treasuries. (68) Is it not better to speak of them than to fill countless volumes in praise of Themista?[51] Let us leave that to the Greeks. We are indebted to them for philosophy and for all higher learning, but there are things that they may do which we should not.

'Consider now the dispute between the Stoics and the Peripatetics. The Stoics argue that there is nothing good except what is moral, the Peripatetics claim that there are certain bodily and external goods as well, even while attributing by far and away the greatest value to morality. Here we have a truly honourable contest, a tremendous clash. The whole dispute centres on virtue and its value. With Epicureans, by contrast, the cruder forms of pleasure seem to dominate the discussion, and Epicurus himself is the leading culprit.

(69) 'Believe me, Torquatus, if you take a hard look at yourself and at your own beliefs and values, you will no longer be able to defend Epicurean doctrines. You will be shamed, I tell you, by that scene which Cleanthes used to depict so skilfully in his lectures.[52] He would ask his audience to imagine a painting of Pleasure, decked out in gorgeous regal attire, sitting on a throne. By her side are the Virtues, depicted as servants who consider that their whole duty and function is to minister to Pleasure and whisper her warnings (if this

---

[49] Two semi-mythical stories from early Roman history, used frequently as illustrations of Roman refusal to knuckle under to arbitrary power.

[50] Public spirit is illustrated by Lycurgus, traditional founder of the distinctive Spartan way of life, and Solon, sixth-century Athenian statesman and reformer. Miltiades and Themistocles are Athenian generals famous in the early fifth-century wars against the invading Persians. For Epaminondas see above, note 46.

[51] Epicurus wrote a eulogy of Themista, an early Epicurean convert along with her husband Leonteus. Cicero is prejudicially contrasting Epicurean praise of uneventful female life with other philosophers' valuation of public spirit and self-sacrifice for the common good. The reference to Cicero's friend Atticus (see book I note 18) is sly: both as a Roman and as a lover of Athens Atticus is treasuring and writing up stories of heroism, while as an Epicurean he should reject them as misguided.

[52] Cleanthes of Assos (*c.* 330–230/29) was the second head of the Stoa (from 262/1). Less original than Zeno's other pupils, Cleanthes was famous for his religious fervour and forceful images, as illustrated here.

can be conveyed pictorially) to take care not to do anything unwittingly which might offend public opinion, or bring her pain in any way. "We Virtues", they cry, "were born to serve you. We have no other business."

(70) 'You will reply – and this is your strong point – that Epicurus denies that one can live pleasantly unless one lives morally. As if I care what he affirms or denies! My question rather is this: what can someone who treats the supreme good as pleasure affirm consistently? Can you explain why Thorius or Postumus of Chios or the king of them all, Orata,[53] should not have had the most pleasant lives imaginable? After all, Epicurus denies, as I said earlier, that an indulgent life is reprehensible unless it is silly enough to be filled with desire and fear. In any case, since he offers a remedy for both these conditions, he is offering a licence for sensual indulgence. Once they are removed, he admits that he finds nothing in a sybaritic life to censure.

(71) 'It is impossible, therefore, to defend or uphold virtue if everything is to be regulated by pleasure. One ought not to be regarded as good and just if one refrains from wrongdoing merely to avoid suffering harm. I am sure you know the verse that begins: "No one is righteous whose righteousness . . ."[b] Regard nothing as truer. Fear does not make one just, or at least keep one so if the fear vanishes. And one will feel no fear if one can keep the wrongdoing secret or has sufficient power to press on with it regardless. We will undoubtedly end up here with a preference to be thought good without being so, over being good but not being thought so. Hence your school – and this is its most shameful aspect – offers us a sham justice in exchange for the genuine article, and teaches us, in effect, to disparage our own trusty conscience and chase after the fallible suppositions of others.

(72) 'The same points are applicable with respect to the other virtues, all of which you base on pleasure's watery foundations. On such a basis, can we even call your great ancestor Torquatus brave? Although my bid to compromise you, as you put it, is doomed, I do take delight in mentioning your family and its name. Damn it all, Aulus Torquatus was a wonderful man and a marvellous friend to me. I have such vivid memories of him. Both you and Triarius are bound to be aware of his conspicuous loyalty and devotion to me at that critical period that everyone knows about. And yet, much as I want to be thankful and to be considered so, I should not have felt thankful had I not discerned that his friendship was given without thought of his own interest. You may of course say that everybody's interest is to do the right thing. But if that is what you say then I have won, since my claim and contention is that duty is its own reward.

(73) 'Your philosopher, however, will not permit this. He insists on squeezing the cash value out of things in the form of pleasure. But let us return to

[53] Famous gourmands of the time.

[b] In view of what Cicero goes on to say, this quotation (whose source is unknown) will presumably have continued 'is based on fear' or some such.

Torquatus of old. Was it for the sake of pleasure that he accepted the Gallic warrior's challenge and fought him in mortal combat on the banks of the Anio? Did he seize those spoils and don that chain that gave him his surname for any other reason than that he considered such action to be worthy of a man of courage?[54] If so, then I cannot consider him brave. Again, if modesty, restraint and a sense of shame – temperance, in a word – are held in place simply through fear of punishment and disrepute, rather than maintained because of their own purity, then every act of adultery, vice and lust will be given free rein just so long as it remains secret, avoids punishment or wins acceptance.

(74) 'As for you, Torquatus, think of how it looks: a man of your name, talent and distinction who dare not reveal in a public forum the real object of his actions, plans and endeavours; the real motive behind all his strivings; his real view about the highest good in life! Soon you will take up office. You will have to announce what principles you will observe in administering the law, and may even decide to follow tradition and say a few words about your ancestors and yourself. As you step up to the podium, would any reward be great enough to induce you to declare that your sole aim in office will be pleasure, and that your whole life has been dedicated to pleasure alone? You will say, "Do not think that I am so crazy that I would speak in this fashion before the ignorant." Well, make the same remarks in a court of law instead, or if you are afraid of the public gallery, then do so in the Senate. You never would. Why? Because such language is disgraceful, though evidently you think that Triarius and I are fit to hear it!

(75) 'This much I grant: the word "pleasure" has no great resonance, and perhaps we do not grasp its significance. You are always saying that we fail to understand what you mean by it. Of course we do – such a difficult and obscure concept! When you talk of "indivisible entities" and "inter-cosmic spaces", whose existence is neither actual nor possible, then we do understand. But pleasure, which every sparrow is acquainted with, we simply cannot grasp. What if I force you to admit that I know not only what pleasure is (it is an agreeable motion of the senses) but what you mean by it too? Sometimes your meaning accords exactly with the definition I have just given, and you call this "kinetic" pleasure, in so far as it is or produces a kind of change. At other times you say that the greatest pleasure is something different, something which cannot be added to. It is present when pain is totally absent, and you call it "static" pleasure.

(76) 'Well, let there be pleasure of this latter kind. Then you can say in any public meeting that the object of all your actions is to be free from pain. If you do not think that this way of putting things is sufficiently dignified or honourable, try saying that both in office and in life you aim entirely at your own advantage, at just whatever is expedient, or, in short, at what is in your own

---

[54] See above, note 44.

interest. Imagine the uproar, imagine your chances of a consulship, which at present you are almost sure of attaining! Are you, then, going to follow a principle that you can express in private and amongst friends, but which you dare not declare openly in a public forum? Indeed it is the Peripatetics and Stoics whose vocabulary is on your lips in the court-room and the Senate: "duty", "fairness", "worthiness", "integrity", "rectitude", "honour", "the dignity of office", "the dignity of the Roman people", "risk everything for your country", "die for your native land". When you utter these phrases, we dupes gasp in admiration. Meanwhile, you are laughing to yourself.

(77) 'Pleasure has no place in the company of such splendid and distinguished words. I refer not just to what you call "kinetic" pleasure and what everyone else – sophisticates, rustics, everyone, in fact, who speaks the language – calls "pleasure". There is no room either for your "static" pleasure, not that anyone apart from you Epicureans calls it pleasure at all.

'Consider, therefore, whether you ought to be using our words with your own meanings. If you were to manufacture some facial expression or way of walking to make you look more important, you would be insincere. Are you, then, to manufacture words and say things you do not mean? Or do you wear your beliefs like clothes – one set at home, another out of doors? You dress up just for show, but the truth is hidden within. I beg you, consider whether this is right. In my view true beliefs are those that are honourable, praiseworthy and noble, the sort which can be openly expressed before the Senate and the people, in every assembly and gathering. You should not be unashamed to think what you are ashamed to say.

(78) 'What room do you leave for friendship? How can one be a friend to others without loving them in their own right? What is love, from which the Latin word for friendship is derived, if not the wish that someone have as many good things as possible irrespective of whether any advantage accrues to oneself? "But", you might say, "it is to my advantage to have such a wish." To appear to have it, perhaps. But you could not actually have it unless you were a friend. And how could you be a genuine friend without feeling genuine love? Love in turn is not created by a rational calculation of advantage. It arises of its own accord, spontaneously. "But expediency is what I pursue." Then your friendships will last just as long as they are expedient, and if expediency brings a friendship into existence then it will destroy it too.

(79) 'What indeed will you do if expediency and friendship part company, as often happens? Do you abandon your friend? What sort of friendship is that? Do you maintain the friendship? Then you are being inconsistent, if you remember what you proposed as your grounds for friendship. "But if I abandon my friend then I might incur disapproval." But what makes such an act deserve disapproval except for the fact that it is base? So let us say that in view of this uncomfortable consequence you do not abandon your friend. You will still wish for his death to release you from an unprofitable tie. What, though, if far from providing any utility, the friendship actually requires you

to sacrifice your own property, run into all sorts of trouble, and even risk your life? Will you even then have no regard for yourself nor entertain the thought that each person is born to serve themselves and their pleasures? Will you offer your own head as hostage on a friend's behalf, as the great Pythagorean did before the Sicilian tyrant?[55] Will you be a Pylades, ready to die for a friend, and say that you are Orestes? Or be an Orestes and rebut Pylades, declaring your true identity? And if you cannot prove it, will you refrain from appealing against death for the two of you together?[56]

(80) 'Torquatus, you, I am sure, would do all of these things. I believe there is no illustrious deed you would forego through fear of pain or death. The question, however, is not what is consistent with your nature, but what is consistent with your philosophical position. The position you defend and the precepts you have been taught and espouse completely do away with friendship, however much Epicurus may, as he does, praise friendship to the skies. "But Epicurus himself cherished his friendships." Let me tell you that no one is denying that Epicurus was a good man, companionable and humane. It is his intellect that is in dispute here, not his character. We can leave to the frivolous Greeks the perverse practice of heaping personal abuse on those whose view of the truth differs from their own. Epicurus may have been a loyal and devoted friend, but if I am right (and I do not claim certainty) his thought lacked a cutting edge. "But he had many followers." (81) Yes, and perhaps deservedly so. But the testimony of numbers carries little weight. In every branch of learning, every field of study and every science, and in the case of virtue itself, what is best is also rarest. Epicurus himself was a good man, and many Epicureans were and are faithful friends who live their whole life through with integrity and dignity, letting duty rather than pleasure guide their decisions. All this goes to show, in my view, that morality is more powerful than pleasure. These people are a living refutation of their doctrines. Others are generally thought to speak better than they act. With these Epicureans it seems to be the other way round.

(82) 'This of course is off the point. Let us examine what you said about friendship. One of your claims I seemed to recognize as a dictum of Epicurus himself,[57] namely that friendship cannot be divorced from pleasure, and should be cultivated for the very reason that no life can be pleasant without it, since without it no life can be secure and free from fear. I have already said

---

[55] A famous story of friendship. Damon of Syracuse stood as surety for his condemned fellow-Pythagorean Phintias so that the latter could make a journey. Ready to be executed by the tyrant Dionysius I (or II; the story is told of both) he was saved by Phintias' last-minute return; the tyrant, impressed, pardoned both.

[56] The legendary friendship of Orestes and Pylades was referred to in book I, 65; here Cicero seems to have in mind a scene from a play on the subject by Pacuvius (see book I, note 4) which is referred to more fully at book V, 63.

[57] This does not correspond exactly to any dictum we possess; perhaps it is a reference to *Principal Doctrine* 27, which claims that friendship is the greatest provision by wisdom for happiness, or to *Vatican Saying* 23, which claims that every friendship is to be chosen (or is a virtue; the text is uncertain) although it takes its origin from benefits to us.

enough about that. You also offered a different, more humane view that originates with more recent Epicureans and not, so far as I know, from the man himself. Thus friends are in the first instance sought for their utility, but as friendships deepen, we come to love our friends in their own right, regardless of any expectation of pleasure. This view can be criticized on several grounds. Nonetheless, I will accept what they are offering, since it suffices for my purposes, though not for theirs. What they are saying is that sometimes right action is possible where pleasure is neither expected nor sought.

(83) 'You also suggested that some Epicureans say that the wise make a sort of pact amongst themselves to adopt the same attitude towards their friends as they have towards themselves, something you say is possible and has actually occurred, as well as being highly conducive to pleasure. If they did succeed in making this pact, then they should also make a pact to love fairness, moderation and all the virtues in their own right, without reward. At any rate, if it is for profit, gain and advantage that we cultivate friendships, and no bond of affection exists to make friendship desirable in its own right and by its own nature, based simply on itself, then surely we ought to prefer land and buildings to friends.

(84) 'You may well at this point remind us once more of those admirable words that Epicurus spoke in praise of friendship. However, it is not what he actually says that I am questioning, but what he is able to say consistent with his system and his principles. "Friendship is sought on the basis of utility." So do you really think that Triarius here could provide you with more utility than you would have if you owned the granaries at Puteoli?[58] Gather in all the usual Epicurean maxims: "Friends give protection." You can protect yourself well enough, the laws can protect you, and ordinary friendships can protect you too. You already have too much power to be easily slighted. You will avoid without difficulty incurring resentment and envy, given that Epicurus lays down rules for doing so. In fact with a handsome income at your disposal with which to demonstrate your largesse, the goodwill of hundreds will ensure you excellent protection and defence, even though you may lack the friendship of a Pylades and Orestes. (85) Who, as the saying goes, will you have to share your thoughts with, be they light-hearted or serious, and your deepest secrets? You will have yourself, best of all, and perhaps some ordinary friends as well. Granted, friendship has its advantages. Still, they are nothing compared to the usefulness of all that money. I hope you see, then, that when friendship is measured by the affection it generates from within, there is nothing to surpass it. If, on the other hand, you judge it in terms of profit, then the rent from a valuable estate will outweigh the closest friendship. So you must love me for myself, not for what I own, if we are to be true friends.

'I am spending too long on the obvious. It has been conclusively proved that if pleasure is the standard by which all things are judged then there is no room

---

[58] Puteoli (modern Pozzuoli) was the main import depot for grain, and the state granaries there represented immense wealth.

for either virtue or friendship. There is nothing much to add. Still, in case it should look like I have failed to respond to all your arguments, I shall make some brief comments on the rest of your exposition.

(86) 'The whole aim of philosophy is to lead us to a happy life. It is for this reason alone that people have turned to philosophy. However, different thinkers have different conceptions of happiness. You Epicureans identify it with pleasure, and likewise conceive of unhappiness entirely in terms of pain. So we must first examine what kind of a life your happy life is.

'You will, I think, grant that if there is such a thing as happiness, then its complete attainment ought to be within the power of the wise person. After all, if happiness, once gained, can be lost, then it cannot be happiness. No one can have confidence in the safe and secure retention of a thing that is fleeting and fragile. Those who doubt that their good is going to endure must of necessity fear that at some point they will lose it and be unhappy. But no one can be happy if worried about the most important thing in one's life. (87) So on this view no one can be happy. We generally speak of happiness not by reference to part of a life but to its whole duration. Indeed we do not strictly speak of a life at all that is as yet unfinished. It is impossible to be happy at one time and unhappy at another, since one cannot be happy if one regards unhappiness as a possibility. Once happiness is achieved, it is as permanent as the wisdom that brings it about. There is no need to wait until the end of our days, as Herodotus tells us that Solon warned Croesus to do.[59]

'You might respond, as you actually did, with Epicurus' view that temporal duration adds nothing to the happiness of a life, and that no less pleasure is enjoyed in a short space of time than in the whole of time. (88) But this leads to great inconsistency. Epicurus holds that pleasure is the supreme good, and yet claims that there is no greater pleasure to be had in an infinite period than in a brief and limited one. Now one who regards good as entirely a matter of virtue is entitled to say that one has a completely happy life when completely virtuous. Here it is denied that time adds anything to the supreme good. But if one believes that the happy life is constituted by pleasure, then one cannot consistently maintain that pleasure does not increase with duration, or else the same will apply to pain. Or are we to say that the longer one is in pain the more miserable one is, but deny that duration has any bearing on the desirability of pleasure? If so, why does Epicurus always speak of the deity as happy and everlasting? If we leave eternity aside, Jupiter is no happier than Epicurus, since both enjoy the supreme good, namely pleasure. "But Epicurus also experiences pain." Yes, but that is nothing to him. He claims that he would cry, "How delightful!" while being burned to death.[60] (89) So

---

[59] Herodotus, *Histories*, book I, 32.
[60] Cicero is unfair here. Epicurus is committed to the thesis that happiness (i.e. static pleasure or tranquillity) once achieved, cannot be increased (e.g., by length of time) but only varied; moreover, once achieved it is not lost merely because of physical pain. However, Diogenes Laertius reports that Epicurean happiness is proof even against the rack, but that the person tortured will scream and groan. Contrast book V, 80 and note 57.

in what respect is the deity superior except by being eternal? But what good has eternity to offer except supreme and everlasting pleasure? It is no use, then, speaking grandiloquently without being consistent.

'Your happy life is constituted by bodily pleasure – I shall add mental pleasure if you like, so long as that too is derived from the body, as you intend. Well now: who can guarantee that the wise person will have such pleasure continuously? The sorts of thing that produce pleasure are not within the wise person's control. Now that happiness does not consist in wisdom itself but in wisdom procuring things that bring pleasure, it becomes a wholly external matter and therefore subject to the whims of fortune. So the happy life turns out to be at the mercy of chance, despite Epicurus' claim that chance hardly affects the wise.[61]

(90) '"This is a minor point", you will object, "since the wise person is endowed with nature's own riches, and Epicurus has taught us that these are easy to obtain." Well said! I have no quarrel with that. Unfortunately, Epicurus' own statements are at odds with one another. He does say that there is as much pleasure to be derived from the humblest of provisions, the meanest food and drink, as there is from a banquet of the most sumptuous delicacies. If this amounted to a denial that the quality of one's supplies has any bearing on the happiness of one's life, then I would agree, enthusiastically so, since he would be speaking the truth. I take seriously Socrates' maxim that the best seasoning for one's food is hunger, and the best flavouring for one's drink is thirst. Socrates of course thought pleasure of no account. But it is hard to take seriously a thinker who makes pleasure his sole aim and lives like Gallonius the gourmet, while talking like Piso the Frugal.[62] He cannot, in my view, be saying what he really thinks. (91) He says that nature's riches are easily obtained, in as much as nature is content with a little. True enough, unless you place a high value on pleasure. "The cheapest things provide just as much pleasure as the dearest," he cries. The man must have lost his taste as well as his wits. Someone who has contempt for pleasure may legitimately claim to find sprats as good as sturgeon. But one who makes pleasure the supreme good is committed to judging everything by sensation rather than reason, and to calling best what gives the most delightful sensation.

(92) 'Let us, though, concede the point. Say he can obtain the highest pleasures at little cost or none. Say there is as much pleasure in the watercress that Xenophon tells us the Persians feed on as there is in the Syracusan banquets that Plato fulminates against so sternly.[63] Let pleasure be as easy to procure as you like. What, then, are we to say about pain? The torments of pain can be so severe as to render a happy life impossible – if, that is, pain is one's great-

---

[61] *Principal Doctrine* 16: chance has only a slight effect on the wise person, for the most important things in his life are organized by his reasoning.
[62] Lucius Calpurnius Piso Frugi, consul 133. He acquired the name 'the Frugal' because of his personal frugality and probity at a time of growing corruption; as tribune in 149 he set up the first enquiries into corruption overseas by Roman officials.
[63] Xenophon, *Education of Cyrus* I, 28; Plato, *Republic* 404d, Pseudo-Plato, *Letter 7*, 326b.

est evil. Metrodorus, who was virtually a second Epicurus, defines happiness in pretty much these words: "Good physical health, and the assurance that it will continue." Can anyone be assured that their good health will continue for a day, let alone a year? Fear of pain, as the greatest evil, is thus ever present, even if pain itself is not. After all, pain could begin any minute. How, then, can one live a happy life when haunted by fear of the greatest evil? **(93)** "Epicurus gives us a formula for disregarding pain." An absurd notion, that one can disregard the greatest evil. Still, what on earth is this formula? "The severest pain is short." What, to begin with, do you mean by "short"? And what, moreover, by "the severest pain"? Excruciating pain can last for weeks if not months. Or perhaps you mean the kind of pain that results in immediate death. Well, who is afraid of that kind of pain? What I want a remedy for is the sort of agony that I saw my dear friend Gnaeus Octavius, son of Marcus, undergo, not just on one occasion and briefly but often and for long spells. Heavens above, what torture he endured! It was as if all his joints were on fire. Yet, though he was undoubtedly suffering, I did not consider him unhappy, because such pain was not the greatest evil. If, on the other hand, his life had been awash with pleasure, but morally disreputable, then he would have been unhappy.

(94) 'I do not understand what you have in mind when you say that severe pain is short-lived and long-lasting pain is light. I see numerous instances of pain that is severe and long-lasting. There is a genuine way of coping with it, but not one that is available to you who do not value morality in its own right. Courage has its rules – they are virtually laws. The brave are forbidden to show weakness in the face of pain. It is therefore considered shameful, not of course to be in pain, which is inevitable from time to time, but to pollute the rock of Lemnos with the cries of a Philoctetes:[64]

> Till he makes the dumb stones utter a doleful sound
> Resonating with his weeping and wailing, his groans and lamentations

Let Epicurus work his magic on one who:

> Poisoned by the viper's bite
> Is racked in his guts by foul distress

'Epicurus will say, "Philoctetes, if your pain is severe it will be short." But Philoctetes has been laid out in his cave for ten years now. "If it is long-lasting it will be light; there will be periods of remission." **(95)** Firstly, this is often not the case. Secondly, what is this talk of remission when the memory of pain endured is still fresh and the thought of its imminent return torments one?" "In that case one should die." Perhaps that is best. But what about your

---

[64] The quotations (and the one at book v, 32) are from *Philoctetes* by Lucius Accius (170–86), prolific poet and dramatist, here probably drawing on the play by Sophocles (book I, note 4). Philoctetes, bitten by a snake on the way to Troy, was left behind on the island of Lemnos because of his agonizing and festering wound, which would not heal. After ten years he was rescued by the Greeks, who had discovered that his bow was necessary for the capture of Troy.

maxim, "There is always more pleasure than pain"? If that is true, consider whether you are not committing a grave wrong in recommending death. Better, then, to say that it is shameful and pathetic to succumb, crushed and broken, to pain. Your maxim "Short if it is severe; light if it is long" makes a nice jingle. But virtue, high-mindedness, courage and endurance are the real remedies for the alleviation of pain.

(96) 'I must not digress. So let me remind you of what Epicurus said on his deathbed, and you will see that his deeds are at odds with his words: "Epicurus sends Hermarchus his greetings.[65] I am writing on the last day of my life, but a happy one. My bladder and bowels are so diseased that they could hardly be worse." Poor man! If pain really is the greatest evil, that is all one can say. He continues: "Yet all this is counterbalanced by the joy I feel as I recall my theories and discoveries. If you are to live up to the goodwill you have shown towards me and towards philosophy since your youth, then be sure to take care of Metrodorus' children."

(97) 'This is a death to match that of Epaminondas or Leonidas. Epaminondas had defeated the Spartans at Mantinea and realized that he was mortally wounded. When the mists cleared he immediately asked if his shield was safe. His weeping soldiers told him that it was, and he asked if the enemy had been routed. When they again gave him the answer he was hoping for, he told them to pull out the spear which had pierced him. In a pool of blood he died, happy and victorious. Leonidas, King of Sparta, had to choose between shameful retreat and a glorious death. With the three hundred troops he had brought with him from Sparta, he confronted the enemy at Thermopylae.

'The death of a general is often glorious. Philosophers tend to die in their beds. Still, it matters how they die. Epicurus considered he was dying happy. Let him be praised. "My agonising pain is counterbalanced by my joy", he said. (98) Epicurus, I take seriously the words of any philosopher, but you are forgetting what you ought to have said. First of all, if the things that you claim bring you joy to remember, namely your writings and discoveries, are true, then you cannot be feeling joy, since what you are experiencing does not have its source in the body, whereas you are always saying that all joy or pain is on the body's account. "I am taking delight in events of the past." And what events are those? If they relate to the body, then I note that it is your theories that were counterbalancing your pain, not a memory of bodily pleasures. If they relate to the mind, then your claim that all mental delight can be traced back to the body is false. Moreover, why are you concerned with Metrodorus' children? What is there in this distinguished act of faithful service (this is how I regard it) that is connected with the body?

(99) 'Twist and turn as much as you like, Torquatus, but you will find nothing in this wonderful letter of Epicurus' that is in agreement with his

---

[65] Hermarchus of Mytilene (*c.* 330–*c.* 250), one of the founding figures of Epicureanism; he succeeded Epicurus as head of the school.

actual doctrines. He is, then, refuted by himself. His very character and probity rebut his theories. His concern for the children, his memory of fond friendship, his observance of his solemn duty even as he drew his last breath: all of this proves that the man had an innate goodness that was free of favour and needed no bidding by pleasure or reward. When we see the loyal service that the dying man rendered, what greater proof can there be that upright and honourable behaviour is desirable in its own right?

(100) 'I do consider the letter I have just translated virtually word for word to be highly laudable, even though it is utterly inconsistent with the central tenets of Epicurus' thought.[66] His will, however, I consider to be at odds not only with the dignity of philosophy but with his own views. He frequently presented the following argument at length, and gives us a plain and concise version of it in the work I mentioned a little while ago: "Death does not affect us. For what has been dissolved has no sensation. And what has no sensation in no way affects us."[67] This might have been more carefully put. The phrase "what has been dissolved has no sensation" does not make it obvious what it is that has been dissolved. (101) Still, I know what he meant to say. All sensation is extinguished at dissolution, that is, at death, and nothing that remains has any effect on us at all. If that is so, what is Epicurus doing when he stipulates so carefully and precisely in his will, "That Amynomachus and Timocrates, my heirs, after consultation with Hermarchus, provide a sufficient sum for the celebration of the anniversary of my birth every year in the month of Gamelion, and provide likewise a sum for a feast to be held on the twentieth day of each month for my fellow students in philosophy, to preserve the memory of Metrodorus and me."

(102) 'I have to admit that these are the sentiments of a good and humane man. But a wise man, and especially a natural scientist, which Epicurus claims to be, should not be thinking that anyone has an anniversary. Can the identical day, once it has occurred, occur time and again? Of course not. A similar day? Not even that, except perhaps after an interval of many thousands of years when all the stars return to their original positions at the same time. It is not the case, then, that anyone has an anniversary. "But the anniversary of his birth is observed!" I am well aware of that! So be it. But celebrated after his death? And provided for in his will when he had issued the oracular pronouncement that nothing affects us when we are dead? This is surely unworthy of someone who with his mind supposedly roamed countless universes and infinite space, without border or limit![68] Did Democritus make a similar

---

[66] However, at *Tusculan Disputations* book 5, 75, Cicero describes this famous letter as hopelessly unrealistic, comparing it to an attempt to deal with overheating by remembering a cold bath.

[67] A famous Epicurean claim, stated in *Principal Doctrine* 2 and *Letter to Menoeceus* 124–5. Epicurus' provisions for being remembered after death are not inconsistent with this; they are to provide future Epicureans with a role model.

[68] Perhaps a reference to lines (book 1, 72–74) from the Epicurean poem (known to Cicero) by Titus Lucretius Carus, in which the 'lively power' of Epicurus' mind is extolled, and said to pass 'far beyond the flaming walls of the world', so that Epicurus 'traversed the immeasurable universe in thought and mind'.

request? – I leave aside others and mention here the one philosopher whom he respected.

(103) 'If you must mark such a day, should it be the day on which he was born rather than the day he became wise? "Well", you will reply, "he could not have become wise had he never been born." By the same token, he could not have become wise had his grandmother never been born. The entire notion of wishing to be commemorated at feasts after one's death is alien to persons of learning. How you actually celebrate these occasions, and the witticisms you attract from those of a humorous disposition, is best left unsaid – we do not want to come to blows. I will say just this: it is more appropriate for you to celebrate Epicurus' birthday than it was for him to stipulate its celebration in his will.

(104) 'I must keep to the point, though. We were discussing pain when we were side-tracked by Epicurus' letter. The whole matter can now be expressed in a syllogism: whoever is afflicted by the greatest evil cannot at that time be happy; the wise person is always happy, though sometimes afflicted by pain; therefore pain is not the greatest evil.

'Now what is meant by saying that the wise person never forgets past goods, but should never remember past evils? Is what we remember really within our control? Themistocles, at any rate, when Simonides or some such person offered to teach him the art of memory, replied, "I would rather learn the art of forgetting. I remember even what I would prefer not to, and cannot forget what I would like to."[69] (105) However great his ingenuity, Epicurus exceeded his authority as a philosopher in instructing us not to remember. You, Torquatus, would be as imperious as your ancestor, or more so, if you commanded me to do the impossible. What indeed if some memories of past evils are actually pleasant? Some proverbs ring rather truer than your doctrines. There is the familiar saying, "A task completed is a pleasant one." Euripides puts it well (I shall try to render it in Latin; you all know the Greek): "Sweet is the memory of labours past."[70]

'Let us return, however, to the topic of past goods. When Gaius Marius was a penniless exile up to his neck in the swamps, he would soothe his distress by remembering his past victories.[71] If this is the sort of thing you had in mind, I would give heed and indeed thoroughly approve. The wise person's happiness could not be perfectly realized if every good thought or action were

---

[69] Simonides of Ceos, a fifth-century poet. Themistocles, an Athenian politician, was one of the architects of the Greeks' defence against the Persian invasion, but was later driven out of Athens and died under the protection of the Persian king; he is the archetype of the politician with a chequered career, not all welcome in memory.
[70] From Euripides' now lost play *Andromeda*.
[71] Gaius Marius (157–86), from Cicero's home town of Arpinum, and like him a 'new man' without established family connections in politics, was a spectacularly successful reformer of the army and general in a variety of campaigns; his military success led to a political career with equally dramatic successes, including six consulships before the flight from Rome referred to here after a coup by his opponent Sulla in 88. Marius returned to wreak vengeance, but soon died. Cicero composed an epic poem about Marius, of which little survives.

wiped out by forgetfulness as soon as it occurred. (106) But as far as you are concerned, it is the memory of pleasures enjoyed that makes for one's happiness, and bodily pleasures at that. Or if not, then it is false that all mental pleasures derive from an association with the body. But if bodily pleasures give delight even when past, then it is hard to see why Aristotle poured such scorn on the epitaph of Sardanapallus in which that famous King of Syria boasts that he has taken all his sensual pleasures with him.[72] After all, how could the kind of pleasure which even in life lasts no longer than the period of its actual enjoyment survive after death? Bodily pleasures are fleeting and fly off in an instant. More often than not they leave us with regrets rather than good memories. Scipio Africanus was the happy one when he addressed his nation with the words, "Rome, the battle is over", and subsequently uttered the ringing phrase, "My struggles have secured your defences."[73] Africanus takes delight in his past struggles, you bid us take delight in past pleasures. Moreover, he is recalling things unconnected with bodily feelings, while you are completely mired in the body.

(107) 'How, then, can you Epicureans defend the claim that every pleasure or pain of the mind is related to a pleasure or pain of the body? Torquatus (I know full well who I am addressing), does nothing ever delight you on its own account? I pass over integrity, morality and the virtues' particular beauty, which I discussed earlier. Let me suggest these more trivial cases: reading or writing a poem or a speech; the study of history or geography; a sculpture or a painting; a beautiful view; the thrill of the games or of the chase; Lucullus' country house[74] – I had better not say yours, else I would give you a loophole, since you could say it had a connection with your bodily pleasure. Do you connect all these examples with the body? Or is there anything that delights you in its own right? If you persist in relating all my examples to the body you will have shown nothing but your stubbornness. If you concede my point, then you will have totally abandoned Epicurus' conception of pleasure.

(108) 'I turn to your contention that the pleasures and pains of the mind are greater than those of the body, since the mind can range over past, present and future, while the body is only aware of the present moment. This is as implausible as claiming that someone who is pleased for me will be more pleased than I am myself. You attempt to ground the wise person's happiness on the notion that wise people experience the greatest pleasures of the mind, and that these are immeasurably greater than the pleasures of the body. But this presents you with an unforeseen consequence, namely that the mental pains they experience will also be immeasurably greater than those of the

---

[72] From one of Aristotle's more popular works, now lost. Aristotle is dismissive of Sardanapallus at *Nicomachean Ethics* I, 5.

[73] Probably from the poem *Annals* by Quintus Ennius (book I note 4). For Scipio Africanus see above, note 41.

[74] Lucius Licinius Lucullus, consul 74, an able general and administrator who won many victories in the East, but was unable to achieve solid influence in politics, and retired into a life of refined luxury which became famous.

body. It follows that those whom you wish always to be happy will on occasions be miserable. Indeed you will never show that they are always happy so long as you judge everything by reference to pleasure and pain.

(109) 'Hence, Torquatus, some other supreme good must be found for human beings. Let us leave pleasure to the animals, whose testimony about the supreme good you generally rely on. Yet even in the case of the animals, there are many activities that their own natures guide them to perform where it is readily apparent that their aim is something other than pleasure. Consider the devotion they show in giving birth to and rearing their young, however great the effort involved. Consider how they love to run free and roam wide. Some are gregarious and form themselves into a kind of civil society. (110) In certain species of birds we see signs of loyalty and of the power of recognition and memory. In many cases we can even observe grief. Are we then to say that semblances of human virtues exist in animals independently of pleasure, yet claim that human virtue is directed at pleasure alone? Are we to say that human beings, in far surpassing other living creatures, have been endowed by nature with no special gifts?

(111) 'Indeed, if it is the case that pleasure is everything, then we are in a far worse state than the animals. The earth pours out an abundance of provisions for them of every kind, with no work on their part, whereas we are able to meet our needs only with difficulty, if at all. However, I cannot accept that humans have the same supreme good as cattle. Consider all the apparatus we devote to the advancement of higher learning, our hive of worthy and honourable pursuits, our intricate web of virtues. What purpose would they serve if we simply sought them in the interests of pleasure? (112) Compare Xerxes, with his huge navy and massed ranks of cavalry and infantry.[75] He cuts through Mount Athos and bridges the Hellespont, marching over sea and sailing across land. He launches a tremendous assault on Greece. He is then asked why he has embarked on such an all out war with such immense forces. Do you suppose he would reply that he wanted some honey from Mount Hymettus? That would hardly explain his vast undertaking. In like manner, our wise person is armed and equipped with every kind of advanced knowledge, but instead of crossing the sea on foot and the mountains in ships, as Xerxes did, the wise person encompasses mentally the whole of heaven, earth and sea. To claim that all this effort is in pursuit of pleasure is to say that Xerxes was after the honey.

(113) 'Believe me, Torquatus, we are born for higher and nobler things. This is shown by the mental attributes we possess: a capacious, and in your case limitless, memory; an ability to predict the outcome of events that falls little short of divination; a sense of shame that moderates our desires; a sense of justice, the faithful guardian of human society; and a disparagement of pain and death that helps us endure suffering and face danger. But, in addition to

---

[75] Xerxes I, king of Persia, led an invasion of Greece in 480, with huge preparations described by Herodotus.

these mental qualities, consider your very limbs and senses. You will realize that, along with the other parts of the body, they are not just the companions but the servants of the virtues. (114) Even in the realm of the body, there is much that is preferable to pleasure, for example strength, health, speed and good looks. Surely, then, you will think this true of the mind, in which the most learned of the ancients located something celestial and divine?

'If pleasure were the supreme good, as you claim, then the ideal would be to spend our days and nights experiencing the most intense pleasure without a break, all our senses aroused and drenched, so to speak, with every delight. But which human being worthy of the name would want to spend even one whole day with that kind of pleasure? The Cyrenaics in fact allow it. Your school is more respectable, but perhaps less consistent.

(115) 'However, we need not survey those greatest of arts we have been discussing, lack of which would have earned one the name "inert" in days gone by. I shall ask instead whether you suppose that Phidias, Polyclitus and Zeuxis, not to mention Homer, Archilochus and Pindar, practised their arts for the sake of pleasure.[76] If not, will an artist have a higher conception of fine form than a good citizen has of fine action? What, then, is the cause of this dreadfully mistaken yet widespread view? It is as follows: the judgement that pleasure is the supreme good is not reached by the part of the mind where reason and deliberation are located, but by desire, the mind's least worthy component. I ask you, if the gods exist, as even your school believes, how can they be happy, given that they cannot enjoy the pleasures of the body? Or if they can be happy without that sort of pleasure, why do you deny that the wise person can experience a similar, purely mental, activity?

(116) 'Read the eulogies, Torquatus, not of the heroes that Homer praises, nor of Cyrus or Agesilaus, Aristides or Themistocles, Philip or Alexander: read instead those of our own heroes, indeed of your own family.[77] You will see that no one is praised for possessing the cunning art of procuring pleasure. This is not what epitaphs convey either. Take this one at the gates of the city: "Here lies one who, many nations agree, was the greatest citizen in the country." (117) Do you think many citizens thought Calatinus the greatest citizen because he had a fantastic ability to secure pleasure?[78] Are we likewise

---

[76] Phidias of Athens, a fifth-century sculptor, who made famous statues of Athena at Athens and of Zeus at Olympia. Polyclitus of Argos, a fifth-century sculptor best known for his *Doryphorus* ('Spear-bearer'). Zeuxis of Heraclea, fourth-century painter famous for his realism. Homer (uncertain date), the author of the two epic poems *Iliad* and *Odyssey*, foundational for Greek culture. Archilochus of Paros, seventh-century poet dealing with personal matters in a variety of metres. Pindar of Thebes, fifth–fourth century composer of hymns and victory odes. Cicero deliberately picks out a variety of genres in both visual and literary arts.

[77] Compare 62 above, with note 46. Cyrus, king of Persia, and Agesilaus, king of Sparta, are the subjects of works by Xenophon. Aristides and Themistocles are Athenian leaders at the time of the Persian wars; Philip was the Macedonian king who established rule over Greek cities, and his son Alexander conquered the Persian empire.

[78] Aulus Atilius Calatinus, consul 258 and 254, was a successful general in the Punic Wars. Cicero also refers elsewhere (*Old Age* 61) to the epitaph on his tomb.

to judge the talent and promise of our youth by how well we think they can serve their own advantage and act in their own interest? It is clear what utter confusion and upheaval would result. All kindness and all thanks will be abolished, the bonds of harmonious co-operation broken. If you lend someone money for your own advantage, that must be regarded not as kindness but as usury. Evidently no thanks is owed to the lender in these circumstances. When pleasure gains the upper hand, all the finest virtues must languish. In fact it will be hard to show that there are not countless vices that the wise person may possess, unless morality by nature has the very highest value.

(118) 'I shall refrain from further arguments, since there are too many to run through. I say that a successful eulogy of virtue must shut out pleasure. But you must no longer expect me to show you this. You must do your own introspection. Scan the contents of your mind, deliberate thoroughly, and ask yourself which you would prefer: to enjoy continual pleasure, experiencing that state of tranquillity that you frequently mentioned and spending your whole life without pain, and even without fear of pain (as you Epicureans generally add, though it cannot happen); or to be a benefactor of the whole human race, enduring even the labours of Hercules to bring it aid and succour in its hour of need? Labours – that was the doleful name that our ancestors gave, even in the case of a god, to unavoidable toil. (119) I would press you on this question and drag an answer out of you. But I am afraid you might reply that the reason Hercules himself suffered all his labours to save the human race was pleasure!'[79]

Here I stopped, and Torquatus said, 'I have authorities to whom I can refer your arguments. I could say something myself, but I would rather leave it to more experienced practitioners.' 'I think you mean our friends Siro and Philodemus',[80] I replied, 'fine and learned men.' 'You are right', he said. 'Very well', I replied, 'but it would be fairer to let Triarius adjudicate our dispute.' 'Objection', smiled Torquatus. 'Triarius is prejudiced on this matter. You are relatively lenient, but he lambasts us like a real Stoic.' 'And I shall be even bolder now', said Triarius, 'with the arguments I have just heard to hand. Still, I shall not attack until I see you properly fitted out by the thinkers you mentioned.'

At that, we finished our walk and our discussion.

[79] The twelve Labours of Hercules (Heracles) form a popular and early myth. The Stoics found in it a moral example of the virtuous person who undertakes efforts for the sake of others.

[80] Prominent Epicureans of the day. Philodemus (*c.* 110–40) was attached to the household of Lucius Calpurnius Piso Caesoninus (Caesar's father-in-law), and, in his speech of 55 attacking Piso, Cicero also attacks Philodemus (68–72 of *Against Piso*). Philodemus' works are known to us from the voluminous fragments of papyrus recovered from a country house at Herculaneum, buried by lava at the eruption of Vesuvius in AD 79.

Book III

(1) If pleasure lacked such tenacious advocates, Brutus, and spoke for herself, I think the previous book would compel her to concede defeat to real worth. How shameless she would be to resist virtue any longer, to prefer what is pleasant to what is good, or to contend that bodily enjoyment and the mental delight that it causes are of more value than a steadfast seriousness of purpose.

So let us dismiss her and order her to stay within her own borders. We do not want the rigour of our debate to be hampered by her seductive charms. (2) We must investigate where that supreme good that we want to discover is to be found. Pleasure has been eliminated from the inquiry, and pretty much the same objections hold against those who maintained that the ultimate good was freedom from pain. Indeed no good should be declared supreme if it is lacking in virtue, since nothing can be superior to that.

We were forceful enough in our debate with Torquatus. But a still fiercer struggle with the Stoics is at hand. The topic of pleasure militates against really sharp or profound discussion. Those who defend pleasure are not well versed in argument, and her opponents are confronting a case that is not hard to refute. (3) Even Epicurus himself said that pleasure is not a matter for argument, since the criterion for judging pleasure is located in the senses. Thus a recollection of pleasure is sufficient; proof is irrelevant. So the debate we held was a simple one on either side. There was nothing involved or abstruse in Torquatus' exposition, and my own speech, so I believe, was perfectly lucid.

The Stoics, on the other hand, as you well know, have a way of arguing which is not so much subtle as obscure, even for the Greek reader, and thus far more so for us Romans who have to find a new vocabulary and invent new terms to match new concepts. This need will surprise no one of even moderate learning once it is recognized that any field of knowledge whose exercise involves a degree of specialization has a large range of new terms set up to designate the subject-matter of the relevant field. (4) Thus logic and physics use terminology unknown even to the Greeks. Geometry and music, as well as grammar, have their own language. Even the art of rhetoric, despite being thoroughly public and familiar, still uses a vocabulary for the purposes of instruction which is pretty much its own.

These refined and noble arts aside, not even artisans could preserve their crafts without using terminology unknown to the rest of us but familiar to them. Agriculture too, a topic which quite resists fine writing, has none the less coined new terms to delineate its themes. How much more, then, does philosophy need to do this! Philosophy is the art of life, and it cannot take ordinary language as the basis for its discussions.

(5) The Stoics have been the greatest innovators of all philosophers in this regard, and Zeno their founder was more an inventor of new words than new ideas.[1] The most learned people, working in a language which is generally considered to be richer than our own, are still allowed to use unfamiliar terms when dealing with recondite material. All the greater is the allowance that should be made for us who are so bold as to tackle these topics for the first time. We have often stated, in the face of complaints not only from Greeks but also from people who would rather be considered Greek than Roman, that our language does not come a poor second to Greek in wealth of vocabulary, and indeed is actually superior. So we must work hard to demonstrate this truth not just in our native arts, but in those of the Greeks themselves. Now there are certain words which by venerable tradition we treat as Latin, such as 'philosophy' itself, 'rhetoric', 'dialectic', 'grammar', 'geometry' and 'music'. One could use Latin alternatives, but these words have been adopted through long usage and we should treat them as our own.

(6) So much for questions of terminology. Turning to the subject itself, Brutus, I am in constant fear that I will be reproached for addressing this work to you, who are such an erudite student of philosophy in general and the best part of it in particular. If I were doing so as if to instruct you, then the reproach would be justified. But that is far from my intention. Nor am I sending you this work to let you know what you already know very well. Rather, I take the greatest comfort in associating it with your name. And I regard you as the most impartial critic and judge in those fields of study where we share an interest. Pay close attention, then, and be the judge in the disagreement I had with your uncle, a wonderful and unique man.

(7) I was in Tusculum, and wanted to consult some books from the library of the young Lucullus. So I went to his villa, as I often did, to take them off the shelves myself. When I arrived, I saw Marcus Cato, who I had not known was there, sitting in the library surrounded by Stoic works.[2] He had a real passion for reading, as you know, and could never get enough of it. After all, he would often scorn the empty mockery of the mob and actually read in the

---

[1] Stoicism was noted for its precise distinctions of terminology; here Cicero couples this point with Antiochus' claim, which will be prominent in books IV and V, that Stoic differences from the Aristotelian tradition are verbal rather than substantial. The issue is raised in 10 and following.

[2] The dramatic date is 52, given by a reference to a 'new' law in book IV, 1. The setting is Tusculum, near Rome, where Cicero has come over from his own country house to that of the younger Lucullus (on Lucullus' father see book II note 71). On Marcus Cato see Introduction, p. xvi.

Senate-house. He did this while the Senate was assembling, so as not to intrude on public business. All the more, then, with total leisure and a huge supply of reading-matter, did he appear to be gorging himself on books, if I may apply this term to so honourable an occupation.

(8) Our meeting being a mutual surprise, he immediately sprang to his feet. 'What brings you here?' he asked. 'I suppose you have come from your villa. If I had known you were there, I would have paid you a visit myself.' 'The games began yesterday', I replied, 'so I left town and arrived in the evening. My reason for coming here was to get hold of some books from the library. Our friend Lucullus should start familiarizing himself with this great collection. I hope he takes more delight in these books than in all the other ornaments of the house. I know this is really your own duty, but I am terribly anxious that he should get an education that will make him the match of his father and dear Caepio and you yourself who are such a close relation. I have good reason for my concern. I cherish the memory of his uncle (you know how highly I rated Caepio – in my opinion he would now be one of our leading figures had he lived). Lucius Lucullus too is at the forefront of my mind. He was a man of enormous distinction. Every attitude and opinion we held cemented the bond of friendship between us.'

(9) 'Your remembrance of these men, each of whom bequeathed their children to your care, does you great credit', said Cato, 'as does your concern for young Lucullus. I am far from shirking what you call my "duty", but I shall enlist you to share it. I would add that the boy has already shown me signs of both modesty and intelligence. But you know how young he is.' 'I do indeed', I replied, 'but still, it is high time for him to get a taste of the skills which will better equip him for the adult world should he imbibe them in his youth.'[3] 'Yes', said Cato, 'and we will discuss these matters more carefully and frequently in the future, and take joint action. But let us sit down, shall we?' And so we did.

(10) Cato then said, 'What is it that you, the owner of so many volumes, need from this place?' 'I came to get some of the Aristotle note-books,[4] which I knew were here', I replied. 'I can read them during what is a rare holiday for me.' 'If only', exclaimed Cato, 'you had made cause with the Stoics! You, if anyone, should surely believe that there is nothing good except virtue.' 'Perhaps you Stoics ought not to have dressed up the same ideas in new terminology', I replied, 'given that there is agreement between us on the point

---

[3] This underlines the pathos of the fact, which Cicero assumes that his readers will know, that the younger Lucullus was killed in the civil war in 42, fighting against Caesar – as was Cato. The younger Lucullus was the ward of Cato, his mother's step-brother, and Cicero seems to have had some informal responsibility for him. The reference to Caepio here is puzzling, and there is some confusion in the manuscripts ('uncle' translates a conjecture for 'grandfather', which produces impossible results). The person meant is probably Quintus Servilius Caepio, Cato's step-brother and uncle to both Brutus and Lucullus, who died young and for whose son Cicero apparently also had some responsibility.

[4] See Introduction, p. xxiii, especially note 20.

of substance. Our arguments coincide; it is merely in their form of expression that our dispute arises.'

'They do not coincide in the slightest', said Cato. 'In saying that anything except virtue is to be sought, or counted as good, you destroy morality itself, the very light of virtue, and you dismantle virtue completely.' (11) 'Splendid words, Cato', I said, 'but are you aware that you share your glory with Pyrrho and Aristo, who declare all things to be equal? I would love to hear your opinion of them.'[5]

'You are asking my opinion?' exclaimed Cato. 'These men were good, brave, just and temperate in public life, as we have either heard told or seen for ourselves. With no systematic doctrine, they followed nature herself, and achieved a great deal that is praiseworthy. In my opinion they were better instructed by nature than they could have been by philosophy, had they adopted any other philosophy than that which holds morality to be the only good, immorality the only evil. All other philosophical systems – some more than others, no doubt, but still all – count something other than virtue as a good or evil. These systems, in my view, not only fail to assist or encourage us to become better, but actually corrupt our very nature. Unless it is maintained that what is moral is the only good, there is no way of establishing that it is virtue that brings about the happy life. And if this is so, then I do not see why we should trouble ourselves with philosophy. If it were possible for a wise person to be unhappy, I fear I would set little value on glorious and wonderful virtue.'

(12) 'What you have said so far, Cato', I replied, 'could equally be said by a follower of Pyrrho or Aristo. You are well aware that this morality we are discussing is regarded by them not just as the highest good but also, in line with your own view, as the only good. And if that is correct, the conclusion that I know you uphold does indeed follow – every wise person is always happy. Are you then commending these philosophers and advising us to follow their line?'

'Not at all', said Cato. 'It is of the essence of virtue that one makes choices among the things that are in accordance with nature. These philosophers make everything equal and collapse all distinctions between alternatives. Hence no selection is possible, and virtue itself is abolished.' (13) 'A very good point', I replied. 'But let me ask if you are not committed to the same position when you declare that nothing is good save what is right and moral, and abandon all means of distinguishing between other things.'

---

[5] For Pyrrho and Aristo, see book II, note 30. Cicero here sketches an argument which will be prominent in book IV: *Either* the Stoics say that virtue is the only good, but that with health, wealth and so on, a life is better, in which case they are saying the same thing as Aristotle, but in different terminology. *Or* they are saying that virtue is the only good, and that health, wealth, etc. do not make a life better – in which case they are following Aristo and others who deny that there is any rational basis for choice among things other than virtue. On either option, the Stoics lack a substantial theory of their own. This claim is put forward to provoke Cato's presentation of just such a theory.

'The answer would be yes', he said, 'if I were guilty of such abandonment. But I am not.' (14) 'How so?' I asked. 'Morality alone is the one thing which you call virtuous, right, praiseworthy and decent (its nature will be better understood if I refer to it by a variety of synonyms). So I ask you, if that is the only good, what else will there be to pursue? On the other side, if the only evil is what is base, vicious, indecent, corrupt and foul (here too a variety of terms will make things clear), what else will you say should be avoided?'

'You well know what I shall say', he replied. 'And I suspect you cannot wait to seize upon some point or other if I make a brief response. So I will not reply point by point. Instead, since we have plenty of leisure, I will expound the whole system of Zeno and the Stoics – unless you would rather I did not.'

'Quite the contrary', I said. 'Your exposition will be of great assistance in resolving the questions we are investigating.' (15) 'Then let us make the attempt', he replied, 'however difficult and obscure Stoic doctrine may be. At one time the terminology used for their new ideas did not seem acceptable even in the Greek language. Long habituation has now made it familiar. But what do you think will happen in the case of Latin?'

'There is no problem whatsoever', I replied. 'If Zeno was allowed to invent a new term to match the discovery of an unfamiliar idea, then why not Cato? None the less, there is no need for an exact word-for-word correspondence when a more familiar term already exists to convey the same meaning. That is the mark of an unskilled translator. My usual practice, where there is no alternative available, is to express a single Greek word by several Latin ones. And I still think we should be allowed to use a Greek word when there is no Latin equivalent. If "ephippia" and "acratophora" are allowed, then "proêgmena" and "apoproêgmena" should certainly be allowed too, even though they may correctly be rendered as "preferred" and "rejected."'[6]

(16) 'I appreciate your help', said Cato. 'I shall use for preference the non-Greek versions you have just given. If you see me in difficulty in other cases, please come to my aid.' 'I certainly shall', I replied, 'but fortune favours the brave, so I bid you press on. What more sublime venture could we undertake?'

'Those whose theory I accept', began Cato, 'have the following view.[7] Every

---

[6] "Ephippia" are saddles, and "akratophora" jars of neat wine. Perhaps these Greek words struck Cicero as being as clumsy as Zeno's coinages "preferred" and "rejected" (or "dispreferred"), introduced to refer to the kind of value possessed by everything other than virtue.

Cato frequently refers to Stoic technical terms in Greek. His presentation is rather like a textbook, well informed but relatively graceless, contrasting with the amateur enthusiasm of Torquatus in book I and the polished rhetoric of Piso in book V.

[7] Cato begins with the Stoic idea of *oikeiôsis* or familiarization (though no term for it). The idea is that of finding something congenial and regarding it as one's own. From 16 to 25 Cato expounds 'personal *oikeiôsis*', which traces our earliest attempts at finding things congenial to our original rudimentary sense of self. As we grow, we come to have more mature conceptions of both what we really are and what is really congenial or akin to us. Development and maturation take us from the baby's primitive self-love to the rational person's recognition that the only good for him, as a rational person, is virtue. ('Social *oikeiôsis*', explicated from 62 to 66, is a corresponding development from primitive concern for others who are 'yours' to moral concern for all rational beings.)

animal, as soon as it is born (this is where one should start), is concerned with itself, and takes care to preserve itself. It favours its constitution and whatever preserves its constitution, whereas it recoils from its destruction and whatever appears to promote its destruction. In support of this thesis, the Stoics point out that babies seek what is good for them and avoid the opposite before they ever feel pleasure or pain.[8] This would not happen unless they valued their own constitution and feared destruction. But neither could it happen that they would seek anything at all unless they had self-awareness and thereby self-love. So one must realise that it is self-love which provides the primary motivation.

(17) 'Most Stoics do not believe that pleasure should be ranked among the natural principles – I passionately agree. If it were otherwise, if nature were thought to have included pleasure amongst the primary objects of desire, then a host of loathsome consequences would follow. As to why we love those objects which by nature we first take up, the following is sufficient explanation: anyone, given the choice, would prefer all the parts of their body to be well adapted and sound rather than of equal utility but impaired and twisted.

'Now cognitions (which we may call graspings or perceivings, or, if these terms are disagreeable or obscure, "catalepses" from the Greek) we consider worth attaining in their own right, since they have within themselves an element that as it were enfolds and embraces the truth. This may be seen in the case of the young, whom we can observe taking delight in having worked something out for themselves even where there is no ulterior motive. (18) We also believe that the sciences should be taken up for their own sake, firstly because what they contain is worthy of adoption, and secondly because they consist of cognitions and embrace a body of work established by systematic reasoning.[9] As for assenting to what is false, the Stoics hold that of all things that are against nature, this is the most repugnant to us.

[['Of the members or parts of the body, some appear to have been bestowed by nature for their own usefulness, such as hands, legs and feet, and also the internal organs, though the extent of their utility is a matter for dispute even amongst doctors. Other parts, though, have no apparent utility and are there as a kind of decoration, for example the peacock's tail, the dove's plumage that changes colour, and the nipples and beard of the adult male.]][a]

(19) 'My exposition has perhaps been rather threadbare. I have been dealing with what might be called the basic elements of nature, and a fullness

---

[8] This anti-Epicurean point has been used in book II, 30; in book V, 24–33 Antiochus agrees. The shared idea is that to explain the appropriateness of an animal's or baby's responses we have to assume that the animal or baby is bringing to the situation some conception of the kind of thing it is, not merely reacting to particular encounters with pleasure and pain.

[9] A cognition is a grasp of a fact, a grasp which could not be wrong (and thus amounts to what we would call knowledge of that fact). As these are linked by systematic reasoning, they build up into the more systematic knowledge that constitutes the sciences or branches of knowledge.

[a] This paragraph is bracketed by the OCT as it has no relevance to its context.

of style is therefore scarcely appropriate. In any case I am not minded to attempt it. Nonetheless, when one discourses on grander themes, the very topic carries the language along with it. The more weighty the content, the more brilliant the style.'

'Just as you say', I replied. 'But still, in my view, when a worthy theme is expounded with clarity, it is thereby expounded with distinction. It is surely childish to want to discuss a topic of the present sort in a rhetorical style. For one of learning and intelligence, a clear and straightforward exposition is the aim.'

(20) 'Then let us move on', said Cato. 'We have been digressing from the natural principles, and it is with these that what follows must cohere. We begin with a classification: the Stoics call "valuable" (this, I think, is the term we should use) whatever is either itself in accordance with nature, or brings about something that is. Worthy of selection, therefore, is whatever has sufficient importance to be worthy of value (value the Stoics call *axia*). On the other hand, they call "non-valuable" what is contrary to the above. The starting-point, therefore, is that things in accordance with nature are to be adopted for their own sake, and their contraries are likewise to be rejected.[10]

'With this established, the initial "appropriate action" (this is what I call the Greek *kathêkon*) is to preserve oneself in one's natural constitution. The next is to take what is in accordance with nature and reject its opposite. Once this method of selection (and likewise rejection) has been discovered, selection then goes hand in hand with appropriate action. Then such selection becomes continuous, and, finally, stable and in agreement with nature. At this point that which can truly be said to be good first appears and is recognized for what it is.

(21) 'A human being's earliest concern is for what is in accordance with nature. But as soon as one has gained some understanding, or rather "conception" (what the Stoics call *ennoia*), and sees an order and as it were concordance in the things which one ought to do, one then values that concordance much more highly than those first objects of affection. Hence through learning and reason one concludes that this is the place to find the supreme human good, that good which is to be praised and sought on its own account.[11] This good lies in what the Stoics call *homologia*. Let us use the term "consistency", if you approve. Herein lies that good, namely moral action and morality itself, at which everything else ought to be directed. Though it is a later

---

[10] Things other than virtue, for the Stoics, are not good, or to be 'chosen', but have their own kind of 'selective' value; we have reason to select (or reject) them, since they are in accordance with our nature (or not). It is in developing the way we select them that we are led to recognize virtue, which is good and to be chosen, having a different kind of value from the kind they have.

[11] We develop from valuing our reasoning as a means to acquiring things with selective value, like health and wealth, to seeing that this reasoning is the only thing valuable in its own right. This attitude is identified with virtue, rather swiftly; as often, the move is more plausible when later seen in the context of other Stoic ideas, such as 'social *oikeiosis*'.

development, it is none the less the only thing to be sought in virtue of its own power and worth, whereas none of the primary objects of nature is to be sought on its own account.

(22) 'What I have called "appropriate actions" originate from nature's starting-points, and so the former must be directed towards the latter. Thus it may rightly be said that all appropriate actions are aimed at our attaining the natural principles. It does not mean, however, that this attainment is our ultimate good, since moral action is not included among our original natural attachments. Rather, such action is a consequence and a later development, as I said. But it too is in accordance with nature and, to a far greater extent than all the earlier objects, stimulates our pursuit.

'Here, though, one must immediately avoid the error of thinking that the theory is committed to there being two ultimate goods. Take the case of one whose task it is to shoot a spear or arrow straight at some target. One's ultimate aim is to do all in one's power to shoot straight, and the same applies with our ultimate good. In this kind of example, it is to shoot straight that one must do all one can; none the less, it is to do all one can to accomplish the task that is really the ultimate aim. It is just the same with what we call the supreme good in life. To actually hit the target is, as we say, to be selected but not sought.[12]

(23) 'Since all appropriate actions originate from the natural principles, so too must wisdom itself. Now it often happens that when one is introduced to someone, one comes to value that person more highly than one does the person who made the introduction. Similarly it is the starting-points of nature which first introduce us to wisdom, but it is no surprise that we then come to cherish wisdom herself far more than we do those objects by which we came to her. The bodily parts that we are given are evidently given to us for some particular way of life. So too our mind's desire – termed *hormê* in Greek – seems given not for any kind of life but for a particular form of living. The same goes for reason and complete reason. (24) Just as actors and dancers are not assigned arbitrary roles or steps but certain fixed ones, so too life is to be led in a certain fixed way, not in any way one pleases.

'This is the way we refer to as consistent and concordant. We do not think that wisdom is like navigation or medicine. Rather it is like the acting or dancing that I just mentioned. Here the end, namely the performance of the art, is contained within the art itself, not sought outside it. Yet even these latter arts are in another way different from wisdom. In their case, when something is rightly done it does not include every aspect of which the art consists. But what we might call – if you approve – either "right actions" or "rightly performed actions" (the Stoics call them *katorthômata*) contain all the meas-

---

[12] The immediate target is to acquire something with selective value. The overall aim is to be a virtuous person; this is a skill like that of being an archer, but one extending over one's life as a whole. Achieving the overall aim is compatible with missing the immediate target, and, since they have different kinds of value, they are not competing goals in life.

ures of virtue. Only wisdom is directed at itself in its entirety; this is not the case with other arts.[13]

(**25**) 'Now it is foolish to compare the goal of wisdom with that of medicine or navigation. Wisdom embraces magnanimity and justice, and judges itself superior to anything which might befall a person. This is not a feature of the other arts. Indeed no one could attain those very virtues that I just mentioned without determining that all things are indifferent and indistinguishable from one another except for virtue and vice.

(**26**) 'Let us now see how evidently the following points flow from what I have just laid down.[14] The final aim (I think you realize it is the Greek word *telos* I have long been translating, sometimes as what is "final", sometimes "ultimate" and sometimes "supreme", though one may also use "end" for what is final or ultimate) – the final aim, then, is to live consistently and harmoniously with nature. This being so, all who are wise necessarily live happy, perfect and blessed lives, with no impediment or obstacle, lacking nothing. The controlling idea behind not only the philosophical system I am discussing but our lives and destinies too is the belief that what is moral is the only good.[15] This idea can be elaborated and dressed up in rhetorical style, with an abundant outpouring of every choice phrase and weighty sentiment. I however prefer the brief and pointed way in which the Stoics express their "consequences".

(**27**) 'Their arguments, then, are summarized in the following syllogism: whatever is good is praiseworthy; whatever is praiseworthy is moral; therefore whatever is good is moral. Does this seem to you a valid argument?[16] Of course it does. You can see that the conclusion is what follows from the two premises. The first of these premises, that whatever is good is praiseworthy,

[margin handwritten note: good / identical / moral]

---

[13] In 24 and 25 (and also in 32, which is out of place in its context but would go well here) virtue is compared to performing skills, where the exercise of skill is the performance, rather than productive skills which result in separable products. The dramatic roles of actors and dancers also illustrate ways in which we develop virtue in performing our social roles (a point probably originating with Panaetius, and with special appeal to Romans). However, a virtuous act is defined by its intention, unlike a performance which is judged by its artistic success.

[14] From 26 to 66 Cato draws out the theoretical consequences and corollaries, particularly for happiness, of the account just given.

[15] This is closely juxtaposed, as in other accounts of Stoic ethics, particularly that in Arius Didymus, to the claim that our final end is to live 'consistently and harmoniously with nature'. Cato takes it that 22 has removed the temptation to think of these as two distinct ends. Our immediate targets are in accordance with nature, but our overall aim is living in a way which is not just in accordance with nature, but is 'consistent and harmonious' with respect to nature in aiming not merely at the targets but at an overall way of living which reasons appropriately about them, which is living virtuously.

[16] 'Syllogism' here covers any deductively valid argument, not just the type familiar to us from the development of Aristotle's logic. (The Stoics were important innovators in logic.) At book IV, 48, Cicero ridicules this argument on the grounds that nobody disinclined to accept the conclusion will grant the first premise. The Stoics, however, may well have been aware of this, and regarded this kind of argument not as a persuasive device but as a compendious and memorable way of encapsulating Stoic doctrines which were argued for on other grounds. See Malcolm Schofield, 'The syllogisms of Zeno of Citium', *Phronesis* 28 (1983), 31–58.

is the one that is normally challenged. There is no disagreement that whatever is praiseworthy is moral. But it would be the height of absurdity for there to be a good that should not be sought; or something to be sought which was not pleasing, or pleasing but not worthy of choice, and so also commendable, and so also praiseworthy; but then it is moral. So it is the case that whatever is good is also moral.

(28) 'Next, I ask, can anyone be proud of a life that is miserable or not happy? It follows that only a happy life is a source of pride. Hence a happy life, if I may put it this way, deserves to be taken pride in, and this can only rightly happen with a life that is moral. So it is the case that the moral life is the happy life. One who justifiably wins praise has outstanding cause for honour and pride; and these in turn are powerful enough to make one happy on their own account. So the life of such a person will quite rightly be called happy. Hence, if a happy life is marked out by its morality, only what is moral should be regarded as good.

(29) 'Moreover, unless it is established that pain is not an evil, it is undeniably the case that no one of steadfast, constant and lofty spirit – such as we call "brave" – could ever exist. One who counts death an evil can never fail to be afraid of it. So with anything, one cannot scorn or disregard what one has decided is an evil. This is a hypothesis that commands universal assent. We also assume that a brave and lofty spirit has no respect or regard for any of the misfortunes likely to befall a human being. This being so, it follows that there is no evil except what is immoral.

'What we are trying to produce, I tell you, the object of our search, is a person noble and distinguished, a lofty spirit, truly brave, who makes light of all human vicissitudes and regards them as insignificant. Such a person must surely have self-confidence as well as confidence in their life both past and future; high self-esteem and the view that nothing bad can befall the wise. From this argument too one can see that what is moral is the only good, and that to live happily is to live morally, that is, with virtue.[17]

(30) 'Now I am well aware that there are differences of opinion amongst the various philosophers who located the supreme good (what I call the ultimate good)[18] in the mind. Some of these philosophers' views are flawed. None the

---

[17] Cato is not claiming that there are actually virtuous people around, but that we do have the ideal of such courage and virtue, so that theories establishing less than this fail to do justice to our considered views.

[18] In 30–1 Cato refers briefly to Carneades' division (see Introduction, pp. xxiii–xxvii). He begins with those who assume that our final good requires reasoning, not just the use of the senses. He rejects final goods which exclude virtue, or include it in combination with another item. He distinguishes the mainstream Stoic view from the excessively intellectual view of virtue held (allegedly) by Erillus, and the alleged view of Aristo, that virtue has value in a way that renders everything else utterly irrelevant for happiness. (See book ii, note 30.) He concludes by insisting that mainstream Stoicism evades the dilemma Cicero suggested at 10–11. The Stoics hold that virtue is the only good, but are not committed to ignoring everything else: virtue is exercised in making choices among things that are naturally preferable for us or not (thus in living consistently with nature).

less, I still rank them above two other classes of philosopher. The first, with three members, regards virtue as distinct from the supreme good, and identifies the latter with pleasure, or freedom from pain, or the primary objects of nature. The second, also numbering three, considers virtue inadequate without some further good; and so adds on one of the three items I just mentioned. Any philosopher, of whatever kind, who locates the supreme good in the mind and in virtue, is to be preferred.

(31) 'It is, however, an absurd philosophical position to declare that the ultimate good is to live knowledgeably; or that all things are indifferent, and the wise person will be happy in not ranking anything above anything else to the slightest degree. Absurd too is the supposed view of the Academy that the final good and supreme duty of the wise person is to resist appearances and resolutely withhold assent to them.

'The usual procedure is to respond at length to each of these latter positions in turn. But obvious ripostes do not need to be long ones. It is perfectly clear that if one does away with the notion of choosing between what is in accordance with nature and what is against, then that highly sought after and hallowed virtue of practical reason will be completely abolished. Hence we eliminate the positions I just set out and any like them. What remains is that the supreme good is to live applying one's knowledge of the natural order, selecting what accords with nature, and rejecting what is contrary. This is what it is to live consistently and harmoniously with nature.

(32) [['Now in the case of the other arts, the term "artistic" should in a sense be considered applicable only subsequent to and as a result of the activity in question – what the Stoics call *epigennêmatikon*. The term "wise", on the other hand, is quite properly applied at the outset of a wise act. Every act that the wise person initiates must be immediately complete in all its parts, since we say that the desirable end is located within the act. Some things are judged wrong by reference to their outcomes – betraying one's country, assaulting one's parents, robbing temples; but fear, grief and lust are wrong without reference to outcome. These latter, then, are wrong not so much in their subsequent effects as in their original and immediate nature. So too an act motivated by virtue should be judged as right at its inception, not its completion.]][b]

(33) 'The term "good", used so much in this discussion, may also be clarified by a definition. The Stoics define it in a number of slightly different ways, which none the less point in the same direction. I side with Diogenes in defining the good as what is complete by nature.[19] Following on from that, he also stated that the "beneficial" (as one might render the Greek *ôphelêma*) is

---

[19] For Diogenes of Babylon see book 1 note 7. Similar definitions of good can be found at Diogenes Laertius 7.94–101, and Arius Didymus in Stobaeus, *Eclogae* 2, 5d–5m. What is good is what benefits in the most basic way. We need rational inference to reach the notion of good, since it has a value which is different in kind from what we have encountered in experience.

[b] This paragraph is bracketed by the OCT as it has no relevance to its context. See n. 13 above.

movement or rest which originates from what is complete by nature. Conceptions of things are formed in our minds by various cognitive processes: experience, association of ideas, analogy, rational inference. Our notion of the good is given by the fourth and last of these. By the process of rational inference our mind ascends from those things which are in accordance with nature to a conception of the good.

(34) 'It is not by addition or extension or comparison with other objects that we have awareness of this good in itself, and call it good, but by reference to its own proper quality. Honey is the sweetest thing; but it is perceived as sweet through its own particular kind of flavour, and not by comparison with other foods. In the same way the good we are discussing is supremely valuable, but its value is a matter of kind, not quantity. Value (the Greek *axia*) is not counted amongst goods nor again amongst evils, so it will remain in its own category, however much you add to it. Hence the particular value of virtue is distinct: a matter of kind, not degree.

(35) 'Emotional disturbances, which make the lives of the unwise a harsh misery (the Greeks call such disturbances *pathê*, and I could have literally translated the word as "illnesses", but it would not suit all cases. One does not usually call pity or indeed anger an "illness", but the Stoics call each a *pathos*. So let our term be "disturbance" – the very name seems indicative of vice.) – all these disturbances fall into one of four categories, each with numerous subcategories. The four are: sorrow, fear, lust and what the Stoics call *hêdonê*, a term applicable to body as well as mind. I prefer to speak of "elation", meaning the sensuous delight of the exultant mind. There is nothing natural about the force that arouses these disturbances; they are all mere beliefs and frivolous judgements. The wise person will always be free of them.[20]

(36) 'The view that anything moral is to be sought for its own sake is one we share with many other philosophers. With the exception of the three schools which do not include virtue in their supreme good, this is the position universally maintained, in particular of course by those who held that nothing else counts as a good except morality. This position has a simple and ready defence. However burning one's greed, however unbridled one's desires, there is no one today, nor was there ever, who would even dream of attaining some goal by an act of wickedness, when the same goal was achievable without such means, even if complete impunity was offered in the former case.

(37) 'Moreover, it is surely no utility or advantage that motivates our desire to discover the secrets of the universe, and the nature and causes of the move-

---

[20] Cato is brief about the *pathê*, passions or emotions, here introduced merely as disturbances in the way of virtue. (Cf. book III, 13 and note 14.) Cicero treats the subject at length in books III and IV of the *Tusculan Disputations*. The wise, virtuous person will be free of emotions because she will not have the attachment proper to virtue to anything other than virtue. Cato refers briefly to the Stoic claim that emotions are beliefs; this is not a claim that emotion is merely an intellectual state, but a shorthand reference to a complex theory which emphasizes the point that belief is central to emotion and determines the other aspects of it.

ments of the heavenly bodies. Whatever barbarian standards one lives by, however absolutely one might be set against scientific pursuits, no one could find such worthy objects of study repugnant in themselves and seek them only as a means to some pleasure or advantage, and otherwise value them at nought. Who can fail to contemplate with delight the noble deeds and wise words of the Maximus and Africanus families, or of my own great-grandfather – a man never far from your lips – and many other outstandingly brave and distinguished men?[21]

(38) 'On the other hand, no one raised in a good family and brought up with decency can fail to be sickened by immoral behaviour in its own right, regardless of whether such behaviour causes oneself harm. It is impossible to regard with equanimity one who lives a sordid and profligate life; impossible to approve of squalid, empty-headed, fickle or untrustworthy people. One must declare that immorality is to be shunned on its own account; otherwise there is nothing to be said against those who act disreputably but do so alone or under cover of darkness. The only deterrent here is that immoral behaviour is hideous in itself. I could go on endlessly in support of this view, but there is no need. Nothing is more certain than that morality is to be sought for its own sake, and immorality likewise avoided.

(39) 'Now we earlier established the point that what is moral is the only good. From this it cannot but be understood that morality has a higher value than those intermediate objects which it procures. We also say that foolishness, cowardice, injustice and intemperance are to be avoided because of what results from them. But this is not a statement which should give the impression of conflicting with the proposition that what is immoral is the only evil. The results we are talking about are not bodily damage but the immoral acts which flow from the vices (these the Greeks call *kakiai*; but I prefer to call them "vices" rather than "bad things"[c]).'

(40) 'How lucidly your language conveys your exact meaning, Cato', I exclaimed. 'You seem to me to be teaching philosophy Latin and, as it were, granting her Roman citizenship. Previously she had looked like a mere visitor to Rome, unable to express herself in our idioms, particularly in the case of Stoic doctrine with its elaborate and subtle use of both ideas and terminology. (I realize that some philosophers could express their doctrines in any language. This is because they have no use for division or definition. Rather, they declare that they only wish to commend views to which nature would give

---

[21] Cato claims that all recognize the Stoic notion of virtue in everyday life, though the Stoics follow up the implications more rigorously. Giving wisdom and courage as examples, he uses Roman examples for the latter. For Cato and his family, see Introduction, p. xvi. For Scipio Africanus the elder, see book II note 41, and for the younger, see book I note 12. The Fabius Maximus family produced many consuls and generals in the third and second centuries, the most famous being Quintus Fabius Maximus Verrucosus Cunctator, consul 233 and 228, died 203, who met Hannibal's invasion of Italy with delaying tactics which eventually produced Roman victory.

[c] The Greek *kakiai* is plural of *kakia*, literally 'badness'.

silent assent. Exposition of such simplistic ideas is hardly a matter of great effort for them.)

'I am concentrating closely on what you say, and committing to memory all of the vocabulary you are using to express your themes. It may well be that I shall have to make use of it myself.[22] In my view your choice of "vices" as the contrary of "virtues" is absolutely right, and in the idiom of our language. Whatever is "vituperable" in its own right is thereby called "vice", or perhaps "to be vituperated" is derived from "vice". If you had rendered "*kakia*" as "badness", Latin idiom would have pointed us towards one particular vice.[d] As things are, vice is the correct contrary for virtue in general.'

(41) Cato then continued: 'With these principles established, there follows a great controversy. It was handled rather weakly by the Peripatetics, whose ignorance of dialectic makes their usual way of arguing somewhat less than acute.[23] Your beloved Carneades, however, with his exceptional proficiency in dialectic and his powerful eloquence, brought the matter to a real head. He would tirelessly contend that on the whole issue known as "the problem of good and evil" there was no dispute between the Stoics and the Peripatetics other than a verbal one.

'To my mind nothing could be more obvious than that the dispute between these schools is substantial rather than verbal. The difference, I assert, between Stoics and Peripatetics is far more a matter of ideas than language.[24] After all, the Peripatetics claim that the whole range of things which, as far as they are concerned, are to be called good, contribute to a happy life; whereas we Stoics deny that a thing's having some value makes it constitutive of such a life.

(42) 'The theory that regards pain as an evil has this certain consequence: the wise person cannot be happy when being tortured on the rack. The theory that does not consider pain an evil carries the equally inevitable conclusion

---

[22] In complimenting Cato on his excellent translations, Cicero is of course congratulating himself. In the months following he was to write several more philosophical works – see Chronology. He also sneers at the style of the Epicureans.

[23] Cato can hardly be referring to Aristotle, who invented logic, or to his pupil Theophrastus, who extended it; he must have in mind later heads of the school, who lost interest in logic – cf. book V, 13–14.

[24] Cato now meets head-on the argument that Stoic and Aristotelian theories differ only verbally. The kind of value, he claims, that the Stoics ascribe to virtue is different from the kind of value that Aristotelians think it has; hence there is a real difference in the way each school thinks that virtue is related to happiness. The Aristotelians think that virtue is not sufficient for happiness, since we also need 'external goods'; thus they accept that virtue and external goods are all good in a sufficiently similar way for the latter to be added to virtue to make a life better. The Stoics claim that virtue is sufficient for happiness, and that 'external goods', which they call 'things according to nature' or (in 53) 'indifferents', having a different kind of value, cannot be added on to virtue and do not contribute to happiness in their own right. It is only the virtuous use of them that contributes to happiness. Cato makes this point after establishing that Stoics do have a use for and rational concern with these things.

[d] The Latin word which Cicero here rejects as a translation is *malitia*, literally 'badness', but also the more specific 'malice'.

that the wise person's life remains happy whatever the torments. The same pain is borne more easily when endured for the sake of one's country than for some less worthy cause. This shows that it is one's attitude, not its own nature, which makes pain more or less intense.[25]

(43) 'The Peripatetic view is that there are three kinds of goods, and that the richer one is in bodily or external goods, the happier. But it is hardly consistent for us Stoics to agree that possession of what is greatly valued with regard to the body makes one happier. The Peripatetics think that no life is completely happy without bodily well-being. We Stoics could not agree less. In our opinion it is not an abundance even of those goods which we really do call good that makes a difference to the happiness, desirability or value of one's life. So when it comes to a happy life, the amount of bodily advantages has no relevance at all.

(44) 'If wisdom and health are both worth seeking, then the two together are more worth seeking than wisdom alone. But if each commands some value, it does not follow that the two together are worth more than wisdom on its own. In judging that health commands a certain value, but not deeming it a good, we thereby consider that there is no value great enough to take precedence over virtue. This is not the Peripatetic position. They have to say that an act that is both virtuous and painless is more worth seeking than a virtuous act accompanied by pain. We think differently. Whether rightly or wrongly is a question to be considered later. But there could hardly be a greater difference between the two views.

(45) 'It is like the light of a lamp eclipsed and obliterated by the rays of the sun; like a drop of honey lost in the vastness of the Aegean sea; a penny added to the riches of Croesus, or a single step on the road from here to India. Such is the value of bodily goods that it is unavoidably eclipsed, overwhelmed and destroyed by the splendour and grandeur of virtue as the Stoic candidate for the highest good.[26]

'Ripeness (this is how I translate *eukairia*) does not increase with length of time, because what is called "ripe" has reached its full measure. In the same way right conduct (this is how I translate *katorthôsis, katorthôma* being an individual right act) – right conduct, as I say, consistency likewise, and goodness itself, which is found in one's being in harmony with nature, do not admit of cumulative enlargement. (46) Like ripeness, these features which I am

[25] Aristotle twice dismisses the idea that virtue is sufficient for happiness (*Nicomachean Ethics* 1, 5 and 7, 13) since this would imply that the virtuous person on the rack would be happy, which he regards as obviously absurd. Cato here regards it as a prima facie objection to a theory that it does *not* hold that the virtuous person on the rack is happy. He thinks it obvious that pain in itself is not significant; it depends on the person's attitude to it and the role it plays in his life.

[26] For the Stoics virtue and conventional 'goods' are in some way incommensurable. The analogies here make it seem as though what this comes to is that they are incomparable in quantity rather than different in kind, although the previous account of how we come to acquire the concept of virtue suggested the latter.

speaking of do not become greater over time. That is why, for the Stoics, a happy life is no more desirable or worth seeking if long than if short. They use the following comparison: a shoe is judged by how well it fits the foot. Many shoes are no better than few, larger no better than smaller. So too where goods are determined solely by their consistency and ripeness, more of them are no better than less, nor the long-lasting better than the brief.

(47) 'The following argument is less than incisive: good health is more valuable the longer its duration; so the wisdom which is exercised over the longest period also has the highest value. This argument fails to grasp that, while the value of good health is judged by its duration, the value of virtue is judged by its ripeness. One might suppose that the proponents of this argument would go on to say that a long-drawn-out death or childbirth is better than a speedy one! They fail to see that some things are of more value if brief, others if long-lasting.[27]

(48) 'Consistent with the theory which states that the highest good (what we call the "final" or "ultimate" good) is capable of increase is the view that one person may have more wisdom than another; and likewise that one person may act more wrongly or rightly than another. We cannot say this, since we rule out any increase in the highest good. When submerged in water one can no more breathe if one is just below the surface and on the verge of getting out, than one can in the depths. A puppy that has almost reached the point of opening its eyes can no more see than one newly born. In the same way one who has made some progress towards the acquisition of virtue is just as unhappy as one who has made no progress at all.[28]

'I realize that all this seems strange. But our earlier conclusions are certainly secure and true, and the present theses follow logically from them. So their truth ought not to be doubted either. However, though the Stoics deny any increase to virtue or vice, they do none the less hold that each in a sense may spread and expand.[29]

(49) 'As for material wealth, Diogenes[30] considers it a power not merely conducive to achieving pleasure and good health, but essential. But he denies it has the same force when it comes to virtue or even the other arts. Money may be conducive to their attainment, but it is not essential. Hence, if pleasure or health count as goods, wealth must also be so regarded, whereas if wisdom is a good, we are not committed to calling wealth a good. Nothing

---

[27] One important corollary of the claim that virtue does not possess the kind of goodness that there is more or less of: a virtuous life is not better just by being longer.

[28] Because there are no degrees of virtue, there is no progress in becoming virtuous (hence, strictly, we are all bad, since nobody is virtuous). There is, however, progress (*procope*) *towards* becoming virtuous, so the Stoics do not hold that it is pointless to try to improve, though they were often misunderstood. Compare book IV, 64–8 and note 36.

[29] For the Stoics, whether an act is virtuous or not has nothing to do with the number of people it affects, or whether it is successful in achieving a target with selective value. However, they can note that a difference is made by such factors as whether many people are benefited, and so on, and this may itself be a difference with selective value, though it does not render the action better, i.e. more virtuous.   [30] Diogenes of Babylon; see book I note 7.

that is not a good can be essential for anything that is a good. Now thought and understanding are the basis of every art and stimulate our desire. But since wealth does not count as a good, it cannot be essential for any art. (50) Even if this point were conceded for the other arts, the case of virtue would still be different. Virtue requires a vast amount of study and experience, which the other arts do not. Moreover virtue demands life-long steadiness, firmness of purpose and consistency, which is evidently not so with the other arts.

'Next I shall expound our principle of ranking. If nothing ranked above anything else, the whole of life would be thrown into chaos, as it is by Aristo.[31] Wisdom would have no role or function, since there would be no difference whatsoever between any of the things that pertain to the conduct of life, and so no method of choosing could properly be applied. It has been well established that what is moral is the only good and what is immoral the only evil, but as for those items which have no bearing on whether one lives happily or miserably, the Stoics then determined a certain ranking among them. Some have positive value, some the opposite, others are neutral.

(51) 'For some, though not all, of the items which are valuable, there is good reason to prefer them to other things, as is the case with health, well-functioning senses, freedom from pain, honour, wealth and so on. Likewise, with the items which are not deserving of value, some offer good reason to reject them – for example pain, illness, loss of a sense, poverty, ignominy and so forth – while others do not. This is the source of Zeno's term *proêgmenon*, and its contrary *apoproêgmenon*. For all the abundance of the Greek language, he still availed himself of new and artificial words, something not allowed us, despite our threadbare Latin tongue – though you are in the habit of saying that Latin is actually more abundant than Greek. None the less, it will not be out of place to explain Zeno's reason for adopting the term *proêgmenon*, since this will make its meaning more readily understood.

(52) 'At court, says Zeno, no one speaks of the king, with regard to rank, as being "preferred" (that is what *proêgmenon* means). The term is applied to those who hold an office which, while lower in order, approaches nearest to the pre-eminence of a king. So too in life, it is not the items that occupy the first rank, but rather the second, which should be called *proêgmena* – that is, "preferred". (This is the term we may use – it is literal. Alternatively, "promoted" and "demoted", or as we have long said, "advantageous" or "superior", and "to be rejected" for the opposite. If the meaning is understood, we should be relaxed about the words we use.)

(53) 'Now everything that is good, we say, occupies the first rank. So what

---

[31] Here Cato presents mainstream Stoicism as rejecting Aristo (see book II note 30 and above, note 5). Rather late in the exposition, he introduces the notion of *indifferent* in the special Stoic sense (in 53), something which, while having a value different from that of virtue, can be preferred or rejected – that is, ranked on a scale of value that gives a rational basis for selection. The analogy of the king and his court may suggest either the king of Persia or the Hellenistic kings who followed Alexander.

we call advantageous or superior must be what is neither good nor bad. Hence we define this as "indifferent" (it occurs to me that I should render their term *adiaphoron* as "indifferent") but with a moderate value. It had to be the case that there were some things left in the middle that would be either in accordance with nature or not. This being so, there were bound to be included among the former category items of some value. And given this, there had to be some things that were advantageous.

(54) 'Thus the distinction we are discussing is a correct one, and the Stoics offer the following analogy to facilitate comprehension: assume (they say) that our final end was to throw the knuckle-bone so that it stayed upright. A knuckle-bone thrown so as to *land* upright will have some advantage with regard to achieving this end; one thrown otherwise some disadvantage. But the "advantage" of the knuckle-bone will not constitute the end I have mentioned. In the same way, the actual advantageous items are certainly relevant to achieving the end, but do not constitute its essence and nature.[32]

(55) 'Next comes the following division: some goods are "constitutive of the final end" (this is how I render what they call *telika*. Here we may decide, as agreed for the sake of intelligibility, to use several words where one cannot serve); some are "productive" (the Greek *poiêtika*), and others are both.[33] The only constitutive goods are moral acts; the only productive good is a friend. But wisdom they declare to be both constitutive and productive. Wisdom is harmonious action, and so is included in the constitutive class that I mentioned. But, in so far as it occasions and produces moral acts, it can be said to be productive.

(56) 'Those items which we call advantageous are in some cases advantageous in their own right, in some cases instrumentally so, and in others both. In the first category will be a certain quality of countenance and expression, a certain bearing, a certain way of moving – these are features that might be advantageous or disadvantageous. Other things, for example money, are called advantageous because they bring about something else. Still others, for example well-functioning senses or good health, are so called on both accounts.

---

[32] The knucklebone example is not very helpful. The point is clear, however: preferred indifferents are relevant to the achievement of happiness (in another Stoic analogy, they are the material for it), but do not form part of what happiness essentially is (it is achieved by virtue, which is the skill of putting materials to use).

[33] Happiness consists in having good things, since these benefit us. Only virtue is good in the proper sense; hence only virtue benefits us and renders us happy. However, the Stoics try to retain, and to transform in their own terms, distinctions ordinarily drawn between ways of being good and types of good. (The rather academic material of which this is an example is much fuller in Diogenes Laertius and Arius Didymus, our other two sources for Stoic ethics.) Something can be good as a means to our final end or as constituting it. Virtuous actions are the only good that constitutes our final end (since that is a life of virtuous activity); wisdom constitutes our final end and is also the means to it, since it produces choices of virtuous actions. The only thing both good, i.e. virtuous, and productive of your final end without also constituting it, is another person (virtuous, it is assumed) whose relationship with you gives you the occasion for virtuous activity.

(57) 'As far as good reputation is concerned (what they call *eudoxia*; it is more suitable in the present context to translate it as good reputation than as honour), Chrysippus himself and Diogenes used to say that, aside from any instrumental benefit it may have, it was not worth lifting a finger for. I absolutely agree. But their successors, unable to handle Carneades, declared that a good reputation is advantageous and worthy of adoption in its own right. One who is free-born and well educated would want to be well thought of by parents, relatives, and good people in general, and this for its own sake, not instrumentally. We are concerned, they add, for the interests of our children for their sake, even if they outlive us. So, too, we should be concerned for our posthumous reputation on its own account, even with all instrumental benefit gone.[34]

(58) 'Now although we say that what is moral is the only good, it is still consistent to perform appropriate actions despite the fact that we regard them as neither good nor evil. This is because reasonableness is found in this area, such that a rational explanation could be given of the action, and so of an action reasonably performed. Indeed an appropriate action is any action such that a reasonable explanation could be given of its performance.[35] Hence one can see that appropriate action is something intermediate, falling into the category neither of goods nor their opposite. Since there may yet be something useful about what is neither a virtue nor a vice, it should not be rejected. Included in this category is also a certain kind of action, such that reason demands that one bring about or create one of the intermediates. What is done with reason we call an appropriate action. Hence appropriate action falls under the category of what is neither good nor the opposite.

(59) 'It is evident that even those who are wise act in the sphere of these intermediates, and so judge such action to be appropriate action. And, since their judgement is flawless, appropriate action will belong to the sphere of the intermediates. The same conclusion is reached by the following argument: we see something that we call right action, and that is complete appropriate action. So there will also be incomplete appropriate action. If returning a deposit duly is a right action, then returning a deposit will be an appropriate action. The addition of "duly" makes it right; so in itself the return of the deposit is merely appropriate.

'Now it cannot be doubted that some of the intermediates should be

---

[34] We have no other evidence of this slight change in Stoic ideas, forced on some by Carneades' arguments. It is of interest that there could be disagreement as to whether good reputation (something particularly important to Romans) had no selective value (apart from its contribution to other ends) or had positive selective value in its own right.

[35] Appropriate action (*kathêkon*, officium), which can be reasonably defended, has already figured at the first stage of moral development (20 above). It is common to the virtuous and non-virtuous; it becomes a virtuous action (*katorthôma*) when performed by a virtuous person with the right intentions and all other requirements of virtue. Appropriate action can be rationally assessed because there are differences of selective value among non-moral items.

adopted, and others rejected. So whatever one does or says in this fashion is included under appropriate action. This shows, since everyone by nature loves themselves, that the foolish no less than the wise will adopt what is in accordance with nature and reject what is contrary. This is how a certain kind of appropriate action is common to both wise and foolish, and it is here that its involvement in what we call intermediates arises. (60) From the latter all appropriate actions proceed; and so it is with good reason that all our deliberations are said to be directed at them, including the question of our departing from life or remaining alive.

'It is the appropriate action to live when most of what one has is in accordance with nature. When the opposite is the case, or is envisaged to be so, then the appropriate action is to depart from life. This shows that it is sometimes the appropriate action for the wise person to depart from life though happy, and the fool to remain in it though miserable. (61) Stoic good and evil, which I have now often mentioned, is a subsequent development. But the primary objects of nature, whether they are in accordance with it or against, fall under the judgement of the wise person, and are as it were the subject and material of wisdom.

'Thus the whole rationale for either remaining in or departing from life is to be measured by reference to those intermediates that I mentioned above. One who is endowed with virtue need not be detained in life, nor need those without virtue seek death. Often the appropriate action for a wise person will be to depart from life when utterly happy, if this can be done in a timely way. The Stoics hold that living happily – that is, living in harmony with nature – is a matter of timeliness.^e And so the wise person is instructed by wisdom to relinquish wisdom herself, if it is opportune. No vice, then, is potent enough to give a good reason for killing oneself. So evidently, even the foolish, despite being unhappy, will act appropriately by remaining alive, so long as they have a preponderance of what we call things in accordance with nature. The fool is equally unhappy dead or alive – prolongation does not make his life more undesirable. So there is good reason for the view that one who can enjoy a balance of natural advantages should stay alive.[36]

(62) 'Now the Stoics consider it important to realize that parents' love for their children arises naturally.[37] From this starting-point we trace the devel-

---

[36] Although virtue is the only good and vice the only evil, it can be reasonable for the virtuous person to commit suicide in sufficiently unfavourable circumstances, which preclude a life of virtuous activity. The topic is particularly appropriate for Cato, who committed suicide himself (see Introduction, p. xvi). See M. Griffin, 'Philosophy, Cato and Roman Suicide', *Greece and Rome 33* (1986), 64–77, 192–202.

[37] A brief account of 'social *oikeiosis*'. We are born with a natural instinct to love our children, who are other humans who are 'ours'. As we mature as rational beings, we extend this concern more widely, in ways which transform it in the process into an attitude of rational concern for all rational beings.

^e 'Timeliness' here translates the same Latin word (*opportunitas*) as 'ripeness' did in paragraph 45 above.

opment of all human society. It should be immediately obvious from the shape
and the parts of the human body that procreation is part of nature's plan. And
it would hardly be consistent for nature to wish us to procreate yet be indifferent as to whether we love our offspring. Even among non-human animals the
power of nature is evident. When we observe the effort they devote to breed-
ing and rearing, it is as if we hear nature's very own voice. Thus our impulse
to love what we have generated is given by nature herself as manifestly as our
aversion to pain.

(63) 'This is also the source of the mutual and natural sympathy between
humans, so that the very fact of being human requires that no human be considered a stranger to any other. Some of our bodily parts – for example our
eyes and ears – are as it were created just for themselves. Others – for example
legs and hands – also enhance the utility of the other parts. In the same way,
certain animals of great size are created merely for themselves. But take the
so-called "sea-pine", with its broad shell, and the creature known as
the "pine-guard", because it watches over the sea-pine, swimming out of the
latter's shell and being shut up inside it when it retreats, as if apparently
having warned the sea-pine to beware. Or take ants, bees and storks – they too
act altruistically. Yet the ties between human beings are far closer. Hence we
are fitted by nature to form associations, assemblies and states.

(64) 'The Stoics hold that the universe is ruled by divine will, and that it
is virtually a single city and state shared by humans and gods.[38] Each one of
us is a part of this universe. It follows naturally from this that we value the
common good more than our own. Laws value the welfare of all above the
welfare of individuals. In the same way one who is good and wise, law-abiding
and mindful of civic duty, considers the good of all more than that of any particular person including oneself. Even to betray one's country is no more des-
picable than to neglect common advantage and welfare for the sake of one's
own. That is why a preparedness to die for one's country is so laudable – it
is right and proper that we love our homeland more than our very selves. It
is thought wicked and inhuman to profess indifference about whether the
world will go up in flames once one is dead (the sentiment is usually articulated in a familiar Greek verse). And so it is undoubtedly true that we must
consider on their own account the interests of those who will one day come
after us.

(65) 'This human affection is the reason why people make wills and appoint

---

[38] The point that the virtuous person extends rational concern to all other rational beings is often
expressed by the idea that rational beings form a community, constituted by humans in so far
as they are rational, and by gods, understood as the divine reason permeating the cosmos. (The
gods of popular religion are seen by the Stoics as a confused expression of this idea.) A human,
in so far as she is rational, will think of herself as part of a rational community rather than as
primarily a promoter of her own interests. Human communities can claim a version of this
commitment to the extent that they embody ideal rationality. The demands of this moral community are seen as having the kind of force that law has; hence the Stoic doctrine of 'natural
law', which Cicero expounds in book I of his *On Laws (De Legibus)*.

guardians for their children when dying. And the fact that no one would choose to live in splendid isolation, however well supplied with pleasures, shows that we are born to join together and associate with one another and form natural communities. Indeed we are naturally driven to want to help as many people as possible, especially by teaching and handing on the principles of practical reason. **(66)** It is hard to find anyone who does not pass on what they know to someone else. Thus we have a propensity for teaching as much as for learning. Nature has given bulls the instinct to defend their calves against lions with immense passion and force. In the same way, those with great talent and the capacity for achievement, as is said of Hercules and Liber,[39] have a natural inclination to help the human race.

'Now we also give Jupiter the names of "Greatest" and "Highest"; we call him our Saviour, our Shelter, our Defender. By this we mean that our security as humans rests on his protection. But it is hardly consistent to ask for the care and love of the immortal gods while despising and neglecting each other! We use the parts of our body before we have learned the actual reasons why we have them. In the same way it is by nature that we have gathered together and formed ourselves into civil societies. If things were not that way, there would be no place for justice or benevolence.

(67) 'But though they hold that there is a code of law which binds humans together, the Stoics do not consider that any such code exists between humans and other animals.[40] Chrysippus made the famous remark that all other things were created for the sake of humans and gods, but that humans and gods were created for the sake of their own community and society; and so humans can use animals for their own benefit with impunity. He added that human nature is such that a kind of civil code mediates the individual and the human race: whoever abides by this code will be just, whoever breaches it unjust.

'Now although a theatre is communal, it can still rightly be said that the seat which one occupies is one's own. So, too, in city or universe, though these are communal, there is no breach of law in an individual owning property.[41] **(68)** Also, since we observe that humans are born to protect and defend one another, it is consistent with human nature for the wise person to want to take part in

---

[39] Moralized versions of Greek and Roman mythology. For Hercules see book II note 79. Liber was an ancient Roman fertility god, regarded as a benefactor for bringing crops and wine to humans.

[40] The Stoic moral community, based on shared reason, excludes non-human animals. Chrysippus drew the conclusion that humans have no duties towards non-human animals, and may use them for their own needs.

[41] The Stoics claim that the moral community of rational beings is compatible with some social conventions, including private property, although it is not clear whether they hold this to be merely permissible, or to have positive (selective) value. See J. Annas, 'Cicero on Stoic Moral Philosophy and Private Property', *Philosophia Togata I*, J. Barnes and M. Griffin (eds.) Oxford 1989, 151–73. The analogy of the theatre seat has weaker conventional implications in the Greek theatre than in the Roman theatre, which was physically divided by social class.

the business of government, and, in living by nature, to take a spouse and to wish to have children.[42] Not even sexual passion, so long as it is pure, is considered to be incompatible with being wise.[43] Some Stoics say that the Cynics' philosophy and way of life is suitable for the wise person, should circumstances arise conducive to its practice. But others rule this out altogether.[44]

(69) 'To preserve society, unity and affection between all human beings, the Stoics deemed both "benefits" and "losses" (what they called *ôphelêmata* and *blammata*) to be shared, the former being helpful, the latter harmful. Nor were they merely shared, but within each category equal to one another. "Conveniences" and "inconveniences" (this is how I translate *euchrêstêmata* and *duschrêstêmata*) they deemed to be shared but not equal. What is helpful or harmful is good or bad respectively, and so must be equal. But conveniences and inconveniences fall under the category of what is advantageous or to be rejected, and the members of each of these categories need not be equal. However, though benefits and losses are held to be shared, right and wrong actions are not so regarded.[45]

(70) 'Stoics consider that friendship should be cultivated, since it falls under the category of what is helpful.[46] Some say that in a friendship the interest of one's friend will be as precious to the wise person as one's own, though others claim that one's own will be more precious. But even these latter declare that it is incompatible with justice, for which we seem to be born, to take something from another for the purpose of enriching oneself. Indeed the school that I am discussing rejects absolutely the adoption or approbation of justice or friendship for utility's sake, since the same utility might ruin or corrupt these. There can be no justice or friendship at all except where sought for their own sake. (71) Now whatever can be described as or called a "law" is so by nature; and it is foreign to the wise person not

---

[42] An ordinary family life can, according to the Stoics, be lived virtuously; so, more remarkably, can some forms of political life. Cato is not explicit here, and Stoics were divided over what kind of political participation could be exercised virtuously, but clearly Roman Stoics felt the pull of Roman traditions of public service.

[43] Some early Stoics thought, like Plato in dialogues like the *Symposium* and *Phaedrus*, that love between an older and younger man could, if non-sexual and educative, guide the younger towards virtue. See Martha Nussbaum, 'Eros and the Wise: the Stoic Response to a Cultural Dilemma', *Oxford Studies in Ancient Philosophy* 13 (1995), 231–67.

[44] Stoicism had an uncomfortable relation to Cynicism, a movement inspired by Socrates' pupil Antisthenes, but generally seen as stemming from Diogenes of Sinope (*c.* 410–*c.* 320), who lived a life 'according to nature' by rejecting social and cultural conventions and living a shamelessly dog-like life ('Cynic' comes from the Greek word for dog.) The Stoics admired the Cynics' uncompromising rejection of conventional ways of thinking, but were also repelled by their anti-intellectual stance and refusal to allow that virtue could be exercised within conventional social roles.

[45] This paragraph seems to be out of place, and would fit better somewhere among the earlier terminological discussions (see para.55 and note 33 above).

[46] For the Stoics a friend unavoidably has the role of a good which is 'productive' of your own happiness (see para. 55 and note 33 above), but they also insist that a friend should be loved for his own sake.

only to wrong, but even to harm, another. Nor can one conspire or collude in a wrong with one's friends or benefactors. Indeed it is maintained with utter severity and truth that fairness and utility necessarily go hand in hand. Whatever is fair and just is also good, and again whatever is good is also just and fair.[f]

(72) 'To those virtues we have discussed they add logic and physics.[47] They call them each a virtue: the first because it provides a method of reasoning that guards against our assenting to anything false and being deceived by the captiousness of probability. It also enables us to protect and preserve all we have learnt about good and evil. Without this skill, they think that anyone might be led away from truth and into error. Given that in all cases rashness and ignorance is a vice, it is right that they call the art that removes them a virtue.

(73) 'The same honour is bestowed upon physics, with good cause. The starting-point for anyone who is to live in accordance with nature is the universe as a whole and its governance. Moreover one cannot make correct judgements about good and evil unless one understands the whole system of nature, and even of the life of the gods, as well as the question of whether or not human nature is in harmony with that of the universe. Those ancient precepts of the wise that bid us to "respect the right moment", "follow god", "know oneself" and "do nothing to excess" cannot be grasped in their full force without a knowledge of physics. This one science alone can reveal the power of nature to foster justice and preserve friendship and other bonds of affection. As for piety towards the gods, and the proper amount of gratitude we owe them, there can be no understanding of such matters without an explanation of the natural world.

(74) 'However, I fear that I am now being carried beyond the scope of my original plan, drawn along by the marvellously systematic way in which Stoic philosophy sets out its doctrines. Heavens above, does it not fill you with admiration? Surely no work of nature (though nothing is more finely arranged than nature) or manufactured product can reveal such organization, such a firmly welded structure? Conclusion unfailingly follows from premise, later development from initial idea. Can you imagine any other system where the removal of a single letter, like an inter-locking piece, would cause the

---

[47] Cato indicates the relation of ethics to the other two parts of Stoic philosophy, logic and physics. Mastery of these is required for someone who hopes to understand Stoic ethics in depth, since logic (or dialectic) enables you to defend your position and meet the arguments of others, and physics provides the metaphysical background which enables the learner to get a better understanding of the demands of ethics. Ultimately all three parts hang together as an organically unified whole. Cato is aware of having put forth considerations only from the ethical part of philosophy; this is what is required for Cicero's project, namely to appreciate the pros and cons of different ethical theories in confrontation with one another.

[f] The word translated, with misgivings, as 'good' in this sentence is *honestum*, whose rendering as either 'moral' or 'honourable' (see Translator's Note, p. xxxviii) would make the sentence virtually tautologous. But a sense of 'good' as 'useful', which would give the sentence point as following on from its predecessor, is not a recognized meaning of *honestum*.

whole edifice to come tumbling down? Not that there is anything here which could possibly be altered.[48]

(75) 'How dignified, how noble, how constant is the character of the wise person drawn by the Stoics! Reason has shown that morality is the only good. This being so, the wise person must always be happy, and the true possessor of all those titles which the ignorant love to deride: more rightly "king" than Tarquinius, who was unable to rule either himself or his subjects; more rightly "master of the people" (for that is what a dictator is) than Sulla, who was in fact master of three foul vices – luxury, greed and cruelty; and richer than Crassus, who would never have crossed the Euphrates without any pretext for war had he truly lacked nothing.[49]

'The one who alone knows how properly to use all things is the owner of all things. Such a person will rightly be called beautiful too, since the soul's features are more beautiful than those of the body; and uniquely free, the servant of no master, the slave of no appetite, truly unconquerable. The wise may have their body put in chains, but you will never chain their soul. (76) The wise do not have to wait any time at all before it can be determined whether they are happy; and they certainly have no need to wait until death crowns the last day of their life, as Solon, one of the Seven Wise Men, unwisely advised Croesus. If Croesus had ever been happy, he would have carried his happy life right through to the funeral pyre that Cyrus built.[50] So if it is the case that no one is happy except the good, and that all the good are happy, then philosophy is to be cultivated above all else, and virtue is the most divine of all possessions.'

[48] Stoic philosophy is holistic in structure; each position can ultimately be understood only in the light of the whole system. (Hence the Stoics are unafraid to put forward claims which in isolation sound odd; they are confident that within the theory as a whole they will be seen to be true and supported.)

[49] The Stoic position that only the wise, virtuous person can rightly have ascribed to him the words we normally use of non-virtuous people; he is the only person who is rich, a king, a householder and so on. This idea (developed at length in other sources) is to shock us into awareness of how much we fail to be aware of the distance between the actual and the ideal; we call someone a king, for example, even though he falls far short of the virtues of a good king. Here Cato claims that the Stoic virtuous person is better entitled to be called a king than Lucius Tarquinius Superbus (534–510), the last king of Rome, who according to tradition was driven out for his pride and cruelty. The virtuous Stoic is more entitled to be called 'master of the people' than the actual dictator Lucius Cornelius Sulla Felix (138–79), who ruled Rome after a period of civil turmoil, imposing autocratic political and administrative changes (see pp. xxxv–xxxvi). Sulla was notorious for the vices Cato names here, and his reforms were not long-lasting. The virtuous Stoic is more entitled to be called rich than the politician Marcus Licinius Crassus, who was notorious for his wealth, and for his ambition which led to his death in battle in 55. (See book II 57 and note 42 above.)

[50] A reference to the main points of the story of Croesus in Herodotus' *Histories* book I. Solon, one of the fabled Seven Wise Men, warned Croesus, king of Lydia, not to consider himself happy until his life had reached its end. Here Cato regards this advice as helping to bring about Croesus' reckless challenge to the Persians under Cyrus, who defeated him and was about to burn him alive when Croesus' telling of his own story made him think better of it.

Book IV

(1) With that, Cato concluded his discourse. 'For a theme so large and obscure', I said, 'your exposition was as accurate as it was lucid. Either I should altogether give up on the idea of responding, or else at least take some time out for reflection. In both its foundations and in the edifice itself Stoicism is a system constructed with great care; incorrectly, perhaps, though I do not yet dare pronounce on that point, but certainly elaborately. It is no easy task to come to grips with it.'

'Is that so?' Cato replied. 'In court I see you, under this new law, delivering the case for the defence on the same day and finishing up within three hours.[1] Do you think I am going to grant you a deferral in this case? Mind you, you will find your brief no sounder than some of those you occasionally manage to win. So handle this one in the same way. Others have, after all, dealt with the topic, as you have yourself often enough, so you cannot be lacking in material.'

(2) To this I replied: 'Steady on! I am not in the habit of mounting reckless attacks on the Stoics. I am by no means in complete agreement with them, but humility restrains me: there is so much in Stoicism that I barely understand.' 'I admit', said Cato, 'that there are some obscure elements. This is not, however, a deliberate affectation on the part of the Stoics. The obscurity is ingrained in the subject-matter.'

'Why is it then', I asked, 'that when the Peripatetics expound the same doctrines I understand every word?' 'The same doctrines?' exclaimed Cato. 'Have I failed to drive home the point that the difference between the two schools is not verbal but a matter of substance at each and every turn?' 'Well', I said, 'if you can establish that, you have a right to claim me as a complete convert to your cause.' 'I did think I had said enough', replied Cato. 'So let us deal with this point immediately, or later if you prefer to start with something else.' 'Actually', I said, 'if it is not an unfair request I would like to use my own discretion in treating each issue as it comes up.' 'As you

---

[1] In 52 a new law, introduced by Pompey, limited the time for the concluding speeches in trials to two hours for the prosecution and three for the defence, both to be on the same day.

please', he replied. 'My suggestion was more appropriate,[2] but each to his own taste.'

(3) 'Here, then, Cato, is my view:[3] Plato's original disciples, namely Speusippus, Aristotle and Xenocrates, and then their pupils Polemo and Theophrastus, put together a system of thought full of richness and refinement.[4] So there was no reason at all for Zeno, as a pupil of Polemo, to dissent from Polemo and his predecessors.[5] I shall set out this system below. If you think that any of my exposition needs correction, then draw my attention to it and do not wait until I have made a complete reply to your own treatment. I suspect that every point of this system will need to be brought into opposition with every point of your own.

(4) 'The philosophers I am discussing realized that we are naturally constituted to be, in general terms, well-adapted for acquiring the familiar and noble virtues of justice, temperance and the rest of that class. (All such virtues are akin to the other arts, and have an edge only in their subject-matter and the way it is treated.) These philosophers also realized that we pursue the virtues with a particularly sweeping passion; that our desire for knowledge is something ingrained or rather innate; and that we are naturally disposed to form societies and to promote community and partnership among the whole human race. These qualities, they held, are most prominent in those with the most developed natures.

'They divided philosophy into three parts, and we may notice that Zeno retained this division.[6] (5) One part they consider is to be used to shape our ethical character. I defer discussion of this part; it is at the heart of our inquiry, and I shall shortly be considering the question of the highest good. For the present, I shall simply mention the topic that I believe is correctly to be

---

[2] Cato is characteristically tactless. The exchange underlines the point that Cicero's charge – that Stoic ethics is merely a pedantic verbal variant on Aristotelian ethics – depends on the account he is about to give, derived from Antiochus, to the effect that Platonic, Aristotelian and Stoic traditions form a unity.

[3] Cicero expounds Antiochus' theory of the essential unity of Platonic, Aristotelian and Stoic philosophy. This will reappear in book v, 9–23 as a prelude to Antiochus' own theory. See Introduction, pp. xiii–xiv. Here Cicero uses it to claim that Zeno introduced nothing substantially new in philosophy generally, before turning to ethics in particular. The arguments in this book, deriving from Antiochus' position, are presented forcefully by Cicero, although in book v he will argue against Antiochus. See Introduction, p. xv, and book v note 54.

[4] Speusippus of Athens (*c*. 410–339) was Plato's nephew and successor in the Academy, succeeded in turn by Xenocrates of Chalcedon (396/5–314/313). Polemo of Athens (see book II note 28) was a later head, not a direct pupil; he moved the Academy towards interest in ethics rather than metaphysics. Aristotle, Plato's most famous pupil, founded his own school, the Lyceum, and Theophrastus (see book I note 8) was his pupil and successor.

[5] Zeno of Citium, founder of Stoicism (see Introduction p. xiii) was a student of Polemo, among others; here Cicero stresses the influence of Polemo in order to minimize other influences, and Zeno's own originality.

[6] In fact the division of philosophy into the three parts of ethics, logic and physics is Stoic, although it was later projected back on to Xenocrates, and Antiochus ascribed it to the unified Platonic - Aristotelian tradition he claimed to find. Without further elaboration it scarcely fits either Plato or Aristotle.

termed political science (the Greek *politikon*), and say that both the early Peripatetics and the Academics handled it fully and carefully. The difference here between these schools was verbal rather than substantial.[7]

'They wrote at truly voluminous length on both politics and the law. They left behind a wealth of valuable rhetorical theory, and plenty of practical examples as well. Even those areas that called for intricate discussion they managed with style and elegance. They used definition and division, and so too do your Stoics. But how much less refined is the Stoic style when compared with their glittering prose! (6) As for subjects that demand ornate and dignified language, their splendid grandiloquence rises to the occasion. On justice, temperance, courage and friendship; on the conduct of life, on philosophy, on statecraft; on all these subjects you will find in their works no Stoic hair-splitting, no picking over the bones, but a style that is ornate when the themes are lofty, and straightforward when they are not.

'Consider, then, their great works of consolation and exhortation, or even the advice and counsel which they addressed to the leading figures of the age.[8] Their rhetorical exercises were in fact two fold, to match the nature of the case. Any question can be debated either universally, without reference to person or time; or, if these factors are taken into account, as a specific point of fact, law or terminology. They practised both forms of discourse, and this training was responsible for their remarkable facility in either style.

(7) 'This whole area was completely neglected by Zeno and his followers, whether through lack of ability or lack of inclination. Cleanthes wrote an "Art of Rhetoric", and so did Chrysippus; these works are perfect reading for those whose burning ambition is to keep quiet.[9] Look how they proceed: coining new words and discarding the tried and tested ones. As for the supposed loftiness of their themes – "the whole universe is our village", for example: it would certainly be a great achievement to persuade the inhabitants of Circeii that the entire universe is their neighbourhood![10] You say that the audience

---

[7] A surprising judgement considering the differences between, say, Plato's *Republic* and Aristotle's *Politics*. Cicero is thinking of the two schools' writings as wholes, taking them to be similar in being seriously concerned with practical politics (as opposed to alleged Stoic indifference to this).

[8] Cicero is thinking of a genre of works now mostly lost or known to us only in part, such as Aristotle's *Protrepticus* or exhortation to Themison, a prince of Cyprus.

[9] Cicero here unifies the Platonic and Aristotelian traditions as accepting, and excelling at, rhetoric; he is thinking of later works, since this is startling if we think of the *Gorgias*, where Plato abuses rhetoric and regards its aim as conflicting with that of philosophy. The Stoics are presented as the exceptions in their pedantry and their attitude to rhetoric. Cicero knows that they accepted it as legitimate (see book II, 17); here he ridicules their procedures, which, considered as attempts to persuade, are dismal failures. The 'syllogisms' he mentions may not have been meant to be persuasive devices (see book III note 16 and below, note 26), but arguably the status of rhetoric is dubious for the Stoics, to whom genuine understanding is more important than superficial communication. See C. Atherton, 'Hand over Fist: the Failure of Stoic Rhetoric', *Classical Quarterly* 38 (1990), 392–427.

[10] Circeii, a coastal town south of Rome, is picked as an example of insignificance, and possibly also philistinism.

will be inspired to believe so. A Stoic inspire anyone? More likely to dampen the ardour of the keenest student.

'True, there are those pithy sayings that only the wise person is king, dictator, plutocrat. You certainly gave them a neat turn of phrase. But then you borrowed that from the rhetoricians. The Stoics' own pronouncements on the power of virtue are poor stuff indeed. Is this what they suppose will bring about happiness through its own intrinsic force? Their petty little syllogisms have all the efficacy of pin-pricks. Even those who accept the conclusions are not converted in their hearts, and leave in the same state as when they came. Stoic doctrines may be true, and they are certainly important, but they are not handled as they should be. The Stoic approach is much too nit-picking.

(8) 'The remaining subjects are the theory of argument and natural science – as I said, I shall consider the question of the supreme good shortly and focus the whole of the discussion on resolving it. There is nothing in these two subjects which Zeno should have been keen to alter. Everything was splendidly arranged in both areas. What had the ancients overlooked in the field of study dealing with argument? They defined a great quantity of terms, and left whole treatises on definition. As for the related science of division into parts, they left both actual examples and rules for how it should be done. The same goes for contradictories, on which construction of genera and the species within genera was based.

'Their system of deductive argument begins from propositions that are evident, and proceeds methodically through to the right conclusion in each individual case. (9) They set out a large variety of methods of deductive argument, none of which bears any relation to the carping syllogistic style of the Stoics. And they frequently issue the pronouncement that we should seek reliability neither in sense-perception without reason nor vice-versa: neither should be separated from the other.

'Furthermore, the material that the dialecticians of today transmit and teach was all put in place by the ancients. Chrysippus may have worked out the subject to its fullest extent, but Zeno's contribution was far less than that of the ancients. In some cases his work was inferior to theirs; many areas he left completely untouched.

(10) 'Now there are two arts which between them completely cover the fields of reasoning and oratory: one is the art of discovery, the other that of argument. Both the Stoics and the Peripatetics dealt with the second of these, but, as for the first, the Peripatetics made an outstanding contribution while the Stoics barely touched upon it. You Stoics had no conception of the notion that one can store arguments in mental "locations" from which they can be taken down for use. Their predecessors, on the other hand, laid out methods and techniques for doing so. This art ensures that there is no need to recite the same arguments on the same topics as if reading a rule-book and never departing from one's notes. One will know where each argument is located and how to lead up to it. However deeply buried, one will be able to dig it up

and always be self-possessed in debate. There may be some of great natural talent who acquire verbal fluency without systematic study. But in this field art is a safer guide than nature. To pour out words like a poet is one thing. To arrange what one says in a methodical and organized manner is quite another.[11]

(11) 'Much the same can be said about natural science. Both the Peripatetics and the Stoics engage in it, and for more than the two reasons which Epicurus recommended, namely to drive out fear of the gods and religious superstition. A study of the heavens brings in addition a certain sense of moderation when one observes the great order and control that obtains among the gods as well. To look upon the gods' works and their acts creates in us also a loftiness of spirit. And we gain a sense of justice when we understand the will, the design and the purpose of the supreme guide and lord to whose nature philosophers tell us that true reason and the highest law are perfectly matched.

(12) 'This same study of nature offers the inexhaustible pleasure of acquiring knowledge. When our business is done, we have a noble and honourable occupation for our hours of leisure.[12] In this entire field the Stoics followed the Peripatetics on almost every major point, in particular that the gods exist and that there are four basic elements of the universe. Then there is the extremely difficult question of whether there is some fifth element from which reason and intelligence are constituted, which involves the further issue of what kind of substance the mind is. Zeno declared that it was fire. There were also some minor points on which he differed from the Peripatetics, but on the central question he agreed that the whole of the universe and its greatest parts were governed by a divine intellect and nature. However, the Stoics leave us with a meagre supply of material on these topics. In Peripatetic works, by contrast, we find a golden harvest.

(13) 'Consider the volume of research they gathered and organized on the classification of animals, and on their reproduction, physiology and life cycles. There is an equal amount dealing with plants. In numerous wide-ranging cases they explain and demonstrate how and why natural phenomena occur. From this great store-house they can draw on a wealth of highly convincing arguments to account for every aspect of nature. So as far as I can understand it, there seems to have been no reason for the change of name. The fact that Zeno did not follow the Peripatetics in every detail does not obviate the fact that he was their disciple. Epicurus too, I consider, in physics at least,

---

[11] The account in 8–10 of the logic part of philosophy greatly understates the originality of the Stoic contribution to logic, especially that of Chrysippus; Stoic logic is a great original achievement, quite distinct from Aristotelian logic. Cicero emphasizes Stoic inadequacy in the more 'applied' area of practical organization of arguments.

[12] Cicero here writes as a Roman for whom the only honourable full-time activity lies in the public arena of politics, and who regards philosophy as a leisure-time occupation – as it is for all the characters in these dialogues, in contrast to the Greek philosophers they are discussing, who devoted their lives to philosophy.

to be a mere pupil of Democritus. He makes a few changes – or many, if you wish. But on the majority of points, and certainly on the most important ones, he does not innovate. The same goes for the Stoics, who fail to acknowledge the extent of their debt to the real pioneers.[13]

(14) 'But enough of these matters. I propose that we now examine the core of philosophy, namely the question of the supreme good. What contribution did Zeno make to justify his break with his pioneering predecessors? On this topic, Cato, you gave a careful explanation of the Stoic highest good and of what they meant by the term. Still, I will also give my own exposition to enable us to detect what innovations Zeno introduced.

'His predecessors, most obviously Polemo, declared that the supreme good was to live in accordance with nature. The Stoics interpret this formula in three ways. Firstly, they say it means "to live applying one's knowledge of the natural order". Zeno himself, they say, held this to be the highest good; it explicates your phrase "to live in harmony with nature".[14] (15) The second interpretation is that it means "to live performing all or most of the intermediate appropriate actions". This does not give the same sense as before. The previous formulation was talking about right action (as you translated *katorthôma*), which is the province only of the wise. The present one refers to a kind of incomplete and imperfect performance, which is available even for some who are not wise.

'The third interpretation is "to live in enjoyment of all or the most important things that are in accordance with nature". This goal does not depend solely on our own conduct. It consists in having the kind of life in which there is virtue to be enjoyed, but also in possessing those things which are in accordance with nature but not in our power. However, the supreme good as set out in this third interpretation, and the life based upon it, is only available to the wise, since virtue is a part of it.[15] This highest good, which we find in the

---

[13] The account of the physics part of philosophy in 11–13 greatly understates the differences between Stoic and Aristotelian physics and metaphysics. (The Platonists are left out here.) Cicero rightly stresses that both schools accept a teleological account of the universe, but fails to mention how diverse these accounts are, and how different are their fundamental metaphysical assumptions and their accounts of time, matter, cause and so on. Cicero mentions, to the Stoics' disadvantage, a familiar contrast: the Aristotelians are more interested in finding explanations, and in finding them over a much wider area.

[14] From here to 44 Cicero argues as follows. The unified 'Old Academy' (Platonist and Aristotelian) traditions declare our final end to be living in accordance with nature. The Stoics repeat this view in their own terms, with no substantial disagreement (14–19). But in two major respects they make it worse. Firstly, their terminology is perverse and misleading (20–3). Secondly, they have a faulty interpretation of human nature and hence of what 'living in accordance with nature' is; they identify human nature with reason and hence with the mind, unrealistically downplaying the important role of bodily and external goods in happiness (20–44).

[15] There are problems in Cicero's rendering of three Stoic definitions of happiness. (1) 'Living in harmony (or agreement) with nature' is ascribed to Zeno, but the explication here is in other sources ascribed to Chrysippus (with 'experience' instead of 'knowledge'). (2) The second definition, as Cicero complains, omits a crucial point: ordinary people live performing appropriate actions, but happiness is attained only by those who do this *virtuously*.

Stoics' own writings, was instituted by Xenocrates and by Aristotle. They expound nature's basic constitution, which was your starting-point too, in something like the following words:

(16) 'Every nature wishes to preserve itself, for its own security and for its conservation in the species. To this end, they claim, various arts are required to assist nature. Chief among them is the art of living, whose purpose is to preserve what nature bestows and supplement what she lacks. As to human nature, these philosophers divided it into mind and body. They held that each of them is valuable in its own right. Hence the virtues of each are valuable in their own right. But they ranked mind as infinitely higher in worth than body, and so they ranked the virtues of the mind above the goods of the body. (17) Wisdom, as nature's companion and helper, they held to be the guardian and protector of the whole person. So they declared the task of wisdom to be aiding and preserving both body and mind, as the protector of a creature that consisted of both.

'To this broad basic outline they added various refinements. They considered that the goods of the body were easy to understand, but they inquired more deeply into the goods of the mind. In particular they discovered that these goods contain the seeds of justice. They were the first of all philosophers to teach that the love of a parent for its offspring is given by nature. They declared that the union of a man and a woman, which is temporally prior and the root of all family affections, is also ordained by nature. From these starting-points they traced the origin and development of all the virtues. Here is where greatness of spirit springs from, providing an easy defence against all the slings of fortune. The most important things are in the wise person's own power. A life run along the lines recommended by these ancient philosophers can readily overcome the inconstancy and unfairness of fate.

(18) 'Moreover, the principles given by nature stir up a great flowering of goods. Partly these spring from the contemplation of the mysteries of the universe. A love of learning is innate to every mind, and from it comes a passion for rational explanation and argument. Also, humans are the only animals born with a sense of shame and modesty and the desire to live in society with their fellow humans. In all that they do and say they are concerned that every-

footnote 15 (*cont.*)

But Cicero (or Antiochus, or his source) has not given us the complete Stoic definition. We have definitions from later Stoics which mention the performance of appropriate actions, but they also add that this must be done *reasonably* (Diogenes) or *invariably and unswervingly* (Antipater). Moreover, these definitions stress that it is not the attainment of the target of the appropriate actions which matters for the performance to be virtuous, but the attempt to achieve the target as part of the overall aim of seeking happiness. (The various definitions can be found in Arius Didymus, 6.) (3)The third definition is also not, as stated, Stoic; they hold that happiness consists in living virtuously, that is, with the right attitude to things that we naturally go for, even if we do not actually attain them. Since Cicero is perfectly aware of this, he (or Antiochus) may be exploiting someone's unfortunate wording to make the Stoic claim sound more like the Aristotelian view which makes bodily goods essential for happiness, thus erasing a crucial difference between the two theories.

thing should take place with honour and decorum. Hence, it is from these starting-points or (as I called them before) seeds bestowed by nature that temperance, moderation, justice and all morality has been developed in full.[16]

(19) 'Here, then, Cato, is the general scheme which the philosophers I have been discussing adopt. My exposition done, I would love to know what reason Zeno had for dissenting from this ancient order, and what view of theirs he actually disagreed with. That all of nature tends to preserve itself? That every animal is well disposed towards itself and so wishes for its safety and security within its species? Surely not the view that the purpose of all arts is to meet some important natural requirement, so that the same principle must apply to the art of life? Or the view that, since we are made out of mind and body, they and their virtues are valuable in their own right? Did Zeno take exception to the pre-eminence they gave to the virtues of the mind? Or to what they say about practical reason, science, the kinship of the human race? About temperance, moderation, greatness of spirit, or virtue in general? No. The Stoics will admit that all these precepts are excellent ones, and were not the reason for Zeno's secession.

(20) 'There are other matters, I believe, about which the Stoics will say that the ancients were mistaken and which Zeno, seeker after truth that he was, simply could not tolerate. What after all could be a more perverse, foolish and insufferable view than that which regards good health, freedom from all pain and possession of well-functioning eyes and other sense-organs as good things? Better surely to say that there is absolutely no difference between them and their opposites! Everything that the ancients referred to as good is actually "preferred", not good. The same goes for the ancients' ridiculous claim that the bodily excellences are to be sought for their own sake. These are to be "adopted" rather than "sought". In short, a life that contains, in addition to virtue, a plentiful supply of the other things that are in accordance with nature, is not more worth seeking, but more worth adopting, than a life consisting of virtue alone. And, although virtue alone ensures that life is as happy as could be, there are still certain things that the wise may need even at their happiest! And so they make it their business to ward off pain, illness and infirmity.

(21) 'Oh, the sheer force of Zeno's intellect! The sheer rightness of the cause that brought a new philosophical school into being! But let us go on. We come next to the doctrine, which you handled with great skill, that every person's foolishness, injustice and other vices are alike; that all wrongdoing is equal, and that those who have progressed, by nature and training, far along the path to virtue, are utterly miserable unless they have attained it. So Plato, that great man, supposing that he was not wise, was no better and lived no happier a life than the most wicked of us.

---

[16] This account of 'Old Academy' ethical theory, from which the Stoics are supposed to deviate, will be given in greatly expanded form in book V. It is in fact Antiochus' amalgam of Aristotelian ideas with Stoic ones.

'Here, then, is evidently our revised and amended version of ancient thought, one which could have no place in the life of the city, the law-courts or the Senate. No one could take seriously anyone who spoke like that, and set themselves up as an authority on the wise and dignified conduct of life while in fact holding the same views as everyone else but inventing new terms for concepts whose meaning is unchanged. The words get altered but the ideas are left intact.[17] (22) Could a barrister conclude the case for the defence by announcing that exile and confiscation of property were not evils? That they are to be "rejected" but not "avoided"? That the judge should not show mercy? Imagine an orator addressing a public assembly, with Hannibal at the gates and spears flying over the city walls. Would the orator declare that captivity, enslavement, death and the loss of one's homeland are not evils? Would the Senate, in granting a triumph to Africanus, be able to state "that by reason of his virtue . . ." or "that by reason of his good fortune . . ." if neither virtue nor good fortune can rightly be said to belong to any but the wise?[18]

'So what sort of philosophy is it that speaks a common language in public, but its own language in its treatises? And this is despite the fact that none of their new terms expresses any new ideas. The same doctrines are preserved, but in a different format. (23) What difference does it make whether you say that wealth, power and health are "good" or "preferred", given that those who call them good rate them no more highly than you who call them preferred? Panaetius, a man with no superior in intellect or high-mindedness, and a worthy member of the famous circle of Scipio and Laelius, wrote to Quintus Tubero on the topic of the endurance of pain. He nowhere makes what ought to have been the clinching point, if it could be proven, that pain is not an evil. Instead he sets out its nature and character, the extent to which it is uncongenial to us, and finally a method for enduring it. Since Panaetius was himself a Stoic, those formulations of theirs seem to me to stand condemned as worthless.[19]

(24) 'Cato, I want to get to even closer grips with your account. I shall press matters home by comparing the position that you just laid out with the one that I prefer. Let us grant those points on which you are in agreement with the ancients, and restrict our discussion to the controversial areas, if that is

---

[17] A Stoic would deny this, claiming that Stoic technicalities are being ridiculed without attention to the theoretical distinctions they mark. This is particularly true of using 'good' only for virtue and 'preferred' and 'rejected' for things other than virtue. This usage marks a crucial theoretical distinction which the Stoics, but not the Aristotelians, find between the kind of value that virtue has and the kind had by other things.

[18] In 211, after a series of victories over Roman armies in Italy, Hannibal began to march on Rome to force the Romans to divert troops engaged elsewhere, but the manoeuvre failed. The speech to encourage the Romans in their darkest hour became a standard textbook exercise. Publius Cornelius Scipio Africanus (see book II note 41) decisively defeated Hannibal at Zama in 202, and was hailed as a saviour of his country.

[19] For Panaetius, Scipio and Laelius see book I note 7 and note 12, and book II note 23. Panaetius communicated Stoic ideas to educated Romans, avoiding the surface harshness and difficulty of earlier texts; but this scarcely shows that earlier Stoic accounts are worthless.

alright with you.' 'It certainly is', said Cato. 'Let us address the issues in a more detailed and, as you say, more "pressing" manner. What you have offered so far is commonplace. From you I want something more refined.'

'Do you now?' I said. 'Well, I shall try, but if little occurs to me I will not shrink from the so-called commonplace. (25) Let it first be granted, then, that we are well disposed towards ourselves, and by nature have the desire to pre- serve ourselves. So far we agree. What follows is that we must give heed to who we are, to ensure that we preserve ourselves in the condition that is proper to us. We are, then, human beings. We are made of mind and body of a certain kind. It is proper for us, as demanded by our primary natural desire, to love these elements and to derive from them our end, the supreme and ulti- mate good. If our premises are correct, this good must consist in our obtain- ing as many as possible of the most important things that are in accordance with nature. (26) This, then, is what the ancients held to be our end. It is living in accordance with nature. I put it at some length, they more concisely. But this is what they took to be the highest good.

'Now I ask that the Stoics, or rather you (since no one is better qualified), tell us how you start from the same principles but manage to end up with the supreme good of "living morally" (since that is what "living virtuously" or "living in harmony with nature" is). How and where did you suddenly abandon the body and all those things that are in accordance with nature but not in our power, finally discarding appropriate action itself? How is it that so many of the things originally commended by nature are suddenly forsaken by wisdom? (27) Even if we were seeking the supreme good not of a human being but of some living creature who had nothing but a mind (let us imagine that there is such a creature, as this will help us discover the truth), then even this mind would not accept the end you are proposing. It would want health and freedom from pain, and would also desire its own preservation as well as the security of those goods I just mentioned. It would establish as its end a life in accordance with nature, and this means, as I said, possession of things that are in accordance with nature, either all of them or as many as possible of the most important. (28) Construct any kind of animal you like, even one without a body as we just imagined, and it will still have mental attributes parallel to the bodily ones. This means there can be no highest good except the one that I set out.

'In his exposition of the different animal species, Chrysippus says that some excel in body, others in mind; and some flourish in both aspects. He regarded the human species as one that excels mentally, but from his defini- tion of the supreme good you would have thought that human beings had nothing but mind, not just that they excelled in it.[20] The only circumstance

---

[20] Cicero here ignores the Stoic position that a human is a psycho-physical unity; when the Stoics extol the life of reason they are thinking of a human life which is rationally ordered overall, not of reason functioning in a mind separable from the rest of the person. Many of the arguments in this book are affected by this misconception, presumably taken over from Antiochus, that Stoic stress on reason alienates the person from their body and the ordinary good things of life.

in which it would be correct to make the supreme good consist solely in virtue would be if our animal which has nothing but a mind also had nothing connected with its mind that was in accordance with nature: for example, health. (29) But any creature one could imagine of that kind would be a walking self-contradiction.

'If Chrysippus is saying that certain things are so small that they are eclipsed or disappear, then I would agree. As Epicurus says of pleasure, the smallest pleasures are often eclipsed and buried. But the bodily assets are too great, too permanent and too numerous to fall into that category. In the case of items which are so slight that they do become eclipsed, we often have to admit that it makes no difference whether we have them or not. So, to quote your examples, lighting a lamp makes no difference in sunshine, nor does adding a penny to the riches of Croesus. (30) But there are some things that are not so easily eclipsed, even though the difference they make may not be great. Thus, say someone who has lived pleasantly for ten years has an equally pleasant month of life added on. That is a good thing – the month's additional pleasure carries some weight. None the less, the life would still have been a happy one regardless of the addition.

'Bodily goods are closer to this latter category. They make a positive contribution that is worth striving for. The Stoics sometimes say that the wise person would rather have an oil-flask and scraper to accompany a virtuous existence than not, but that one's life would not be happier on that account. I think they must be making a joke. (31) The case is hardly comparable. One should dismiss it with a laugh rather than a speech. To care about whether one has a flask or not is fully deserving of mockery. On the other hand, one who alleviates bodily deformity or agonizing pain earns great gratitude. Imagine your famous wise person sent to the rack on tyrant's orders. Would we observe the facial expression of one who has just lost a flask? I think not. Rather, the expression would be of one embarking on a great and difficult challenge. Realization dawns that one's adversary is the mortal enemy, pain. All one's principles of courage and endurance are summoned up. With their protection one enters the tough, serious battle I spoke of.

'Our question, again, is not what is so small that it is eclipsed or destroyed, but what is of sufficient significance to contribute to the whole. Any one pleasure will be swamped by the swarm that makes up the life of pleasure that I mentioned earlier. But still, however small, it is a part of that life which is based on pleasure. A penny is swamped by the riches of Croesus, but it is still a part of those riches. Hence, though what we refer to as things in accordance with nature may be swallowed up in a happy life, they are still a part of the happy life.[21]

---

[21] Contrast the Stoic view at book III paras. 42–6: things other than virtue are not part of the happy life because they have a different kind of value from virtue, not because they have the same kind of value but not much of it.

(32) 'We must agree that there is a certain natural desire for things that are in accordance with nature. If so, then all such things should be formed into some kind of whole. If this is granted, we can then discuss at leisure questions about the importance of the individual items and the significance of their contribution to the happy life; and even the question of which items are so trivial that they are swallowed up and all but disappear, or actually do disappear.

'Now what about an issue on which there is no disagreement? No one will dispute that the final goal, the ultimately desirable objective, is similar for all natures. All by nature have self-love. There is none that ever abandons either itself, or any part of itself, or any disposition or power of such a part; or indeed anything, whether process or state, that is in accordance with its nature. What nature ever forgot its own original constitution? Surely there is none that fails to retain its essential character from beginning to end? How is it, then, that human nature alone should abandon itself, forgetting the body and placing the highest good not in the whole but in a part of itself? (33) How indeed shall one maintain that the ultimate good that we are investigating is, as even the Stoics declare and as is universally acknowledged, similar for all natures? It could only be so if, in the case of the other natures, the ultimate good lay in the area where each excelled.

'This in fact is the Stoic idea of the ultimate good. (34) Why hesitate, then, to change your view of the principles of nature? Instead of saying that every animal, as soon as it is born, is devoted to loving itself and is concerned with its self-preservation, why not rather say the following? Every animal is devoted to the best part of itself and is concerned with the security of that one part; no other nature has any other aim than to preserve whatever is best in itself. But why even "best" if no other part is good? And if the preservation of the other parts *is* desirable, then surely the ultimately desirable objective is the attainment of one's desire for them all, or as many as possible of the most important ones?

'A great sculptor like Phidias can start a work from scratch and carry it through to completion, or can take over an unfinished work from someone else and perfect it. Wisdom corresponds to the latter case. It did not itself generate the human race; it took it over, unfinished, from nature. So it ought to watch nature closely and perfect her work as if it were a statue.

(35) 'What is the character of human beings that nature left incomplete? And what is the task and function of wisdom? What is it that it must polish and perfect? If there is nothing to be perfected except a certain operation of the mind, namely reason, then the ultimate good must be to live in accordance with virtue. Virtue, after all, is the perfection of reason. And if there were nothing except the body, then health, freedom from pain, beauty, and so on, would be the supreme goods. (36) But as things are it is the supreme good of the human species that we are investigating. Let us then not hesitate to investigate the product of its whole nature.

'It is generally agreed that wisdom's duty and task is centred on the cultivation of the human person. Now some thinkers (in case you are imagining it is only the Stoic position that I am opposing) maintain the view that the supreme good is located in the class of things that are beyond our control, as if they were discussing a creature without a mind. Others, on the other hand, show concern for nothing but the mind, as if human beings had no body. This despite the fact that the mind is not some strange immaterial entity (a concept I find unintelligible) but is itself a species of body. It is not therefore satisfied with virtue alone but also desires freedom from pain.

'Each of these propositions protects one flank but leaves the other exposed. They are analogous to Erillus' championing of abstract thought and neglect of action within the area of the mind. In picking and choosing what to follow every view of this kind leaves out so much, and thus presents a lop-sided outlook. A complete and fully rounded system is to be found only in those philosophers who left no human element unprovided for, be it mind or body, when they investigated the supreme human good.

(37) 'Virtue, we all admit, occupies the loftiest and most distinguished position in human life. Those who are wise we all consider to be whole and complete. And so you Stoics, Cato, try to blind our mental vision with the dazzling splendour of virtue. In every living creature – dogs, horses – there is an element that is supreme and best; but they do not for that reason lack the need to be free from pain and to be healthy. It is the same with human beings, who attain their greatest glory in that aspect which is their best, namely in being virtuous. And so you do not seem to me to pay sufficient attention to the sequential way in which nature advances. True, in the case of corn, nature guides it through from blade to ear and then discards the blade as of no value. But it is not the same procedure with the human species, when nature has guided us through to the acquisition of reason. Where something new is added, it is never at the cost of the withdrawal of an earlier gift. (38) Thus reason was linked to the senses, and the senses were not discarded when reason was created.

'The art of viticulture has the purpose of ensuring that the vine and all its parts are in the best possible condition. Let us at any rate understand things in the following terms – one may, as you often do, create a thought-experiment for the sake of instruction. Imagine, then, that the art of viticulture resided in the vine itself. It would, as before, wish to bring about everything that pertains to the cultivation of the vine. But it would rank itself above every other part and would consider nothing else about the vine to be superior to itself. Similarly, when a creature acquires sense-perception, the latter protects the creature but also itself. But when reason is acquired, such is its dominion that all the primary elements of nature fall under its guardianship.

(39) 'So reason never ceases to take care of all these elements placed under its charge. It has a duty to guide them for the whole of a lifetime. The inconsistency of the Stoics here causes me endless amazement. They determine that natural desire – what they call *hormê* – and appropriate action, and even

virtue itself are all things that are in accordance with nature. Yet when they wish to arrive at the supreme good, they skip over everything else and leave us with two tasks instead of one – to "adopt" some things, and "seek" others, rather than including both of them under a single end.

(40) 'You may say that virtue cannot be secured if there exists anything apart from virtue that is conducive to a happy life. But it is completely the other way round. Virtue cannot be brought into play at all unless everything that it chooses and rejects is related to a single all-embracing good. If we completely neglect our own nature, we shall make the same errors and mistakes as Aristo, and overlook those very elements that we laid down as the origins of virtue herself. If we do not neglect these elements, but still fail to relate them to the domain of the supreme good, then we shall be straying close to the frivolity of Erillus. He set up two separate ultimate goods which, to be genuinely ultimate, ought to have been combined. As things are, they are so disconnected as to be mutually exclusive, which is the height of perversity.

(41) 'And so it is the complete opposite of what you say: virtue cannot be secured at all unless it takes the primary objects of nature to pertain to the supreme good. We are seeking a virtue that does not abandon our nature but protects it. Yet virtue as you advocate it protects one part but abandons the rest.

'The human constitution itself would declare, if it could speak, that its first incipient burgeonings of desire were directed at preserving itself in the natural condition in which it had been born. True, nature's chief intent had not yet been revealed. Well, let it be revealed. What else are we to understand by that except that no part of our nature should be neglected? If our whole nature were nothing but reason, then let the highest good lie in virtue alone. But if we also have a body, then the revealing of nature on the Stoic account will actually make us abandon what we had held to before it was revealed. Hence to live in harmony with nature will be to abandon nature.

(42) 'There are philosophers who began with the senses but then saw a grander and more divine vision, whereupon they abandoned the senses. So, too, the Stoics moved on from original desire to the beautiful vision of virtue, and cast aside all that they saw apart from virtue. But they forgot that in its entirety the nature of what is desirable has a very wide scope, from starting-points to final ends. And they failed to realize that they were undermining the foundations of those beautiful objects of their admiration.

(43) 'Thus all who declared that the highest good is to live virtuously are, in my view, wrong, though some are more wrong than others. Pyrrho was clearly the most mistaken. His conception of virtue leaves no room for any object of desire whatsoever. In second place is Aristo. He lacked the audacity to leave us with nothing. Instead he introduced, as the motive force of the wise person's desire, "whatever may enter one's head", and "whatever may occur to one".

'Aristo is better than Pyrrho in that he did give us some kind of desire, but worse than everyone else, since he departed utterly from nature. The Stoics resemble these philosophers in that they locate the highest good in virtue alone. They are an improvement on Pyrrho, given their attempt to find a foundation for appropriate action. And in avoiding imaginary "occurrences" they are better than Aristo. But they say that certain things are suited to nature and should be adopted in their own right, yet these form no part of their highest good. In this respect they abandon nature and are somewhat similar to Aristo. The latter invented these strange "occurrences". The Stoics present us with the primary objects of nature but distinguish them from our ends and our supreme good. These objects are "preferred" and so a certain principle of choice is admitted. To this extent the Stoics appear to be following nature. But the denial that they have any relevance to the happy life is again an abandonment of nature.[22]

(44) 'Up to this point, Cato, I have been explaining why Zeno had no good reason to depart from the teaching of his predecessors. Now let me deal with the remaining issues, unless you wish to make a reply to what I have already said, or I am taking too long.' 'Neither', said Cato. 'I would like to see your argument completed, and no discourse of yours could seem long to me.'[23] 'Excellent', I replied. 'Nothing could be more of a pleasure for me than to debate virtue with Cato, that champion of all the virtues. (45) Consider, first, a point about that most important of your doctrines, the veritable head of the Stoic household, namely that what is moral is the only good and that the highest good is living morally. This doctrine you will have in common with all those philosophers who locate the highest good in virtue alone. Moreover, your view that there can be no virtue if anything other than morality is included in it will be held by those thinkers I was just mentioning.

'Now Zeno agreed with Polemo about what the principles of nature were. It would have been fairer, then, in his dispute with Polemo, for Zeno to have begun with these shared first principles and then to have indicated where he took a stand and where the cause of the controversy arose. Instead, he lined himself up with philosophers who actually denied that their supreme goods derived from nature, yet he employed the same arguments and the same doctrines that they did.[24]

---

[22] Cicero has argued that the Stoics are driven to the unorthodox views of Aristo and Erillus by their allegedly overnarrow conception of rational human nature. This is held to result from taking seriously the Stoics' *distinctive* understanding of human nature, that is, taking their view to be *not* a mere verbal variant on Aristotelian ethics. Thus, either the Stoic theory is a trivial variant on Aristotelianism, as originally claimed, or, if given a distinctive interpretation, it is forced to a position they themselves regard as unacceptable. Either way, it is not an acceptable theory. (See para. 78 which concludes the argument of the whole book.) On the theories of Pyrrho, Aristo and Erillus see book II note 30.

[23] The break in exposition marks the end of a concerted attempt to show that the Stoics are caught in a dilemma by beginning their account of our final end from human nature but then allegedly narrowing this to include only rational concern for virtue (see last note). From here to the end of the book, apart from one major complaint about Stoic method, Cicero presses arguments which are consequences of this point.

[24] Zeno, though, on this account, sharing the alleged unified Platonic–Aristotelian tradition, supposedly departs from it in defining our final end in ways that sever it from the development

(46) 'Here is another point to which I take great exception. You show, at least to your own satisfaction, that what is moral is the only good. You then claim, however, that there are starting-points laid before us which are adapted and suited to our nature, and that it is in selecting from among these that virtue may arise. It was wrong of you to have located virtue in an act of selection, since it means that the ultimate good will itself be in pursuit of some further thing. The sum total of goods must include everything worth adopting, choosing or wishing for, or else the ones who possess it will still want something more.

'For those whose supreme good lies in pleasure, observe how obvious it is what actions should be done or not done. No one can deny in what direction their every appropriate action lies, in both pursuit and avoidance. Assume, alternatively, that the ultimate good is the one that I myself currently uphold. It is then immediately obvious what the appropriate duties and actions are. But you Stoics propose as your good nothing other than rightness and morality. You cannot on this basis find any principle of duty or action.

(47) 'All of you who are looking for such a principle will return to nature, including the proponents of following whatever comes into one's head or occurs to one, and you Stoics yourselves. To you all, nature will make the following just riposte: it is wrong to seek the standard for a happy life elsewhere, while seeking the principles of conduct from nature herself; there is a single unified system encompassing both principles of conduct and ultimate goods. Aristo held that there is no difference between one object and another, and that there is no significant distinction between anything except the distinction between virtues and vices. This theory has been exploded. In just the same way Zeno was wrong to claim that nothing other than virtue carries any weight in the attainment of the supreme good; wrong too to claim that nothing else has any effect on the happy life, yet that other things can affect our desire. As if this desire of ours were not aimed at attaining the supreme good! (48) It is completely *in*consistent of the Stoics to say that one returns to nature to seek out a principle of appropriate action and duty once one has grasped what the supreme good is. Considerations of action and duty do not motivate us to desire the things that are in accordance with nature. Rather, the latter are what motivate our desires and our actions.[25]

of human nature, and lines up with philosophers who deny that our final end does derive from human nature. Who are these? Aristo and Erillus are Stoics, even if unorthodox by later standards, and cannot have denied that virtue is a development of human nature. Perhaps the claim unfairly generalizes a claim about Pyrrho, the sceptic, who is alleged to have said that it was difficult (but our aim) to strip off human nature (Diogenes Laertius 9, 66). However, Cicero's usual understanding of Pyrrho does not stress the sceptical side.

[25] The Stoic account of our final good, it is claimed, cannot account, as other theories can, for rational selection among everyday things. Since nothing but virtue contributes to happiness, our rational selection of things that are naturally good for us becomes severed from pursuit of our final end. (Contrast the claim at book III, 22, that the Stoics are *not* committed to two separate final ends.)

'I now turn to those examples of Stoic brevity that you called "consequences"[26]. Here, firstly, is one that could hardly be more concise: "Everything good is praiseworthy; everything praiseworthy is moral; therefore everything good is moral." What a rusty sword! Who would admit your first premise? (In fact if that is admitted, there is no need for the second, since if everything good is praiseworthy, then everything good is moral.) **(49)** No one would admit it except Pyrrho, Aristo and the like, and you do not even accept their views. Aristotle, Xenocrates and the whole of their school will refuse to grant it. They call health, strength, wealth, honour and many other things good without calling them praiseworthy. At least they rate virtue higher than anything else, even though they reject the view that the highest good consists solely in virtue. But what do you think the response will be from those who completely separate virtue from the highest good: Epicurus, Hieronymus and whoever claims to support the end propounded by Carneades? **(50)** Callipho and Diodorus could not grant your premise either, since they combine morality with another element from a different category.

'So, Cato, are you content to draw any conclusion you please from premises that are not agreed? The following is a sorites, which you hold to be a particularly fallacious form of argument:[27] "What is good is worthy of choice; what is worthy of choice is worth seeking; what is worth seeking is praiseworthy." The rest follows, but I shall stop here. As before, no one will grant to you that what is worth seeking is praiseworthy.

'As for the following argument, it hardly ranks as a "consequence". Indeed it is exceptionally heavy-going, though that is the fault of the Stoic founders, not yours: "The happy life is something we should be proud of; but it could not be the case that in the absence of morality one could be justly proud of anything." **(51)** Polemo would grant Zeno this, as would Polemo's teacher and the whole of that tribe. So, too, would any philosopher who values virtue far above all other things but combines it with some further element in arriving at a definition of the supreme good. Now if virtue is something to be proud of (as it is), and ranks so far above everything else that one could hardly put

---

[26] From 48 to 53 Cicero criticizes Stoic method. He mentions arguments such as the one at book III, 27, complaining that they are ineffective, since no opponent would concede their premises. (The list of opponents is drawn from the place-holders in Carneades' division, rather than any actual debates.) The complaint is then generalized: Stoic philosophy, with pedantic, far-fetched terminology, fails in moral philosophy's task of engaging with the listener and making a difference in her life. The arguments attacked, though, may have been intended as memorable encapsulations of doctrine, rather than to persuade non-Stoics (who were to be convinced by overall, mutually supporting considerations such as Cicero mentions in 53 (echoing Cato in book III, 74)). See book III note 16.

[27] A sorites argument, from the Greek word for 'heap', proceeds from a premise which the opponent accepts, through individual steps each of which he also accepts, to a conclusion which he does not. This form of argument was much used by the Academic Sceptics against the Stoics. The Stoics thought it legitimate to stop at a point at which the item did not *clearly* fall into the class in question. For the argument and Stoic responses, see Jonathan Barnes, 'Medicine, Experience and Logic', pp. 24–68 of J. Barnes and others (eds.), *Science and Speculation*, Paris/Cambridge 1982.

the difference into words, then Polemo could be happy if he possessed virtue alone, and lacked the rest. Yet he still would not grant to you that only virtue is to be counted a good. Moreover, those whose supreme good does not include virtue will probably not concede that the happy life is something which we might justly take pride in, though sometimes they do actually regard pleasures as things to be proud of.

(52) 'You can see, then, that you are helping yourself to points that either have not been agreed, or have been agreed but are of no use to you. With regard to the whole lot of these syllogisms, I would have thought that an aim worthy of both philosophy and ourselves was that they should change our lives, our plans and our wills, not just our terminology. Yet could anyone change their view on the basis of hearing these brief, pointed arguments which you say you love?

'People come eagerly expecting to hear why pain is not an evil. The Stoics tell them that pain is a tough, unpleasant burden, contrary to nature and hard to bear – but not an evil, because it involves no wrongdoing, dishonesty or vice, no blameworthiness or cause for shame. Will anyone who hears this know whether to laugh or cry? They will certainly not leave any more resolute in enduring pain than when they arrived.

(53) 'Moreover you say that no one who thinks pain an evil can be brave. Yet why should one be any more brave for thinking, as you would admit yourself, that pain is tough and hard to bear? Cowardice is based on facts, not words. You claim that if one letter of the Stoic system were altered, then the whole thing would collapse. Do you think that I am altering a letter, or whole pages? Let us grant what you praise, namely the methodical ordering of their system and the way all its parts are mutually consistent and connected (that was your description). One still ought not to adhere to a set of interlocking and thematically focussed propositions if they are derived from false premises.

(54) 'Your founder Zeno abandoned nature in framing his constitution. He located the supreme good in that excellence of character which we are calling virtue. He declared that there was no other good except what was moral, and that there could be no conception of virtue if any of the other things were better or worse than one another. He then held rigorously to the conclusions that followed from these premises. But the conclusions are so false that the premises from which they spring cannot be true.[28]

(55) 'Logicians teach us, as you know, that if whatever follows from a premise is false, then the premise from which it follows is itself false. Hence we get the well-known syllogism which is not only true but sufficiently

---

[28] The major Stoic theses that virtue is the only good, and is sufficient for happiness, lead to conclusions which are obviously false, but which the Stoics try unsuccessfully to disarm (54–8). The proper response to a clearly false conclusion, Cicero claims, is to reject the premise (if the argument is valid). In 55 he supports this with one of the 'unprovable' principles of Stoic logic, the principle we call *modus tollens*. (He is using Stoic logic against the Stoics, although downplaying its originality in 9.)

evident for the logicians not to deem it in need of proof: if A then B; but not B; so not A. So if your conclusions are overturned, then so are your premises. 'What, then, are your conclusions?[29] That all who are not wise are equally miserable; that all who are wise are supremely happy; that all right acts are equally right and all wrongdoing is equally wrong. These maxims sound wonderful on first acquaintance, but become less convincing on mature reflection. Common sense, the facts of nature, and truth herself proclaimed the impossibility of being persuaded that there was really no difference between all the things which Zeno made equal.

(56) 'Consequently, your hero Zeno, as crafty as only a little Phoenician can be (as you know, your clients from Citium are descended from the Phoenicians),[30] started playing with words. He was, after all, losing his case, given nature's opposition. So first he conceded that those things which my school calls goods might be considered valuable and suited to nature. Then came the beginnings of an admission that even for the wise – that is, supremely happy – person, it might be nicer to possess some of those items which he admitted were suited to nature, without having the courage to call them good.

'He denied that Plato, even if he were not wise, was in the same condition as the tyrant Dionysius. The latter's best option was to die, since there was no hope that he would become wise. For Plato there was a hope; so it was best for him to stay alive. Moreover some acts of wrongdoing can be tolerated, others not at all. This is because some transgress many aspects of one's duty, others just a few. Again, some people are so foolish as to be utterly incapable of attaining wisdom, while other fools might do so if they worked at it.

(57) 'Zeno's language was unique, but his thoughts were commonplace.[31] He really did not set any lower value on the objects which he denied were goods than did those thinkers who called them goods. So what on earth was his purpose in changing the labels? He ought at least to have reduced their importance and put a slightly lower value on them than the Peripatetics did, to give the appearance that the thought and not just the description was different.

'Well now, what do you have to say about the happy life, which is the aim of all else? You deny that it requires the satisfaction of all our natural desires,

---

[29] 55 and 56 list Stoic theses which in isolation sound counter-intuitive, and claim that the Stoics are illegitimately evasive in saying that the theory has resources to render them acceptable.

[30] In 58 Cato was in charge of taking over Cyprus from its Greek rulers, the kings of Egypt. Having supervised its annexation as a Roman province, he became its Roman patron, and the Cypriots his clients. Citium in Cyprus is Zeno's birthplace; it was a Greek city, and Zeno may have been Greek, native Phoenician or a mixture. He is called Phoenician here to suggest that his philosophical moves are shifty; the Romans saw Phoenicians as untrustworthy, a stereotype fortified by their long struggle with the Phoenician city of Carthage.

[31] From 57 to 60 Cicero argues that Zeno's account of happiness implies indifference to rational selection of what is naturally advantageous to us, but that he evades the obvious falsity of this by regarding these natural advantages, in relation to virtue, in just the same way as his opponents do.

and instead locate it entirely in virtue. Now every dispute tends to revolve around either facts or terms. Ignorance of facts or misuse of terms will lead to one or other form of dispute. Where neither is the case, we must make every effort to employ the most familiar and appropriate terminology, namely that which reveals the facts. (58) There can be no doubt that the ancients had a more suitable terminology, assuming they were right about the facts. I shall return to the question of terminology later.

'The ancients say that desire is aroused in the mind when something appears to it to be in accordance with nature. Everything that accords with nature deserves a certain value, and the value is to be proportionate to the importance that each item has. Of the things which accord with nature, some, namely those which are called neither moral nor praiseworthy, have nothing in and of themselves to stir up the desire I just mentioned; but there are others which are objects of pleasure for every living creature, and for humans objects of reason too. Those items that are suited by being objects of reason are called moral, beautiful and praiseworthy; the earlier ones are merely termed natural, though when joined with the moral goods they produce a life of complete and perfect happiness.

(59) 'Now the ancients attribute no more value to all these natural advantages than Zeno does, though they call them goods and he does not. What is moral and praiseworthy forms by far the most important category. None the less, if one is offered the choice between morality with good health and morality with ill health, there is no doubt about which option nature herself will lead us towards. Yet such is the power of morality, such is its pre-eminence and superiority over everything else, that neither punishment nor reward can deflect it from what it has decreed to be right. Every apparent hardship, every difficulty and adversity, can be crushed by the virtues that nature has equipped us with. Such hardships are not to be derided as easily borne (where would that leave the power of virtue?), but should result in our judging that they are not the most important determinant of whether life is happy or unhappy.

(60) 'In sum, the things that Zeno says are to be valued and adopted and accord with nature, the ancients call goods. The happy life for them is one that is constituted by these aforementioned goods, either all of them or as many as possible of the most important ones. Zeno on the other hand will only call good what has its own unique lustre that makes it desirable, and the only happy life is the life spent virtuously.

'If, Cato, we are to discuss facts, then there can be no disagreement between you and me. Not one of our views is different, once one alters the terminology and compares the actual substance. Zeno was well aware of this, but was seduced by the glorious grandeur of language. If he had intended to use his terms with their real meaning, there would have been no difference between him and Pyrrho or Aristo.[32] But if he did not go along with them, why did he

---

[32] See above, note 22.

bother to get involved in a verbal dispute with thinkers he concurred with on matters of substance?

(61) 'Imagine that those pupils of Plato, and their followers in turn, were to come back to life and address you in the following manner:[33] "Marcus Cato, most devoted student of philosophy, most just of men, most honourable of judges, most scrupulous of witnesses, as we listen to you we wonder what your reasons might be for preferring the Stoics to us. After all, the Stoic views on good and evil are those which Zeno learned from Polemo here, while their terminology is at first sight remarkable, and then, when the matter is understood, ridiculous. If you were persuaded by these views, why did you not maintain them in their own proper terminology? Or if you were simply swayed by authority, did you really prefer that nobody to all of us and to Plato himself?

'"In particular, you intended to play a leading role in public life, and we were just the people to have armed and equipped you to protect the state and to maximize your own honour. We founded the study of statecraft; we created its form, its vocabulary and its rules. We have written exhaustively on every variety of government; on stability and revolution; and on the laws, institutions and traditions of nations. Oratory is the greatest asset of the political leader, and we hear that you are an outstanding orator. But a study of the records of our oratory would have made you all the greater."

'Well, Cato, what response could you make to the words of men like these?' (62) 'I would request', said Cato, 'that having put this speech into their mouths you make one on my behalf too. In fact I prefer to listen to you, and I intend to reply to these distinguished figures – meaning to yourself – on another occasion. Otherwise I would have asked you to give me a little breathing-space to make my reply.'

'Then if you wanted to make a truthful reply, Cato, this is what you would have to say: notwithstanding that these were men of great intellect and authority, you were not persuaded by them. Instead, you noticed that the Stoics had seen things which they, on account of their antiquity, had missed. The Stoics discussed the same topics with greater insight, and their judgements had more depth and boldness. After all, to begin with, they declared that good health was not worth seeking, but worth selecting, and this latter not because being healthy is a good, but because it has a certain value (not that those who had no doubt that it was a good placed any higher value upon it).

'You simply could not bear it that those bearded old coves (as we generally call our ancestors)[34] thought that a morally good life which also had health, reputation and wealth would thereby be a preferable, better and more desir-

---

[33] From 61 to 68 Cicero claims that Stoic pedantry is particularly unworthy of a Roman public figure like Cato, who needs the oratory and study of politics supplied by the Aristotelians rather than verbal nitpicking. Moreover, it is perverse for a straightforward Roman like Cato to be attracted by verbal ingenuities and evasions.

[34] Greek and Roman adult males normally wore beards until the period following Alexander the Great, when it became the norm for men to be clean-shaven (except for philosophers, who continued to wear beards).

able life than one which was equally moral but, as with Alcmaeon in Ennius,[35] was "beset on all sides by illness, exile and poverty". (63) Those ancients, dimwits that they were, believed that the first life was more desirable, superior and happier. The Stoics, on the other hand, consider that this life is merely to be preferred in one's choices, not because it is a happier life but because it is more suited to nature. Furthermore, those who are not wise are all equally miserable.

'The Stoics had evidently noticed a point which eluded their predecessors, namely that those who are steeped in crime and treason are no more unhappy than people who lead lives of blameless integrity but without attaining to perfect Stoic wisdom. (64) At this point you would introduce those utterly disanalogous analogies that the Stoics love to use.[36] Everyone knows that when a number of people are trying to get out of some deep water, then however close you are to the surface and to being able to breathe, you can no more actually breathe than someone far beneath you. So, in simply making progress towards virtue, as progress towards the surface, without actually reaching it, you are as utterly miserable as before. And puppies who are about to open their eyes are still just as blind as newly born ones. So Plato, who did not attain the vision of wisdom, must have been as mentally blind as Phalaris.[37]

(65) 'These are cases in which, however much one progresses, one remains in the same state that one is trying to get out of until one finally emerges. But they are not good analogies for virtue. The swimmer cannot breathe before breaking the surface; the puppies are as blind just before opening their eyes as they would be if they were to remain always in that condition. Here are some better analogies: one person has blurred eyesight, another a weak body. By applying a remedy they improve day by day. Every day, one gets stronger, the other sees better. It is like this for every keen seeker after virtue. Their faults and their errors are gradually cured.

'Or do you consider that Tiberius Gracchus the elder was no happier than his son?[38] The father worked hard to maintain the stability of the state, the son to undermine it. To be sure, the father was not a wise person. Who is?

---

[35] See book I note 4.
[36] Contrast book III para. 48, with note 28. Cicero here fails to allow that the Stoics can allow progress towards virtue, even if there are no degrees of virtue itself.
[37] Phalaris was a legendary tyrant of Acragas, famous for cruelty, in particular for roasting people alive inside a bronze bull. 'Phalaris' bull' was a stock example of the torments that can be inflicted on the virtuous, and is so referred to at book V, 85.
[38] Tiberius Sempronius Gracchus the elder, consul in 177 and 163, was a prominent and successful Roman general and politician. His son Tiberius Sempronius Gracchus, as tribune in 133 introduced a much-needed agrarian reform, which, however, led to unprecedented forms of constitutional impasse and eventually to Gracchus' murder by a group of senators. These events mark the beginning of the breakdown in the working of Roman Republican political institutions which finished only with the end of the Republic. Cicero prejudicially regards the younger Gracchus and his brother (see next note) as wickedly aiming to destroy a stably functioning constitution, and as responsible for the breakdown of the Republic.

When, where and how? But because he sought praise and honour, he made great progress in virtue. (66) Compare your grandfather Marcus Drusus with Gaius Gracchus, who was about the same age.[39] The former tried to heal the wounds that the latter had inflicted on the state. If nothing makes people so miserable as being impious and wicked, then even if all who are not wise are miserable (as assuredly they are), none the less it is less miserable to serve the interests of one's country than to wish it destroyed.

'Thus those who make some progress towards virtue see at the same time a great reduction in their vices. (67) The Stoics allow that there is progress towards virtue, but deny the reduction in vice. The argument that these clever people use to prove the point is well worth examining. It goes like this: where the boundaries of a field of knowledge can be extended, then the boundaries of its opposite can also be extended; but virtue has a fixed boundary; therefore vice, which is the opposite of virtue, cannot admit of increase either.

'Well now: should the evident clarify the doubtful or be refuted by it? This at any rate is evident, that some vices are worse than others. Whether or not what you call the supreme good admits of any increase is open to doubt. But you Stoics try to overturn the evident with the doubtful, when you should be illuminating the doubtful with the evident. (68) Hence you will founder by the same reasoning that I used just now. If the justification for the view that no vice is worse than any other is that what you conceive of as your highest good cannot admit of any increase, then you should change your conception of the highest good, since it is evident that not everyone's vices are equal. We must hold to the principle that when a conclusion is false, its premises cannot be true.

'So what has landed you in these dire straits?[40] The pride and vanity which went into the construction of your supreme good. In declaring what is moral to be the only good, you do away with concern for one's health, care of one's household, public service, the conduct of business and the duties of life. Ultimately morality itself, which you regard as everything, must be abandoned. Chrysippus took great pains to make these very points against Aristo. Here, then, is the difficulty which led to this "false-speaking trickery", to quote Accius.[41] (69) Wisdom had nowhere to stand once all appropriate action was done away with; and it was done away with when every form of choice and distinction was abolished. This, in turn, required the levelling of all objects until there was no difference between them, and from this parlous state came a set of principles even more bizarre than those of Aristo.

---

[39] Gaius Sempronius Gracchus, brother of Tiberius Gracchus the younger, was tribune in 123 and 122. He revived his brother's reforms, and, like him, was driven to extreme constitutional measures and eventually killed by a group of reactionary senators. Marcus Livius Drusus, tribune in 122, opposed Gracchus' proposals. He went on to become consul in 112, dying in 109. His daughter was Cato's mother.

[40] 68 to 73 repeat the charge alleged to pick out the Stoics' difficulties. Their conception of happiness as consisting in virtue alone either gives no basis for rational choice among non-moral things, or reduces to a verbal variant of Aristotle's view.

[41] From an unknown play by Accius; see book II, note 64.

'At least Aristo's are straightforward; yours are convoluted. Ask Aristo whether he thinks the following are goods: freedom from pain, wealth, health. He will say no. Well then, are their opposites evils? Similarly, no. Now ask Zeno the same question, and his reply will be the same. In our astonishment, we ask both philosophers how it will be possible to live a life if we think it makes no difference to us whether we are well or ill, free from pain or in agony, able to stave off cold and hunger or not. Aristo says we will live great and glorious lives, doing whatever we think fit, without sorrow, desire or fear.

(70) 'What does Zeno say? That Aristo's doctrine is a monstrosity; no life can be lived by such a rule. His own view is that there is a huge, an utterly immense, gap between morality and immorality, but that between all other things there is no difference whatsoever. (71) So far, this is still the same as Aristo. Hear the rest and choke back your laughter if you can.

'"These intermediates", says Zeno, "all of which are indifferent, none the less comprise some which should be chosen, some which should be rejected and others which should be altogether ignored. So, some you will want, others you will not want, and for the rest you will not care either way." But Zeno, you just said that the whole lot of them were indifferent. "And that is still what I say", he will reply, "but I mean indifferent with respect to the virtues and vices."

(72) 'Well, everyone would agree with that, but let him continue: "Those things that you mentioned, health, wealth and freedom from pain, I call not good but in Greek *proêgmena*, in Latin 'brought forward' (though I would rather use 'preferred' or 'pre-eminent' as more acceptably smooth renderings). On the other hand I call disease, poverty and pain not evil but, if you please, worthy of rejection. So in the case of the former category I speak not of seeking but of selecting, not of wishing for but of adopting; while its opposite one does not avoid but as it were sets aside."

'What do Aristotle and the other pupils of Plato have to say? That they call all things which are in accordance with nature good, and all those against nature evil. Note, then, that your leader Zeno agrees verbally with Aristo, but differs in substance, whereas he agrees in substance with Aristotle and the others while differing merely in words.[42] Since there is agreement in substance, why not prefer the standard terminology? Or else let him demonstrate that I will be more ready to despise money if I regard it as preferred rather than good, and more courageous in enduring pain if I call it harsh, difficult to bear and contrary to nature, rather than evil.

(73) 'Our friend Marcus Piso[43] used his ready wit on many targets, particularly the Stoics on this present point. "Well now", he would say, "you claim that wealth is not good but preferred. What use is that? Do you thereby diminish avarice? In what way? If it is a question of words, then to begin with,

---

[42] Compare book III, 41–4 and note 24.
[43] Marcus Pupius Piso Frugi Calpurnianus, the defender of Antiochus' theory in book V. See Introduction, pp. xvi, xxxiv.

'preferred' is actually a longer word than 'good'." "That is irrelevant." "Fine. But it is certainly a more impressive word. I do not know the derivation of 'good', but 'preferred' means, I believe, what is 'put before' other things, and this, I would have thought, must be something special."

'So Piso would maintain that Zeno held wealth in higher regard by classifying it as preferred than did Aristotle in calling it a good though not a great good, something to be despised and looked down upon in comparison with uprightness and moral goodness, and not worth spending much effort in pursuing. On the general theme of all these terminological changes that Zeno made, Piso would contend that he came up with more attractive names for the objects he denied were good than the names we use, and less attractive names than ours for the objects he denied were evil.

'This is how Piso dealt with the Stoics. He is an excellent man, and, as you know, a devoted admirer of yours. Let me add just a few words to his, and then finally draw to a conclusion. It would take too long to reply to all your points.[44]

(74) 'The same sort of verbal trickery gives rise to your kingdoms, your empires and your riches, riches so vast that you claim the wise person owns everything in the world. Moreover, only the wise person is beautiful, only the wise person is free, only the wise person is a citizen. The foolish have all the opposite characteristics, and you declare that they are insane as well. The Stoics call these views *paradoxa*, and we may describe them as startling.[45]

'What, though, is so startling about them on closer inspection? I will consult with you over the meaning you attach to each term, so there will be no dispute. You say that all wrongdoing is equal. I will not now repeat the joke I made on this subject when I was defending Lucius Murena and you were prosecuting. I was addressing a non-specialist audience then, and played a little to the gallery.[46] Now I must take a more subtle approach.

(75) '"All wrongdoing is equal." How so? "Because nothing is more moral than morality, nor more immoral than immorality." Explain further, since this is a point of great controversy. Show me the precise arguments for the thesis that all wrongdoing is equal. "Imagine", comes the reply, "that a number of lyres are all strung in such a way as to be out of tune. They will all be equally

---

[44] Cicero's arguments in this book have been general and systematic (reflecting the use Antiochus made of Carneades' arguments). In 74–7, however, Cicero does argue closely against one specific point in Stoicism, returning in 78 to a summary of the general argument that has played so major a role.

[45] In his short work *Stoic Paradoxical Theses*, dedicated to Brutus and written in 46, before Cato's death, Cicero takes six such theses, claims which in isolation are strikingly counter-intuitive, and tries to make them plausible by rhetorical means. Two of these appear here, 'only the wise person is rich' (beautiful, free, and so on), alluded to at book III, 75, and 'all wrongdoings are equal', mentioned at book III, 46–8. Rather than try sympathetically to bring out the point of them, as in his shorter work, Cicero here argues against the second.

[46] In 63 Cicero defended Lucius Licinius Murena, who was being prosecuted by Cato for malpractice in the election in which he had been elected consul. The defence speech *In defence of Murena* says little about the charges (usually taken as a sign that Murena was guilty) and ridicules Cato (61–3) as a Stoic who lives by wildly unrealistic ideas (such as that all wrongdoings are equal) and is thus out of touch with the real world. Murena was acquitted.

out of tune. So too all wrongdoing, in so far as it is disharmonious, is equally disharmonious."

'This trades on an ambiguity. It is equally the case that all the lyres are out of tune. But it does not follow that they are all equally out of tune. So this comparison of yours is no help. If we were to say that every case of greed was equally a case of greed, it would likewise not follow that we should also declare every case to be of equal greed.[47]

(76) 'Here comes another of those disanalogous analogies: "A ship's captain", it is said, "will be equally culpable whether the ship goes down with a cargo of straw or a cargo of gold. So too it is an equal offence whether one assaults one's parents without good cause or one's slave." But this fails to grasp that the kind of cargo a ship is carrying has no bearing on the skill of the captain! So whether its cargo was straw or gold is irrelevant to the question of the ship's being steered well or badly. But the distinction between a parent and a mere slave can and must be recognized. When it comes to ship's captaincy, then, the category of the victim of the offence makes no difference. In the sphere of moral action it makes all the difference.

'Even in the case of captaincy, if the ship goes down due to negligence, then a greater offence has been committed with gold on board than with straw. We maintain that the virtue generally known as practical reason is a characteristic of any art, and so every good practitioner in whatever field ought to possess it. So even from this perspective it is not the case that all wrongdoing is equal.[48]

(77) 'But the Stoics press on and refuse to let up. "Every act of wrongdoing", they say, "is a sign of weakness and inconstancy; these vices are present to an equally large degree in all foolish people; therefore all wrongdoing must be equal." They speak as if it were agreed that all foolish people have an equal amount of vice, and that Lucius Tubulus had the same level of weakness and inconstancy as Publius Scaevola, who brought in the bill for his condemnation.[49] As if, in addition, the circumstances in which wrongdoing is committed make no difference, whereas the seriousness of a wrongful act varies in proportion to the importance of the circumstances which surround it.

(78) 'Hence (and here I conclude my discourse) your Stoic school seems weighed down above all by one particular flaw, namely that of believing that they can uphold two opposing views. Nothing could be more contradictory than claiming that what is moral is the only good, and at the same time that we have a desire, which springs from nature, for the things that are conducive

---

[47] A Stoic is committed to the equality of wrongdoings by the thesis that virtue is not the kind of thing that comes in degrees or amounts that can be quantitatively compared.

[48] Stoics can allow that the consequences of an act may reasonably affect some aspects of the way it is judged; they are committed to the thesis that such consequences do not affect the issue of whether the act is right or wrong. In his explication of this Stoic paradox in his short work on them, Cicero uses the example of the cargoes of straw and gold to make the point that difference in consequences does *not* affect the rightness or wrongness of an action.

[49] See book II, 54 and note 38.

to life. When they want to maintain views that are consistent with the first principle they turn out like Aristo. When they seek to avoid this position, they are actually defending the same thesis as the Peripatetics while clinging doggedly to their own terminology. Unwilling once again to cast such terminology from their ranks, they become ever more uncouth, harsh and rough, not just in their discourses but in their way of life.

(79) 'Panaetius rejected this depressing harshness of theirs. He had no time either for the severity of their views or their tortured way of arguing for them. His doctrines were gentler, and his style more lucid. As his own writings show, Plato and Aristotle were always on his lips; Xenocrates, Theophrastus and Dicaearchus too.[50] Indeed I strongly advise you to study these authors with care and diligence.

(80) 'However, evening is drawing in and I must return home. Enough, then, for now. I hope we shall often return to these subjects.' 'Indeed we shall', said Cato. 'There is no finer pursuit. The first favour I shall ask of you is to hear my refutation of your arguments. Remember, though, that you actually accept all of our doctrines, rejecting only our new terminology, whereas I accept none of yours.'[51] 'That is quite a parting shot', I remarked, 'but we shall see.' With these words I departed.

---

[50] For Panaetius, see book I note 7. He wrote on Stoicism in a way that communicated better than the early Stoics to a non-professional audience, and also showed interest in the ideas of Plato and his follower Xenocrates, and Aristotle and his followers Theophrastus and Dicaearchus. (Dicaearchus of Messene flourished *c.* 320; he had wide empirical interests.)

[51] Cato's parting shot utterly rejects the book's main argument. How, though, can Aristotelians be committed to Stoic ideas if Stoics reject Aristotelian ideas? Presumably Cato means that a clarification of Aristotelian ideas leads to Stoicism, whereas Stoics have arguments against Aristotelian ideas.

Book V

(1) I had been listening, Brutus, as I often did, to a lecture by Antiochus with Marcus Piso.[1] It took place in the public building known as the Ptolemaeum.[2] With us were Quintus my brother, Titus Pomponius and Lucius Cicero,[3] whom I loved like a brother, though we were actually cousins. We decided to take our afternoon stroll in the Academy, mainly because there would be no crowds at that time of day. We all met at Piso's place, at the appointed hour, and occupied ourselves with various topics of conversation on the walk, just over half a mile, from the Dipylon Gate. We arrived at the Academy's justly famous grounds to find that we had the place to ourselves, as we had hoped.

(2) Piso then remarked: 'I cannot say whether it is a natural instinct or a kind of illusion, but when we see the places where we are told that the notables of the past spent their time, it is far more moving than when we hear about their achievements or read their writings. This is how I am affected right now. I think of Plato, who they say was the first philosopher to have regularly held discussions here. Those little gardens just nearby not only bring Plato to mind, but actually seem to make him appear before my eyes. Here come Speusippus, Xenocrates and his pupil Polemo, who sat on that very seat

---

[1] For the setting, see Introduction, pp. xi and xvii. The dramatic date is 79, much earlier than the preceding two dialogues. The setting is Athens, where the youthful Cicero and friends are attending philosophy lectures and visiting historic sites. For Piso, see Introduction, p. xvi, and for Antiochus, pp. xiii–xv.

[2] The building is named after one of the Greek rulers of Egypt in the Hellenistic period. Although Antiochus claims to return to the tradition of the 'Old Academy' he does not teach in the Academy itself, which is not in use. The philosophical schools were outside the city walls, and had probably been damaged in the siege of Athens by Sulla eight years previously.

[3] Cicero's younger brother Quintus (c. 102–43), less gifted a politician and much less intellectual, was moderately successful as a soldier and administrator. For Titus Pomponius see book I, note 18. His becoming called 'Atticus' because of his love for Attica (Athens) is referred to in 4. Lucius Tullius Cicero, son of Cicero's uncle Lucius, was brought up with his cousins Marcus and Quintus, and was especially close to Marcus, whom he helped, in Sicily, in his prosecution of the corrupt governor Verres in 70. He died young in 68, which adds pathos to the prominent concern the older friends have here for his proper development. (Compare the concern in book III for young Lucullus, likewise prematurely dead.)

we can see over there.[4] Even when I look at our own Senate-house (I mean the original old Hostilia; its enlargement seems to me to have diminished it[5]), I often think of Scipio, Cato, Laelius and above all my grandfather.[6] Such is the evocative power that locations possess. No wonder the training of memory is based on them.'

(3) 'That is quite true, Piso', said Quintus. 'While on my way here just now, I could not help noticing the famous site of Colonus, and it brought Sophocles, who lived there, before my eyes. As you know, I feel great admiration and love for him. In fact a still more ancient vision moved me, bringing to mind Oedipus arriving there and asking in those wonderfully tender verses, "What place is this?" – an idle vision, no doubt, but still it moved me.'[7]

'As for me', remarked Pomponius, 'my devotion to Epicurus incurs your constant attacks, and I do spend a lot of time with Phaedrus, whom you know to be my dearest friend, in Epicurus' garden, which we just passed. But I follow the old proverb, "Remember the living". Still, I could hardly forget Epicurus, even if I wanted to. The members of our Epicurean family have his likeness not only in paintings, but even engraved on their cups and rings.'

(4) 'Our friend Pomponius seems to be displaying his wit', I said. 'And perhaps that is as it should be. He has stationed himself so firmly in Athens that he is almost one of the Attic tribe. I have a feeling he might even take on the name "Atticus".[8] But I agree with you, Piso. It is a fact that the stimulus of place considerably sharpens and intensifies the thoughts we have about famous individuals. You remember when I once came to Metapontum with you that I could not go to my lodgings until I had seen the exact place where Pythagoras died, and the chair that he sat on.[9] Every part of Athens is filled with reminders of great men in the actual places they lived. Still, at this moment it is that alcove over there that is affecting me. Not long ago it was Carneades' stage. I think I see him now (his likeness is well known), and I

---

[4] Speusippus, Xenocrates and Polemo are the direct successors of Plato as heads of the Academy. See book IV note 4.

[5] The original Senate House was ascribed to Tullus Hostilius, sixth king of Rome. Piso refers deprecatingly to its rebuilding and enlargement (to contain his expanded Senate) by the dictator Sulla in 81.

[6] Scipio here is probably Scipio Africanus, defeater of Hannibal; see book II note 41. Cato here is Marcus Porcius Cato the Censor (234–149), great-grandfather of the Cato of books III and IV, Roman politician noted for his stern and unbending nature. For Laelius see book II note 23. Piso's grandfather is Lucius Calpurnius Piso Frugi; see book II note 62. Piso, after evoking the glorious Athenian philosophical past, at once matches it with the glorious Roman political past.

[7] In his last play Sophocles, the Athenian dramatist (see book I note 4) brings Oedipus, the blinded king of Thebes, to his own village of Colonus. Quintus quotes the play's opening lines.

[8] As he did. Despite his long friendship with Atticus, Cicero here presents his Epicureanism as ridiculously deferential and unintellectual. On Phaedrus see book I note 17.

[9] Pythagoras of Samos came to the Greek colonies in Italy in the mid sixth century. Traditionally he was driven out of Croton, where he had founded Pythagorean societies, and died in Metapontum. Very little can be safely established about Pythagoras' life, but his legend gave rise to such relics.

think that the very seat where he sat misses his voice and mourns the loss of a towering intellect.'

(5) 'Well', said Piso, 'since we each have our own special place, what about our friend Lucius? Does he enjoy visiting the spot where Demosthenes and Aeschines used to wage their verbal battles? It is our own particular area of study that especially influences us.'

'Do not ask', blushed Lucius. 'I have actually been down to the Bay of Phalerum where they say that Demosthenes used to practise declaiming against the waves, to train his voice to overcome the roar of a crowd. And just now I turned off a little to the right to visit the tomb of Pericles.[10] Indeed there is no end to it in this city. Wherever we go, we are walking on historic ground.'

(6) 'These enthusiasms of yours, Lucius', said Piso, 'are worthy of a genuine talent if their purpose is the emulation of great individuals. If, however, they serve merely to acquaint you with memorials of the ancient past, that shows no more than inquisitiveness. We all urge you – though I trust you are already up and running – to strive not only to learn about these figures but to imitate them as well.'

'As you are aware, Piso', I interjected, 'he is already putting your precepts into practice. None the less, I thank you for your encouragement.' 'Let us all', replied Piso, with his usual graciousness, 'join forces to promote this young man's development. Above all, let him devote some of his studies to philosophy, either in homage to you whom he adores, or to equip him better in his own field. But Lucius,' he went on, 'do you need our encouragement or are you already leaning towards philosophy of your own accord? You are going to Antiochus' lectures, and seem to be pretty attentive.'

'I suppose so', replied Lucius, in a timid or I should say modest tone. 'But have you heard any talks on Carneades? I find him alluring, though Antiochus pulls me in the other direction, and there is no one else to hear.'[11]

(7) 'Perhaps', said Piso, 'desertion will be impossible while our friend here (meaning me) is around. None the less, I shall venture to draw you away from the New Academy to the Old. As you heard Antiochus say, the Old Academy contains not only those who are known as Academics – Speusippus, Xenocrates, Polemo, Crantor and the rest[12] – but also the early Peripatetics,

---

[10] Lucius, a budding politician, has been visiting sites associated with famous Athenian politicians. Pericles (495–429) is the leading Athenian political figure of the fifth century. Demosthenes (*c.* 384–322) and Aeschines (*c.* 397–322) are competing fourth-century politicians.

[11] Lucius sees the only real philosophical options as the two rival traditions of Platonism. One is the sceptical Academy, represented by Carneades, for which the true task of philosophy is to inquire into and criticize others' claims in search of understanding; the other is the revived 'Old Academy' tradition represented by Antiochus, which takes Platonism to be a system of ideas, into which the insights of other great thinkers can be integrated. In this book Cicero defends the sceptical Academy against Antiochus; in book IV he used Antiochus' position to argue against the Stoics, but this is perfectly consistent for an Academic (see Introduction, p. xv, and below note 54.)

[12] Crantor of Soli (c. 336–276/5), important figure among Plato's successors, though not head of the school. He wrote commentaries on Plato's works, particularly the *Timaeus*, and a famous work *On Grief*.

headed by Aristotle, who should perhaps be called the chief of all philosophers, with the exception of Plato. I beg you, change your allegiance over to
them. In their writings and teachings is to be found a complete liberal education, a complete history, and a complete manual of style. In fact such is the
variety of their accomplishments that no one who fails to make use of their
resources can be sufficiently equipped for any of the more illustrious pursuits.
They have produced orators, generals and political leaders. To turn to the lesser
occupations, a stream of mathematicians, poets, musicians and doctors has
flowed from what one might call their production line of all the professions.'

(8) 'You know, Piso, that I agree with you on this', I said. 'Still, you have
raised the subject at an opportune moment. My cousin Lucius is keen to find
out the views of the Old Academy that you mention, and also of the
Peripatetics, on the question of the highest goods. We think that you are the
one to explain them most fluently, since Staseas of Naples has been a member
of your household for many years, and we know that you have been pursuing
the same topic with Antiochus in Athens these past few months.'[13]

'Alright, alright', said Piso with a smile, 'You wanted me all along to start
off our discussion. Let me see if I can give the young man a lecture. Since the
Academy is deserted, I have the chance to discourse in it like a philosopher,
which I would never have believed possible had even a god foretold it. But I
do not want to bore you while I am indulging the young man.' 'Bore me?' I
replied. 'It was I who made the request!'

Quintus and Pomponius also gave their assent, and Piso began. Please con-
centrate, Brutus, and see if his talk adequately captures the philosophy of
Antiochus. I know that you are a particular adherent of his views, and have
often heard lectures by his brother Aristus.

(9) This is what Piso had to say: 'I have already said enough, as concisely
as I could, about the richness of the Peripatetic tradition.[14] Formally, their
system has three divisions, like most others: one is concerned with nature,
another with argument, and the third with the conduct of life. They investigate nature with a thoroughness that misses out no part of sky, sea or earth,
to put it poetically. In fact, in discussing the basic elements of the universe as
a whole, they argue not merely on the basis of likelihood but bring to bear the
binding force of mathematical reasoning. A great mass of material based on
direct research is applied to the discovery of hidden realities.

---

[13] Staseas of Naples, the first Aristotelian philosopher known to have settled in Rome.
Aristocratic Romans often had philosophers in their households; the Stoic Diodotus lived in
Cicero's. In ethics, Antiochus' 'Old Academy' synthesis owes most to Aristotle. However,
Cicero points out at 75 below that an Aristotelian like Staseas cannot agree with Antiochus on
one major point: the sufficiency of virtue for happiness.

[14] From 9 to 15 Piso expounds the supposed 'Old Academy' tradition defended by Antiochus,
but with a marked Aristotelian slant, the focus being ethics, where Antiochus is most dependent on Aristotle. Compare book IV, 4–14. In both passages we find the projection back onto
earlier philosophers of the Stoics' three parts of philosophy; praise of the Peripatetics for their
broad interest in explanation; stress on their concern with rhetoric as well as logic; and focus
on practical politics.

(10) 'Aristotle gives a thorough account of the birth, nutrition and structure of every living creature. Theophrastus did the same with regard to the nature of plants and gave a scientific explanation for virtually everything that grows from the ground. The knowledge this provided facilitated research into even the most arcane areas of reality. As for argument, the Peripatetics laid down rules not just for dialectic but for rhetoric too. Aristotle their founder began the practice of presenting both sides of every argument, with the purpose not of contradicting everything like Arcesilaus, but of revealing every point which could be made on either side of any question.

(11) 'The third division of philosophy is concerned with rules for living well, and here the Peripatetics were interested not only in the organization of one's private life but in the good conduct of public affairs as well. The traditions, institutions and systems of every state, Greek and non-Greek, we can discover from Aristotle, and their laws from Theophrastus.[15] Both philosophers laid down the suitable qualifications for a political leader, and both wrote often on the question of the best form of the constitution. Theophrastus discusses particularly fully the nature of political change and crisis, and how it can be controlled when circumstances demand.

'The way of life that they most commended was one spent in quiet contemplation and study. This is the most god-like of lives, and so most worthy of the wise person. Some of their most noble and distinguished writing is to be found on this theme.[16]

(12) 'Their discussions of the supreme good sometimes appear inconsistent. This is because they wrote two different kinds of work, one more popular which they called "exoteric", the other more specialized, which took the form of note-books.[17] In fact there is no variation in the main body of their thought, either within the works of the individual thinkers I have mentioned, or between them.

'However, there does appear to be a certain divergence and uncertainty amongst them when it comes to the question of the happy life, and in particular the issue which philosophy ought to consider and pursue above all else, namely the following: is happiness entirely in the power of the wise person, or can it be diminished or destroyed by external misfortune? A paradigm case of this divergence was Theophrastus, whose book *On the Happy Life* gives a

---

[15] Aristotle and his pupils produced historical accounts of the constitutions of many states; one of these, the *Constitution of Athens*, has survived. Theophrastus produced a long collection of laws from Greek and non-Greek states.
[16] A recognition that some Aristotelian passages claim that the best life is one of theoretical contemplation rather than of active virtuous living. One has come down to us as part of the last book of our *Nicomachean Ethics*. Despite the obvious problem in reconciling this with the rest of Aristotelian ethical and social thought, and the existence of a debate in Aristotle's school, between Theophrastus who favoured the contemplative and Dicaearchus the practical life (of which Cicero is aware; see his letter to Atticus, II, 16, 3), Piso drops the issue. Perhaps we are meant to note this as an example of bland harmonizing of different views, ignoring philosophical difficulties.   [17] See Introduction, p. xxiii, and note 20, and book III, 10.

leading role to good and bad fortune. If this were correct, then wisdom could not guarantee a happy life.

'This position, though, seems to me, if I may say so, too soft and delicate to do justice to the power and weight of virtue. So I shall confine myself to Aristotle and his son Nicomachus. Now the elaborate treatise on ethics is attributed to his father, but I do not see why the son should not have matched the father. We can still follow Theophrastus on many points, provided that we allow virtue a more robust strength than he did.[18]

(13) 'Let us rest content with these thinkers. Their successors, though better in my view than the representatives of other philosophical schools, were so inferior to their forebears that you would have thought they had given birth to themselves. First there was Theophrastus' successor Strato, who wanted to be a natural scientist and was a distinguished one at that, but his many innovations included almost nothing on ethics. Strato's successor Lyco had an opulent style but rather threadbare content. Finally, we have Lyco's successor Aristo: refined and elegant, but without the authority required of a great philosopher. His writings are copious and polished, to be sure, but they lack a certain weight.

(14) 'I pass over a number of thinkers, including the clever and charming Hieronymus. I am not sure why I even call him one of the Peripatetics. He declared the supreme good to be freedom from pain, and in breaking ranks over the supreme good he breaks ranks with their whole philosophical system. Critolaus tried to imitate the ancients. He comes pretty close from the point of view of weightiness, and has a flowing style, but not even he remains true to the teachings of his ancestors. Diodorus, his pupil, combined freedom from pain with moral goodness. He, too, goes his own way, and in disagreeing about the supreme good cannot really be called a Peripatetic.[19] My own teacher Antiochus seems to me to follow the views of the ancients with the most care, and he tells us that the positions of Aristotle and Polemo were the same.

---

[18] Theophrastus' *On The Happy Life* was famous for stating that virtue is not sufficient for happiness, which can be lost through misfortune. This is awkward for Antiochus, who claims that Aristotelians agree with Stoics that virtue is sufficient for the happy life (though not the supremely happy life). Hence we find that he gives a privileged place to the *Nicomachean Ethics*, though he takes it to be written by, rather than dedicated to, Aristotle's son Nicomachus (an unlikely author since he died young in battle). However, although possibly Antiochus supported his view by an interpretation of passages at the end of chapters 8 and 10 of the first book, the work also contains two passages (1, 7 and 7, 13) which strongly reject the sufficiency of virtue for happiness, so the problem of how Antiochus' view relates to Aristotle's writings remains, as Cicero points out in 75.

[19] A rapid survey of the later heads of Aristotle's school supports Antiochus' dismissal of it and retention only of Aristotle's and Theophrastus' ideas, together with those of the Platonist Polemo. The characterizations given here of Strato of Lampsacus (died *c*. 268), Lyco of Troas (*c*. 300–*c*. 225) and Aristo of Ceos (active *c*. 225–200) are borne out by their fragments. Critolaus of Phaselis (probably old in 156/5) defended Aristotle's ideas against the Stoics; his major innovation may be an attack on rhetoric. Hieronymus and Diodorus are both said to diverge from the Aristotelian tradition in their definitions of our final end. Almost nothing is known about either (see book II, 8 and note 9, and 19 and note 19) except that they occur in Carneades' classification as the holders of two of the views there.

(15) 'Our friend Lucius, then, is well advised in wanting principally to learn about the supreme good. When this question is settled, so is every question in philosophy. On other issues, an incomplete or uncertain grasp is harmful in proportion to the value of the topic where the neglect occurs. Ignorance of the supreme good, however, is necessarily equivalent to ignorance of how to plan one's life. And this may take one so far off course that one loses sight of any haven to provide shelter. Once, however, we understand the highest ends, once we know what the ultimate good and evil is, then we have a path through life, a model of all our duties, (16) to which each of our actions can thereby be referred.

'Now this is a subject of great controversy. So let us adopt Carneades' classification, which my teacher Antiochus is also happy to use.[20] Carneades surveyed all the philosophical theories that had been propounded to date concerning the supreme good, and all those that could possibly be propounded as well. He declared that no branch of knowledge could be based on itself. There is always something external to it that it comprehends. There is no need to dwell on this point with examples. It is obvious that no branch of knowledge is concerned with itself. We have the particular branch of knowledge on the one hand, and its object on the other. Thus medicine is the art of health, navigation the art of steering a ship. Similarly, practical reason is the art of living, and it is necessary that it too have as its basis and starting-point something external.

(17) 'It is almost universally agreed that what practical reason is concerned with and wants to attain must be something that is well suited and adapted to our nature, something that is attractive in itself and capable of arousing our desire (what the Greeks call *hormê*). There is less agreement, however, on what it is which moves us in this way and is the natural object of our desire from the moment we are born. In fact it is at precisely this point of inquiry into the supreme good that philosophical controversy rages. The origin of the whole dispute about the highest goods and evils, and the question of what among them is ultimate and final, is to be found by asking what the basic natural attachments are. Discover these, and you have the source from which the rest of the debate about the supreme good and evil can be traced.

(18) 'Some, then, consider that our basic desire is for pleasure and our basic aversion is to pain. Others hold that it is freedom from pain that we are first drawn to, and pain that we first shun.[a] For others, the starting-point is what they call the primary things in accordance with nature, among which they number the sound preservation of all the parts of the body, good health, well-functioning senses, freedom from pain, strength, beauty, and so on.

---

[20] The exposition goes from 16 to 23. See Introduction, pp. xxiii–xxvii.

[a] This sentence is bracketed out by the OCT, perhaps because freedom from pain recurs a few lines below as one of the items in the category of things in accordance with nature. The sentence is none the less retained in the translation since in paragraph 19 below freedom from pain is explicitly treated by Cicero as forming by itself one of the three categories of basic goods.

Analogous to these are the primary mental attributes, which are the sparks and seeds of virtue. It is one or other of these three classes which first moves our nature to desire or repulsion. It cannot be anything outside these three. It must be the case, then, that every right act of avoidance or pursuit is aimed at one of them. Hence practical reason, which we described as the art of living, will be concerned with one or other of these three categories, and from it the beginnings of our whole way of life can be derived.

(19) 'Now practical reason will determine what it is that first arouses our nature, and that in turn will result in a theory of what is right and moral, a theory that should be able to tie in with one or other of our three categories. Hence it will be moral to aim all one's actions either at pleasure, even if one is unable to secure it, or at freedom from pain, even if it cannot be attained, or at procuring the things that are in accordance with nature, even if they cannot be won. So it turns out that there is a difference of opinion over the first principles of nature corresponding exactly to the dispute over the highest goods and evils. Other thinkers in turn, starting from the same elements, will make the standard of right action the actual attainment of pleasure, or freedom from pain, or the acquisition of those primary things that are in accordance with nature.

(20) 'I have, then, now set out six views on the supreme good. The three latter ones have the following authors: for pleasure Aristippus, for freedom from pain Hieronymus, and for the enjoyment of what we called the primary things in accordance with nature Carneades, though he did not so much originate the view as defend it for the sake of argument. The three earlier views might be held, but only one of them has actually been defended, and vigorously at that. No one has ever said that all our actions should aim at pleasure, and that even if we did not attain it, we should still pursue the plan of action for its own sake as the only moral and good option. Nor has anyone thought that avoidance of pain was worth pursuing in its own right independently of whether one actually did avoid it. However, the Stoics do say that we should direct all our actions towards acquiring the things that are in accordance with nature, whether or not we actually obtain them. This, they say, is what morality is and the only thing desirable and good in its own right.

(21) 'Here, then, are six simple views about the supreme good, two of them without a sponsor, four actually upheld. There are also three complex or dual theories of the supreme good. There could not be more than three, if you examine the nature of the case closely. With morality one can combine either pleasure, as Callipho and Dinomachus did, or freedom from pain, for Diodorus, or the primary natural things, the view of the ancients, as we call both the Academics and the Peripatetics.

'Now I cannot lay out everything at once, so note for the present that pleasure must be excluded, since we are born for greater things, as I shall shortly explain. One can say pretty much the same about freedom from pain. (22) Nor need we look for any further arguments against Carneades' view. Any exposition of the supreme good that leaves out morality has no place in its theory for duty, virtue or friendship. Moreover the conjunction of morality with pleasure or lack of pain debases morality in attempting to embrace it. Our actions are being referred to two standards, one of which declares that the greatest good consists in being without evil, while the other concerns itself with the most frivolous part of our nature. That is to dull all the brilliance of morality, if not to defile it. There remain the Stoics, who borrowed everything from the Peripatetics and the Academics, and reached the same conclusions using different terminology. It would be best to argue against these positions one-by-one. But now I must press on. We can return to them if we please.

(23) 'Democritus' freedom from care, or tranquillity of mind, which he called *euthumia*, must also be excluded from this discussion, since that very tranquillity is actually identical with the happy life, and we are asking not what the happy life is, but what is its source.[21] The theories of Pyrrho, Aristo and Erillus do not fall within the circle I have drawn. Long discredited and discarded, they were never worthy of application.[22] The whole question of ends, and as it were of the outer limits of good and evil, begins from what we described as being well suited and adapted to our nature, that is, the primary object of our desire in its own right. But such a conception is completely done away with by those who deny any scope for the exercise of preference among objects which are neither morally good nor bad, and who hold that there is absolutely no difference among such objects. As for Erillus, if his view was that knowledge is the only good, then he has removed the whole basis of rational planning and of the discovery of right action.

'Thus I have eliminated the views of every other philosopher. Since there are no possible views apart from these, the theory of the ancients must prevail.[23] Let us then follow the tradition of the old schools, one that the Stoics also utilize, and begin in the following way:

(24) 'Every living creature loves itself,[24] and as soon as it is born strives to preserve itself. For the purpose of its life-long protection, nature bestows on it from the beginning a desire for self-preservation and for maintaining itself

---

[21] Hitherto Democritus has appeared as a philosopher of nature (book I, 17–21, book II, 102–3, book IV, 13). His passion for philosophy is mentioned below at 50 and 87; his ethical ideas are mentioned only here and below at 87–8. It is not clear why he is brought in, since he has no place in the Carneadean classification, and at 87–8 it is claimed that what he said about virtue was brief and unsystematic. Later thinkers recognized that Democritus' ethics can be interpreted as an early version of eudaimonism, but the first systematic concern with happiness and virtue is ascribed, at any rate by Cicero and his sources, to Socrates (88).

[22] See book II note 30.

[23] Antiochus has used Carneades' classification to rule out all ethical theories but his own, which is now expounded from 24 to 74. It begins, as does the Stoics', with a developmental account of human nature from the cradle, but differs in that it regards virtue, goods of the body and external advantages as all being good, and concludes that our final end is not simply a life of virtue, but a life which is lived virtuously and also contains bodily and external goods.

[24] Like the Stoics, Antiochus begins from self-love, which involves a self-conception as having a certain kind of nature, and expands as the creature develops. He pays more attention than they do to the details of the process.

in the best possible state according to nature. At first this arrangement is vague and uncertain, so that the creature merely gives itself some basic protection regardless of what species it belongs to. It has no understanding of what it is, or what it might become, or what its own nature is. Then it develops a little, and starts to realize how things affect it and are related to it. It gradually begins to acquire self-awareness, and to grasp the reasons why it possesses the desire that I spoke of. So it sets about pursuing the things which it perceives to be suited to its nature, and shunning their opposites. The object of every living creature's desire, therefore, is to be found in what is adapted to its nature. Hence we arrive at the highest good, to live in accordance with nature in the best and most suitable natural condition possible.

(25) 'Now every living creature has its own nature, while all necessarily share the goal of fulfilling their nature. (There is no reason why all non-human animals should not share some common features, nor why humans should not have some things in common with them, since they all share a common nature.) But those ultimate and supreme goods that we are investigating will be distributed variously from species to species. Each species will have its own particular ones, suited to the requirements of its particular nature. (26) So when we say that the goal of them all is to live in accordance with nature, we should not be saying that they all have precisely the same goal. In the case of the arts, it might rightly be said that they all have the common feature of being concerned with some kind of knowledge. Yet the knowledge that pertains to each individual art is distinctive. In the same way, all living creatures have the common goal of living in accordance with nature. But their natures are diverse – a horse's nature is different from that of an ox, which is different from that of a human being. None the less, there is a common aim not just among animals but with everything that nature nourishes, develops and protects.

'So we observe that even the plants that grow from the earth can be said to undertake a number of activities by their own power which conduce to their life and growth, and this enables them to reach the ultimate goal of their species. Hence we may embrace the whole living world under a single heading, and unhesitatingly declare that all of nature preserves itself, and has before it the ultimate goal of maintaining itself in the best possible condition appropriate to the particular species. Every single product of nature, then, has a similar but not necessarily identical goal. And so we must infer that for human beings too the ultimate good is to live in accordance with nature, interpreted as follows: to live in accordance with human nature as fully realized and needing nothing. (27) This notion requires elucidation, and your forgiveness if the explanation is rather long. But it is perhaps Lucius' first exposure to the subject and we must allow for his youth.'

'Absolutely', I said, 'though the manner of your discourse so far is appropriate for an audience of any age.'

'Well then', he said, 'having explained what it is that defines the category of desirable things, I must next demonstrate why things are as I have claimed. To this end, I shall go back to my previous starting-point, which is in fact the starting-point in reality: let us understand that every living creature loves itself. This fact cannot be doubted. It is a fundamental feature of nature, which we can grasp just by using our senses. Anyone who wished to deny it would be ignored. However, for completeness' sake, I think I should also offer some arguments for the thesis. (28) Yet how could one form an intelligible conception of a creature that hated itself? The very notion is self-contradictory. Such a creature's desire will deliberately set about drawing something harmful to it, given that the creature hates itself. Yet, since it will be doing this for the creature's own sake, it will hate itself and love itself at the same time, which is impossible. Moreover any humans who hated themselves would have to think of goods as evils, and evils as goods, and avoid what is desirable and desire what should be avoided, and that would unquestionably result in life being turned completely upside-down.

'One can find some who sought the noose, or other forms of departure from life. Then there is the character in Terence who (in the playwright's own words) "decreed that the more he made himself suffer the more he would alleviate the wrong he had done to his son".[25] None of these, however, should be considered self-haters. (29) Some are driven by grief, others by passion. Many are carried away by rage, and deliberately rush headlong towards disaster, thinking that they are acting in their own best interests. They will declare unhesitatingly: "This is right for me. Whatever you need to do, do." If such people had really declared war on themselves they would want days of torture and nights of anguish and would not reproach themselves for having misjudged their own interests. Such regrets are a sign that one cares about and loves oneself. Hence, however often it may be said that some set no value on themselves, feel self-hatred and hostility, and even long for death, one should realize that there is an underlying explanation of the above sort which will reveal, in the very cases at hand, that everyone loves themselves.

(30) 'Indeed it is insufficient to say that no one hates themselves. One must also realize that no one considers their own condition to be a matter of indifference to themselves. There are certain issues of genuine neutrality where we lean neither to one side nor the other. But if we have to regard the state we ourselves are in as a matter of indifference to ourselves, then all desire would be abolished.

'It would also be the height of absurdity for anyone to wish to say that we do love ourselves, but that this love is essentially directed towards some other object, not towards the actual person maintaining the self-love. This point might be made about friendship or duty or virtue, but whether sound

---

[25] Terence (book I note 4), *The Self-Tormentor* lines 147–8. The quotation in the next paragraph is line 80 of the same play.

or not it would at least be intelligible. But in the case of our love for our own selves it is not even intelligible that this be directed elsewhere, for example at pleasure. It is for the sake of ourselves that we love pleasure, not the other way round.

(31) 'Indeed it is perfectly obvious that we not only love ourselves, but do so with a passion. There are very few of us, if any, who can face our impending death and not "feel our blood chill and our face grow pale with ghastly fear".[26] It may well be a failing to be so terrified of the dissolution of our nature. A similar fear of pain is equally reprehensible. But the fact that we pretty well do all feel this way is sufficient proof that our nature recoils from its own destruction. In fact those cases of excessive fear, justly though we may criticize them, also help us to realize that they are merely outgrowths of a reaction which in its more moderate form is natural.

'Notice that when I speak of death I am not referring to specific categories of people: those who think that death will deprive them of the good things in life, those who are haunted by terror of the after-life, those who fear dying in pain. These are all reasons given for fearing death; but even small children, who think nothing of all that, often become extremely scared if we playfully threaten to drop them from a height. And as Pacuvius says, "Wild animals who lack the intelligence to be on their guard none the less shiver with fright" when the fear of death possesses them.[27]

(32) 'Surely even a wise person who has decided that it is time to die will not be unmoved at leaving friends and family, and even the very daylight, behind? This whole area reveals more clearly than any the power of our nature. Many will endure being beggars just so that they can live. People worn out with old age still suffer mental torment at death's approach. Others we can see experiencing what Philoctetes goes through in Accius' play. Though racked with unbearable pain, he kept himself alive by catching birds – "Slow himself, he shot the swift; standing, he shot those that flew" – and made a shirt for his back by weaving their feathers together.[28]

(33) 'Why just speak of the human race or even the whole of the animal world? Trees and plants have virtually the same nature. Some distinguished thinkers have held that this power is bestowed on them by some great and divine cause. Or maybe it is just fortuitous. At any rate we can see how everything that grows from the ground is kept secure by bark and roots, which perform the same function that the distribution of the sense-organs and the arrangement of the limbs does for animals.

'On this issue I tend to agree with the view that the whole system is regulated by nature, on the grounds that, if nature stood by, she herself would be unable to survive. But I am happy for those of an opposing view to think as

---

[26] A line from Ennius' *Alcmaeon*, a play also quoted at book IV, 62 (see book I note 4).
[27] For Pacuvius see book I note 4. He is quoted also at book II, 79 and below at 63.
[28] Accius' play *Philoctetes*, probably based on Sophocles' play, has also been quoted at book II, 94; see note 64 there.

they will.[29] Whenever I speak of human "nature" they may take me to be referring to the human person. It makes no difference. Either way, one can no more lose one's desire for what is conducive to one's own interest than one can lose one's very self. Hence our greatest authorities have been quite right to seek the foundation of the supreme good in nature, and to hold that the desire for what is suited to nature is innate in everyone, a consequence of the natural attraction that makes people love themselves.

(34) 'It is now sufficiently clear that everyone by nature loves themselves. We must next examine the question of what human nature is, since that is the object of our search. Evidently human beings consist of mind and body, but the mind and its components are primary, the parts of the body only secondary. We may also observe that the human body has a configuration superior to that of all other creatures. The human mind, for its part, has a constitution that provides it not only with sense-perception but with the dominant element, intellect, which the whole human person by nature obeys. Intellect encompasses the wondrous powers of reason, understanding, knowledge and all the virtues. The parts of the body, however, while lacking any importance comparable to the components of the mind, are easier to understand. Let us begin, then, with them.

(35) 'It is evident how well adapted to our nature the parts of our body are, as well as its shape, structure and bearing in general. It is equally easy to grasp the particular usefulness to human beings of the forehead, eyes, ears and other parts. Of course they must be healthy, strong and capable of exercising their natural movements and functions. Nature requires that none of them be missing, or be sick or disabled. There is also a certain way of using the body which keeps its movements and postures in harmony with nature. These can go wrong if there is some distortion or deformity, or an abnormality in movement or posture. For example, someone who walked on their hands, or backwards instead of forwards, would plainly be trying to escape from their own self and to strip themselves of their human nature, in apparent loathing of it. So, too, there are particular ways of sitting or moving, with a slouched or languid posture, that are contrary to nature. These are usually the mark of a decadent or weak personality, a mental flaw manifested as a bodily perversion of human nature. (36) In the opposite case, if we maintain, carry and use our bodies in an orderly and well-balanced way, then this gives the appearance of being in harmony with nature.

'As far as the mind is concerned, it must not just exist but have a certain character. All of its component parts should be unimpaired, and all its virtues present. Each of the senses has its own virtue too, namely the unimpeded exercise of its proper function, the quick and efficient perception of sensible

---

[29] Note the focus on human nature, bracketing the issue of whether nature as a whole is teleologically ordered, as Aristotle and the Stoics think, or is the product of fortuitous collisions of atoms, as the Epicureans think. Although Antiochus supports the Stoics and Aristotelians it is interesting that he allows ethical issues a relative autonomy from metaphysical ones.

objects. The mind itself, and that principal part of the mind known as the intellect, has many virtues, though they fall into two main categories. The first category is implanted by its own nature and is called "non-volitional". The second is located in the realm of volition and is generally called "virtue" in the more proper sense.[30] It is here that the mind attains its highest and greatest glory. The first category includes quickness to learn and good memory. Nearly everything that belongs in this category can be grouped under the single heading of "ability". The possessors of these virtues are termed "able". The other category contains those great and genuine virtues that are termed volitional, for example practical reason, temperance, courage, justice and others of the same sort.

(37) 'Here in brief is what needed to be said about body and mind, enough to give an outline of the requirements of human nature. We love ourselves and want every aspect of mind and body to be perfect. This shows that we love all these aspects on their own account, and that they are of the greatest importance in determining whether we live well. Whoever aims at self-preservation must also love each of their parts, all the more so the more perfectly developed and admirable those parts are within their own category. We seek a life in which the virtues of both mind and body are fully realized. This is where the supreme good is to be found, since the latter ought to represent the upper limit of what is desirable. Once this is understood, it cannot be doubted that humans love not only themselves, in their own right and of their own accord, but also cherish and desire in their own right and for their own quality all the component parts of body and mind, and all that is manifested in the processes and states of both.

(38) 'From these results we may readily infer that our most desirable components are those that possess the highest worth. Hence the most desirable virtue will be that which belongs to the best part of us, a part desired for its own sake. It follows that the mind's virtue will rank more highly than that of the body, and that the volitional virtues of the mind will come in ahead of the non-volitional. The former are virtues properly so called, and are far superior because they spring from reason, the most divine part of the human being.

'Now of all the things that nature creates and protects, the supreme good is bodily for those that have no mind or hardly a mind. I find the observation about the pig well made, that here is a creature whose mind functions like salt, to preserve it for eating.[31] But some animals do have a semblance of virtue, for example lions, dogs and horses. In these creatures, unlike pigs, we see not only bodily movement but some kind of mental activity too. In humans, however,

---

[30] In Latin, as in Greek and English, the word for virtue can be used widely for kinds of excellence, including intellectual excellences, and also more narrowly, in a way that sounds more correct, for states which are voluntary or up to us to develop, which are the virtues proper.

[31] This unpleasant comment comes from Chrysippus; the Stoics, who stress the rational unity of all humans, are insensitive to non-human animals. Antiochus, however, also accepts, with the Aristotelians, that animals have a lot in common with humans; he combines these views by regarding pigs as lower animals.

the mind, and especially reason, is absolutely paramount. Reason is the source of virtue, and virtue is defined as the perfection of reason.[32] This is a point that the ancients believe should be spelled out again and again.

(39) 'Plants too develop and mature in a way not dissimilar from animals. So we speak of a vine as living and dying, of a tree as young or old, flourishing or declining. Hence it is correct to suppose that for plants as well as for animals there are some things suited to their nature, and others alien to it, and that there exists a method for procuring their growth and nature, namely the art and science of agriculture. This art, with its trimming, pruning, straightening, raising and propping, helps ensure that the plant reaches its natural goal. If a vine could speak, this is how it would say it should be handled and preserved. In fact – speaking specifically of the vine – what preserves it is external to it. There is insufficient power within it to bring it to its optimal state without further cultivation.

(40) 'But imagine that the vine acquired senses, and so a degree of desire and self-motion. What do you think it would do then? Surely it would seek by its own endeavours to procure for itself the same results that had previously been sought by the vine-keeper? But notice that now it would have also acquired a concern to protect its senses and the capacity for desire that they afford, as well as any other organs it may have developed. So, in adding these new features to those it already had, the vine would not have exactly the same objective as the vine-keeper did. It would want to live in accordance with its newly acquired nature. Hence its highest good will be similar to what it was before, but not the same. It will be seeking not the good of a plant but the good of an animal.

'Now what if it had not only been given senses but also a human mind? It must be the case that its original features would still be there, in need of care. But these later additions will be of far more value, and most valuable of all will be the finest components of its mind. In fully realizing this aspect of its nature, it will attain its end, its supreme good. After all, intellect and reason are by far the outstanding elements. Let this represent the limit of all that is desirable. Starting from an initial natural affection, we have ascended many steps to reach the summit, the combination of full bodily integrity with the perfection of reason.

(41) 'This, then, is an outline of our nature. Suppose, as I said at the outset, that at the moment of our birth each of us were able to recognize and determine our essential nature both as a whole and in its individual parts: in that case we would immediately comprehend, without the possibility of error, the object of our search, the supremely and ultimately desirable goal. As things stand, our nature is strangely hidden from us at first, and cannot be grasped or understood. But, as we get older, we gradually, slowly, come to know our own selves. Hence the initial natural affection that we feel for ourselves is

---

[32] A Stoic rather than Aristotelian definition.

vague and obscure. Our earliest desires have no other aim than to keep us safe and sound. Then, however, we begin to look around us and become aware of what we are and how we differ from the other animals. At this point we start to pursue the real objectives for which we were born.

(42) 'We observe a certain similarity to this process in the other animals. At first they do not move away from the place they were born. Subsequently, desire moves each of them on. We see little snakes crawling, ducklings swimming, blackbirds flying, oxen using their horns and scorpions their stings. In short, we see how nature guides each to its own life. The similarity with the human race is clear. New born children just lie there as if completely inanimate. Once they acquire a little strength, they start to use their mind and their senses. They try to stand upright and use their hands; they recognize those who are caring for them. Next they find pleasure in the company of their peers. They love to mix with them and take part in games. Listening to stories enchants them. They enjoy sharing their abundant energy with others, and take a more active interest in what goes on in their house. They begin to reflect and to learn, and want to know the names of those they meet. When they beat their friends in a contest they are overjoyed; when they lose, they are depressed and disheartened.

'One must suppose that all this happens for a reason. (43) Nature seems to have generated the human spirit to enable us to acquire every virtue. That is why children, without instruction, are stirred by semblances of the virtues, which contain within themselves the seeds of virtue. These seeds are the basic elements of our nature, and they grow and blossom into virtue. We are endowed at birth with the capacity to act, and to show affection, generosity and gratitude. We have a mind that is receptive to knowledge, to practical reason and to courage, and unreceptive to their opposites. This, then, is why we see the sparks of virtue I was talking about in children. These sparks must kindle the light of philosophical thought, a light we must follow as a divine guide to discover nature's final goal. As I have now said many times, in the years of immaturity and intellectual weakness the power of our nature can only be glimpsed as if through a mist. When our mind develops and gains strength, it comes to recognize that power, but recognizes at the same time that it has great scope for enlargement and is as yet in itself incomplete.

(44) 'So we must delve into the workings of nature and reach a deep understanding of what it requires. If not, we cannot know ourselves. This precept seemed too lofty to have a human origin and was therefore assigned to a god. Hence the Pythian Apollo bids us to know ourselves.[33] But the only way to gain this knowledge is to understand the powers of our body and our mind, and to follow the life that utilizes them to the full. Now our desire from the beginning was to possess these parts in their fullest natural perfection. When

---

[33] The temple of Apollo at Delphi (where Apollo was called Pythian) displayed, among other sayings, 'Know yourself'.

our desire is fulfilled, then, it must be admitted that this is as it were the stopping-point, where nature rests. Here is the supreme good. This end as a whole must surely be desired on its own account and in its own right, since we proved earlier that each of its individual components is desirable in its own right.

(45) 'It might be thought that our enumeration of the bodily advantages overlooked pleasure. Let us postpone this question for another time. The issue of whether pleasure belongs in the category of what we described as the primary things in accordance with nature is not relevant to the present argument. If I am correct in thinking that pleasure adds nothing to the sum of natural goods, then it was right to overlook it. If, on the other hand, it does count (as some maintain), then its neglect in no way impedes our understanding of what the supreme good is. If we add pleasure to the roll of nature's primary elements, then we have simply added one more bodily advantage. We have not altered the basic structure of the supreme good.

(46) 'The entire theory as so far advanced has been based on primary natural affection. Now, however, I shall adopt a different line of reasoning. Each part of our nature, both bodily and mental, has its own particular power, and it is for this reason, and not just through self-love, that our supreme concern is automatically with these parts. To begin with the body: have you noticed how people with deformed or disabled or withered limbs try to hide them? They go to great trouble and effort to eliminate, or at least minimize to the best of their ability, the appearance of a bodily defect. They even undergo very painful treatments to restore the appearance of a limb to its natural condition, even though such treatments, far from improving the use of the limb, can actually have a detrimental effect. We all by nature think of ourselves as desirable in our entirety, and not on account of some other thing but on our account. So it must be the case that where a whole is desired on its own account, its parts are too.

(47) 'Moreover, there are aspects of the body both in motion and at rest that nature herself judges to be of importance. How one walks, or sits, one's countenance and expression, are all features that we consider can be either worthy or unworthy of a free citizen. Many people are deemed worthy of disapprobation for appearing to violate a rule or law of nature in some movement or posture. And since people try to rid their body of such defects, what reason is there not to count beauty also as desirable in its own right? If we think that bodily deformity and impairment is to be avoided on its own account, then surely we should also seek for its own sake, and perhaps even more so, to have an impressive figure? We avoid postures and bodily movements that are ugly, and so there is no reason not to pursue beauty. Health, too, strength and freedom from pain we shall seek not just for their utility but for their own sake. Our nature wants all of its parts to be fully realized, and therefore seeks on its own account a bodily condition that maximally accords with that nature. If our body is ill or in pain or weak, then our whole nature suffers.

(48) 'Let us now examine the components of the mind, which provide an altogether nobler array. The more lofty they are, the more certainly they indicate the presence of nature. Human nature has an innate love of learning and knowledge, such that no one could doubt the strength of its passion for them, irrespective of the further inducements of gain. Notice how not even punishment is sufficient to deter children from looking into the world around them and exploring it. Drag them away, and they go right back. Acquiring some bit of knowledge fills them with joy. They cannot wait to share it! Processions, games and any similar kind of spectacle will grip them. Hungry or thirsty, they keep watching.

'Observe too the case of those who love the higher forms of intellectual pursuit. Look how they neglect their health and household, so captivated by their advanced studies that they will endure any hardship, the sole compensation for all their toil and effort being the sheer pleasure derived from learning. (49) I believe that Homer took this point well in his portrayal of the songs of the Sirens. It was not apparently the sweetness of their voices that used to summon back those who were sailing by. Neither was it the originality and variety of their songs. It was their declaration of great knowledge that fired sailors with the hope of learning, and drew them towards their rocky shore. Here is their invitation to Ulysses (this is one of various passages of Homer that I have translated):

> Ulysses, glory of Argos, turn your ship around
> You will be able to listen to our song
> None has ever sailed this sea-blue course
> Without stopping, entranced by our sweet voice
> Greedy soul filled with all manner of music
> Then to glide away and return home wiser
> We know the dire struggle and clash of war
> That Greece waged on Troy by divine will
> We know every last detail on the face of the earth

'Homer realized that his story would lack plausibility if some little ditty had ensnared his hero. It was knowledge that the Sirens were promising, and it is not incredible that a lover of wisdom should hold this even dearer than home.[34] Now a desire to know anything no matter of what sort is simply a mark of inquisitiveness. But one who is led to a desire for knowledge by the contemplation of higher things should be considered the very finest example of a human being.

(50) 'Consider how great Archimedes' passion for study must have been. He was absorbed in a diagram he was drawing in the dust, and did not even notice the capture of his city! Think of the enormous intelligence that Aristoxenus lavished on the study of music, or the time that Aristophanes

---

[34] Cicero is translating Homer's *Odyssey* 12, 184–91. The philosophical interpretation is not to be found in Homer.

must have devoted to the pursuit of literature. One need hardly mention Pythagoras, Plato or Democritus. We are told that their desire for knowledge propelled them to the four corners of the earth.[35] Those who cannot understand this have never loved any great and worthy object of knowledge.

'At this point one hears the objection that the studies I have mentioned are pursued for the sake of mental pleasure. This fails to grasp that they are desirable for their own sake precisely because the mind takes delight in them in the absence of any utility, and finds joy in pure knowledge even if it should be practically disadvantageous. (51) There is little purpose in inquiring further into such an obvious matter, as will be clear if we ask ourselves the following questions: why are we so fascinated by the motions of the stars, and by contemplation of the heavenly bodies and all of nature's hidden secrets? Why do we like history so much? We enjoy pursuing the smallest points, worrying over areas we have left blank, and trying to fill in what is incomplete.

'Now I am quite aware that history is useful as well as pleasurable. (52) But what about fiction, which we read with pleasure even if no utility can be extracted from it? What about our wish to discover the names of those who performed famous deeds, and their parents, their country and much else of minor importance besides? How do we explain that the humblest of people, even artisans, may be enthusiasts for history, though they have no hope themselves of a career in public life? Indeed we may note that the keenest to hear and read about public affairs tend to be those rendered unfit to partake in public business themselves due to the infirmities of old age. We must therefore conclude that the attractions of learning and study are contained within the very things that we learn and study.

(53) 'Philosophers of old picture what kind of life the wise will have on the Isles of the Blest: freed from every trouble, and requiring none of the accessories and equipment that are necessary for life, they will simply devote all their time to investigating and researching nature. As for us, we can see that such study may provide not only diversion for those who are happy, but alleviation of unhappiness too. That is why many people who find themselves in the hands of an enemy or a tyrant, or in prison or exile, have eased their pain by study. (54) Demetrius of Phalerum, a ruler of this city, was unjustly driven from his homeland and took himself to the court of King Ptolemy of Alexandria. Demetrius was a distinguished proponent of the philosophical system that I am recommending, and a pupil of Theophrastus. In the leisure

---

[35] Archimedes of Syracuse (*c.* 287–212), a famous mathematician, is said to have been killed, as the Romans captured his city, by a soldier irritated by his refusal to look up from his diagram. Aristoxenus of Tarentum (*c.* 370–*c.* 300), a student of Aristotle, wrote widely on music theory and harmonics. Aristophanes of Byzantium (*c.* 257–180), head of the Alexandrian library, and a diligent scholar of literature. For Pythagoras, see note 9 above, and for Democritus note 21 above. They and Plato are said to have travelled widely, but this may not be historical; later tradition thought of them as finding the origins of their philosophy in foreign countries. See below, 87.

granted by his misfortune he wrote many fine treatises. These had no practical use for him, since he was debarred from practical business.[36] Their composition cultivated his mind, providing a kind of nourishment for his humanity. Indeed I often heard Gnaeus Aufidius, an erudite man who served as praetor but lost his sight, say that he missed the daylight more than the usefulness of being able to see.[37]

'Next consider sleep. Were it not for the fact that it provides us with bodily rest and a kind of remedy for our exertions, we would think its existence contrary to nature, since it deprives us of sensation and the ability to act. Hence we would have no problem if nature did not need rest, or could obtain it by some other means, given how often we virtually violate nature already in staying awake to pursue some business or to study.

(55) 'Here are some even clearer cases from nature – in fact absolutely obvious and indubitable ones – of the desire, most evident in humans but also present in animals, for constant activity. Continual rest is unendurable under any circumstances. This is readily seen in children of even the most tender age. I hope I am not concentrating too much on this group, but all the ancient theories, especially the one I espouse, visit the cradle, in the belief that the easiest way of understanding nature's intentions is to look at early childhood. We note, therefore, that not even infants are capable of keeping still. When not much older, they start to enjoy even quite boisterous games, and are hardly deterred by punishment. This desire for activity continues to grow as they do. And so none of us would choose the sleep of Endymion, even if we were given the sweetest dreams to go with it. We would consider this a fate as bad as death.

(56) 'Even the laziest people, as extravagantly idle as they may be, can none the less be seen in constant activity, both physical and mental. Once they have any unavoidable business out of the way, they still call for the dice-board or look for a game to play or someone to gossip with. Lacking the nobler delights of intellectual pursuit, they seek out any kind of company or social gathering instead. Even the animals that we keep caged for our amusement find captivity difficult. Despite the fact that they are better fed than they would be in the wild, they miss being able to move about and roam freely as nature allows.

(57) 'Thus the more able and accomplished one is, the less one would even want to live at all if prevented from going about one's business, however well provided one may be with pleasures to graze on. One chooses either a life of private pursuits, or, if more ambitious, aspires to a public career and the authority of office. Alternatively, one devotes oneself entirely to intellectual study, a life far removed from that of the pleasure-seeker. Indeed those who

[36] Demetrius of Phalerum (*c.* 355–280), a member of Aristotle's school, was given supreme power in Athens in 317 by Cassander, one of Alexander's successors, but after a decade was expelled by another Macedonian ruler. In exile in Alexandria he took to intellectual pursuits.
[37] Gnaeus Aufidius, praetor in 107, presumably comes into this intellectual company because he wrote history (in Greek); he is mentioned also at *Tusculan Disputations* 5, 112.

take this course endure worry, anxiety and sleeplessness as they exercise the cutting-edge of their talent and intellect, the finest element of a human being, and one that should be considered divine. Such people have no desire for pleasure, nor any aversion to hard work. Indeed their activity is ceaseless, be it wondering at the discoveries of the ancients or undertaking original research. Their appetite for study is insatiable. They forget everything else and never think a mean or unworthy thought. Such, indeed, is the power exerted by these pursuits that even those who claim to have a quite different highest good, defined for example by utility or pleasure, may yet be seen to spend their whole life in the investigation and exposition of nature.

(58) 'It is evident, then, that we are born to act. There are many forms of activity, however: so much so that one may lose sight of the trivial amidst the more important ones. As to the most important, it is my view and that of the thinkers whose system I am discussing, that these are: the contemplation and study of the heavenly bodies, and of the mysterious secrets of nature that rational thought has the power to uncover;[38] the administration of public affairs, or perhaps knowledge of its theory; and a way of thinking that displays practical reason, temperance, bravery and justice, and which manifests the other virtues too and the actions that flow from them. We may sum up this latter category under the single heading of "morality". When we are fully mature, nature herself gives us the cue that leads us to understand and practise it. Everything has small beginnings, but grows greater by gradual progress. The reason for this is that when we are born we possess a certain delicacy and weakness which prevents us from seeing and doing what is best. The light of virtue and happiness, the two most desirable possessions of all, dawns rather late; and much later still a clear understanding of what they are. Plato puts the point very well: "Happy the one who even in old age has managed to acquire wisdom and true beliefs!"[39] I have said enough about the basic natural advantages. Let us now examine what comes later, which is more important.

(59) 'The human body, as created and shaped by nature, has some parts fully developed at birth, and others that are gradually fashioned as we grow up; and nature has little use in this process for external assistance. Now the mind's development is in most respects analogous to that of the body. Nature equipped us with senses well suited to perceiving their objects, and needed little or no help in bringing them to maturity. But the noblest and best human element was neglected. True, nature gave us an intellect that has the capacity to acquire every virtue. She implanted in it at birth and without instruction small inklings of great things to come. She even initiated its education, introducing, so to speak, the building blocks of virtue. But as for virtue itself, nature only began to develop it, nothing more.

(60) 'Thus it is our function – and when I say "our" I mean the function of

---

[38] The place of study and contemplation in our final good is left very unclear; cf. note 16 above.
[39] *Laws* 653a.

a particular skill – to strive to build on the foundations we were given until we reach our desired goal. This goal is far more valuable, and much more desirable in its own right, than the senses or the bodily assets I spoke of. The wondrous perfection of the intellect so surpasses these goods that the gulf between them is scarcely imaginable. That is why honour, admiration and enthusiasm are directed exclusively at virtue and at actions consistent with virtue. That is why all mental states and processes of this kind are given the single name "moral".

'I shall shortly examine the conceptual basis of all the virtues, and the meanings conveyed by the terms that are applied to them, as well as their individual powers and natures. (61) For the present I shall simply explain that what I am calling morality is desirable in its own right and not just because we love ourselves. This is shown by the case of children, where we can see nature at work as clearly as in a mirror. Consider how keen their rivalries are, and how fierce the contests where those rivalries are pursued! Consider their elation at winning and their shame in defeat; their aversion to blame and their love of being praised; their willingness to endure anything so long as they come out on top! Consider how well they remember those who have shown them kindness, and their own eagerness to repay it. These traits are most apparent in the best characters, where what we understand as the moral qualities are already being drawn in outline by nature.

(62) 'So much for childhood. The picture is not filled in until the age of maturity. No human being is so peculiar as to lack feelings of revulsion at immorality, and approval at its opposite. No one feels anything but aversion to those whose formative years are corrupt and debauched. On the other hand, regardless of personal connection, we are all delighted when a young person is modest and steady. Everyone hates Pullus Numitorius of Fregellae, the traitor, even though he did our own country a service.[40] We all lavish praise on Codrus, the saviour of this city, and on the daughters of Erectheus.[41] The name of Tubulus generates universal odium,[42] the memory of Aristides universal respect.[43] Let us not forget either the emotional impact which acts of piety, friendship or magnanimity have on us when we hear or read about them.

(63) 'I need not merely appeal to our own reactions. We are, after all, born, raised and educated to aspire to honour and glory. But even ordinary, uneducated people at the theatre raise the roof with their cheering at the words "I

---

[40] In 125 the city of Fregellae rebelled against Rome, but was betrayed to the Roman commander Lucius Opimius by Quintus Numitorius Pullus. A debate as to whether Pullus' former revolt should be excused by his treachery (which Romans particularly despised) is mentioned at Cicero's *On Invention* 2, 105.

[41] Mythical examples from Athenian history. The Dorians invaded Athens, having had an oracle that they would win only if King Codrus were not killed. Learning the oracle, Codrus disguised himself and provoked the enemy till they killed him; the Athenians then drove them out. Erechtheus was a mythical king of Athens, with many legends; this is probably a reference to a lost play by Euripides, in which Erechtheus was commanded by an oracle to sacrifice his youngest daughter to save his country from an invasion. In the play the daughter accepted her fate, and her sisters committed suicide. [42] See book II 54 and note 38.

[43] See book II, 116. Aristides was known as 'the Just'.

am Orestes" and at the reply "It is I, let me tell you, who am Orestes." Then, when each offers the same solution to the puzzled, confused king – "Then, pray, kill both of us together"[b] – the applause is never less than tumultuous, however often this scene is played.[44] This example shows that the attitude of mind that wins everyone's praise and approval is one that, far from seeking advantage, maintains loyalty even at the cost of disadvantage.

(64) 'Examples like these fill the pages not just of fiction but of history too, and the history of our own nation in particular. It was we Romans who chose our finest citizen to receive the sacred emblems from Ida. It was we who provided guardians for royal princes. Our generals gave their lives to save their country. Our consuls warned the king who was their bitterest foe of the plot to poison him, even as he was closing in on the city walls. In our nation we find the woman who took her own life to atone for the dishonour that was forced upon her. In our nation we find the man who took his daughter's life to save her from dishonour. Consider all these acts and countless others besides.[45] No one can fail to see that their performance was inspired by the sheer splendour of a noble cause, with no thought of personal advantage. So, too, it is for no other reason than their sheer moral worth that we praise them.

'My exposition of these points has been brief. I have not offered as full an account as I might have, since the present issue is not a matter for doubt. From these cases alone one may draw the immediate conclusion that all the virtues are desirable in their own right, as is the morality which both arises from them and inheres in them.

(65) 'Now in the whole moral field that we are discussing there is nothing so noble or wide-ranging as society between human beings, that alliance, so to speak, of shared interests, and the mutual affection of the human species.[46] It arises from the moment of procreation. The new-born are loved by their

---

[44] The play *Orestes* by Pacuvius (see book I note 4) has been referred to already at book II, 79 (and the poet has been quoted above at 31). Orestes and his friend Pylades prefer to die together rather than have either of them save his own life by saying that the other is Orestes.

[45] A selection of patriotic Roman stories. In 204 Publius Cornelius Scipio Nasica was chosen as an exemplary Roman to receive the image of the Great Mother goddess Cybele, whose worship centred on Mount Ida, as her worship became officially established in Rome. The 'guardian' to princes is Marcus Aemilius Lepidus, who is said to have been sent to Egypt as guardian of the young king Ptolemy V after his father's murder in 205. The claim that Roman generals give their lives to save their country may have particular reference to the Decii, who 'devoted' themselves to death to ensure Roman victory; see book II, 60 and note 45. In 278 the consuls Gaius Fabricius Luscinus and Quintus Aemilius Papius revealed to the invading Greek king Pyrrhus his doctor's offer to poison him. The two final examples are Lucretia and Verginius, already referred to at book II, 66.

[46] We now turn to concern for others. Unlike the Stoics, Antiochus' account does not draw a sharp distinction between the development of our mature self-conception as rational beings and the development of our mature recognition of others as worthy of our concern. Rather, he regards the latter as an extension of the former, since he has made a single principle, of self-love, the foundation of his theory; he appeals in the next paragraph to the idea that human nature is social to make this move plausible.

[b] The text of this quotation is corrupt. I adopt Madvig's reading.

parents, and the whole household is united by the bonds of marriage and family. From there affection spreads gradually outwards, first to blood relatives, then to relations by marriage, next friends, then neighbours, and then to fellow-citizens, and friends and allies in the public sphere. Finally, it embraces the whole human race.

'This is an attitude of mind that assigns each person their due. It preserves with generosity and fairness the cohesion of human society that I am speaking of. That is why it is called justice, which is connected with service, kindness, open-heartedness, goodwill, friendliness and other attributes of the same sort. But, although these belong especially to justice, they are shared with the other virtues too. (66) Human nature is so constituted as to have an innately civic and social character – what the Greeks call *politikon*. So whatever the business of each virtue, none will be averse to community and to the affection and society between human beings that I have been expounding. Justice in turn needs the other virtues, as much as it flows through them itself. It can only be protected by the brave and wise. Morality itself, then, has just this quality of concordant union between the virtues that I am speaking of, given that morality either is actually virtue or is virtuous behaviour. A life that is in accordance with all of this, and which answers to the virtues, may be judged upright, moral, consistent and in harmony with nature.

(67) 'This complex interweaving of the virtues may, however, be unpacked by philosophical analysis.[47] True, their mutual interconnectedness is such that every virtue has a share in every other, and this makes actual separation impossible. None the less, each retains its own function. Thus courage is discernible particularly in cases of great effort or danger, temperance in the forgoing of pleasure, practical reason in one's choice of goods and evils, and justice in allocating each person their due. Every virtue, then, possesses as it were an outward looking concern, in that it reaches out to and embraces other people. It follows that our friends, our siblings, our relations by blood and then marriage, our fellow-citizens, and finally – since we declare that humankind is a single community – all people, are valuable in their own right.

'Yet none of these ties falls into the category of the highest and ultimate good. (68) Thus we find that there are two separate categories of things that are valuable in their own right. The first is where the ultimate good is realized, namely in the category of mind and body. The second is the class of external goods, namely those that belong neither to mind nor body, such as friends, parents, children, relatives and one's own country. These are indeed valued in their own right, but do not fall into the same class as mind and body. In fact if all these external goods, however desirable, were included in the supreme good, then the supreme good could never be attained.

---

[47] A vague reference to the idea that the virtues form a unity of some kind, which seems to mean that they differ in their areas of application but share a common practical reasoning. This has not been argued for, but the (even stronger) Stoic thesis of the unity of the virtues has not been a topic of concern in book III; perhaps the issue was lacking in contemporary interest.

(69) 'How, then, you will ask, could everything be subordinate to the supreme good if friendship, family ties and the other external goods are not included in it?[48] Here is the obvious reason: external goods are what we preserve by performing the duties that derive from the class of virtue specific to each. Someone who performs the duty of looking after a friend or a parent is benefited by the very fact that its performance is a right action; and right actions derive from the virtues. Now the wise seek the virtues with nature's guidance, while people who are imperfect but endowed with outstanding abilities are often motivated by honour, which has the appearance and image of morality. Morality itself, though, is in every way perfect and complete, a single object of absolute splendour, the most glorious of all things. If only they could gaze upon it directly, how joyously these people would embrace it, given the delight they take in a shadowy impression!

(70) 'We surely do not think that mere devotees of pleasure, however consumed by the flame of passion, could feel such elation in obtaining the objects of their heart's desire as Africanus the Elder did when Hannibal was defeated, or Africanus the Younger when Carthage was destroyed. No one has ever felt more joy in voyaging down the Tiber on the festive day as Lucius Paullus did when he journeyed along that river with the captive King Perses in tow.[49]

(71) 'Come now, Lucius, construct a mental picture of the virtues' lofty grandeur. You will then be left in no doubt that those who possess the high-minded character and the uprightness to attain them live happy lives. Such people realize that, in a contest with virtue, all the whims of fate, all the changes that time and circumstance bring, are but foolish trifles. It is true that what we count as bodily goods do make a contribution to the happiest life. But a happy life can exist without them. What they add in the way of good is so slight and insignificant that they are lost in the glow of virtue, like starlight in the rays of the sun.[50]

(72) 'So it is right to say that these bodily advantages have only small importance for the happy life; but it is too impulsive to say that they have none at all. Those who object to this point seem to me to forget those very principles of nature that they themselves established. Some weight must be given to these goods, so long as you realize what the right amount is. Philosophers who seek

---

[48] Here Antiochus' account is explicitly committed to the foundational point that happiness, our final end, must be complete – that is, everything we do is done ultimately for its sake. (See Introduction pp. xvii–xviii.) See below, at 77–86.

[49] Piso's examples of morality are very Roman and triumphalist. For Scipio Africanus (the elder) see book II note 41; for Scipio Aemilianus (the younger) see book I note 12. King Perses or Perseus of Macedonia, after an attempt to rival Roman power, was defeated in 168 and led in triumph in 167 by Lucius Aemilius Paullus (consul 182 and 168), on a holiday normally marked by river festivities.

[50] This paragraph attempts to unite the Stoic view that virtue is not merely necessary but sufficient for happiness, with the Aristotelian view that happiness requires bodily and external goods as well as virtue. It does so by holding that virtue is sufficient for the *happy* life, but that the *happiest* life requires bodily and external goods as well. This position is criticized below, at 77–86.

truth rather than glory will refrain from valuing at nothing what even our glorious objectors themselves declare to be in accordance with nature. They will, none the less, recognize the full force of virtue, and the full authority (so to speak) of morality, which make the remaining goods insignificant enough to look like nothing, even though they are not. This is the language not of one who rejects everything except virtue, but who extols virtue with its own due praise. In short, here is in every way a complete and finished exposition of the supreme good, even though other philosophers have endeavoured to grab small parts of this system, each wanting to give the impression of presenting their own view.[51]

(73) 'Knowledge for its own sake was often admirably praised by Aristotle and Theophrastus. Erillus was so captivated by this one point that he maintained that knowledge is the supreme good and nothing else is desirable in its own right. The ancients had much to say about how ordinary human affairs were worthy of disparagement and contempt. Aristo fastened on this one point and denied that there was anything worth avoiding or pursuing except the vices and virtues. Members of our own school included freedom from pain amongst the things that are in accordance with nature; Hieronymus said that this was the supreme good. Then again Callipho, and after him Diodorus, despite being enamoured of pleasure and freedom from pain respectively, could neither of them do without morality, which our school values above all else.

(74) 'Even the very proponents of hedonism themselves resort to contortions and have virtue constantly on their lips. They declare that pleasure is only desired initially. Subsequently, habit creates a kind of second nature, which drives people to do many things that do not include seeking pleasure. There remain the Stoics. They have transferred not one or other small part of our philosophy over to themselves, but the whole of it. Thieves generally change the labels on the items they have taken. So the Stoics have changed the names that stand for the actual things in order to treat our views as their own. It is therefore our system alone which is worthy of the student of the liberal arts, worthy of the learned and distinguished, worthy of princes and of kings.'

(75) At this point Piso paused a little, and then said, 'Well now. Do you think I have done enough to justify dinning your ears with this recital?'[52] To which I replied, 'Piso, today, as on many other occasions, you have shown yourself so well acquainted with these doctrines that I think we would have no need of assistance from the Greeks if only we had more opportunity to hear from you. Your speech won my approval all the more because Staseas of Naples, your teacher and a Peripatetic of unquestionably high repute, used to give a somewhat different account of the system. He would side with those who gave importance to fortune good or bad, and to bodily goods and evils.'

---

[51] Rival ethical theories are now presented as overemphasizing different parts of this 'system'. The philosophers named are largely place-holders in Carneades' classification, and this is a rational reconstruction of sources of disagreement rather than a record of any actual debates.
[52] After Piso's speech he and Cicero exchange preliminary badinage in 75 and 76, and from 77 to 86 Cicero produces a devastating criticism of the theory.

'Quite so', said Piso, 'but our dear Antiochus gives a much better and bolder account of these matters than Staseas did. It is not, however, your approval that I am seeking, but that of our friend Lucius here, since I am eager to steal him away as a disciple from you.'[53]

(76) 'I am completely won over', exclaimed Lucius, 'and I believe that my cousin is too.' 'Well then, does the young man have your consent?' Piso asked me. 'Or do you prefer that he learn a system which will leave him knowing nothing when he has mastered it?' 'I give him his head', I replied, 'but are you forgetting that it is quite legitimate for me to bestow my approval on what you have said? After all, who can fail to approve what seems probable?' 'Yet who can approve anything that is not the subject of perception, comprehension or cognition?' he replied.

'There is no great disagreement here, Piso', I said. 'There is only one thing that makes me deny the possibility of perception, and that is the Stoics' definition of the faculty. They claim that nothing can be perceived except that which is true and could not be false. So it is with the Stoics that disagreement arises, with the Peripatetics evidently not. But let us put this matter to one side, since it will involve a rather long and pretty contentious debate.[54]

(77) 'However, your claim that all the wise are happy appears to me to be too quick. Somehow or other it slithered by in the course of your speech.[55] But unless the claim is made good, I am afraid that Theophrastus will be vindicated in his view that no life can be happy if it involves ill fortune, sorrow or bodily anguish. For it is a violent contradiction for a life to be happy and yet weighed down with many evils. I quite fail to understand how this position is coherent.'

'What is it, then, that you take issue with?' asked Piso. 'That virtue has such power that it is sufficient in itself for a happy life? Or, if you accept this, do you deny that those who possess virtue can be happy even when suffering certain evils?'

'I wish to attribute the greatest possible power to virtue', I replied. 'Let us leave the question of just how much for another occasion. For now, the

---

[53] Cicero first makes the point that Antiochus' theory, in trying to combine Aristotelian ethics with the Stoic claim of the sufficiency of virtue for happiness, is untrue to the actual Aristotelian tradition, represented by Staseas (see above, note 13), which insists that virtue is *not* sufficient for happiness. Piso brushes the point aside elegantly; it is hard to see how he could meet it.

[54] Piso, overjoyed that his speech has converted young Lucius to the 'Old Academy' tradition of Antiochus (see above para. 6 and note 11), asks Cicero why he would prefer Lucius to join the sceptical New Academy tradition, which would leave him knowing nothing. Cicero reminds Piso that an Academic can approve of a theory as being plausible (Cicero himself has adopted Antiochus' theory as plausible to argue against the Stoics in book IV; see Introduction p. xv). Piso replies that plausibility is not good enough; we demand certainty and knowledge. Cicero replies that this is a Stoic demand, which does not spring from the Aristotelian kind of theory Piso has presented; but he postpones epistemological disputes (they are the subject of his *Academica*). The exchange establishes Cicero as philosophically quicker and more sophisticated than Piso.

[55] From here to 86 Cicero makes a devastating point which Piso fails to rebut. Cicero surely intends us to see a contrast between 'Old Academy' edifying rhetoric and the sceptical Academy's insistence on probing all claims by argument.

question is whether virtue's power could be so great if anything outside virtue is counted as a good.'[56]

(78) 'And yet', said Piso, 'if you concede to the Stoics that the presence of virtue by itself is sufficient to make a life happy, then you are also conceding this to the Peripatetics. The Stoics do not have the courage to call evils things that they admit are harsh, troublesome, worthy of rejection and alien to our nature. We do call them evils, albeit trivial and almost vanishingly small ones. Hence one who can be happy in the midst of things that are harsh and worthy of rejection can also be happy in the midst of minor evils.'

'Piso', I said, 'in court there is surely no one better than you at grasping the real nub of an issue. So please give me your attention. It may be my fault, but you have not as yet caught the point of my question.' 'I am all ears', he said, 'and I am awaiting a reply to my questions.'

(79) 'My response will be', I replied, 'that I am not at this time asking what virtue can do, but what account of it is consistent, and what self-contradictory.' 'What do you mean?' asked Piso. 'Zeno', I replied, 'makes the magnificent and oracular utterance that "Virtue is sufficient in itself for a happy life." To the question "Why?" his response is, "Because nothing is good other than what is moral." I am not now asking whether this is true. But I do say that his statements are manifestly self-consistent.

(80) 'Imagine Epicurus to have stated the same thing, that the wise person is always happy – he does occasionally have the habit of babbling to this effect. Indeed he says that a wise person when racked with the greatest pains will cry, "How sweet it is! How unconcerned I am!" I will not quarrel with the man about the particular view he holds on the nature of the good. But I would urge that he fails to grasp what he should be saying, given his view that pain is the greatest evil.

'I have the same story to tell against your account. Your claim about what is good and evil exactly matches the views of people who, as the saying goes, have never seen so much as a picture of a philosopher. So health, strength, physical stature, good looks and the proper functioning of every part from head to toe – these are all goods; ugliness, disease and disability are evils. (81) You maintain caution about the external goods. But, given that you regard the bodily attributes as goods, you will surely regard what conduces to them as goods too, namely friends, children, relatives, wealth, honour and power. Note that I have nothing to say against this. My point is that if the things you mentioned as able to afflict a wise person are evils, then being wise will not be sufficient for a happy life.'[57]

[56] How can virtue be sufficient for happiness if we reject the Stoic claim that only virtue is good, and allow, with the Aristotelians, that bodily and external advantages are also good? In allowing this we thereby allow that their loss can render a happy life unhappy (as Theophrastus saw).

[57] Cicero caustically points out that Piso's answer at 78 is off the point. It is consistent for the Stoics to hold that virtue is sufficient for happiness, since they explicitly deny that anything but virtue is good. But the Aristotelian view holds that bodily and external advantages are

'Being wise is indeed insufficient for the happiest life,' replied Piso, 'but is certainly enough for a happy life.'

'I noticed that you made this move a little while ago', I said, 'and I know that our teacher Antiochus often says the same thing. But the idea of being happy but not sufficiently happy is highly implausible. Anything added to what is sufficient is too much; no one has too much happiness; therefore no one is happier than happy.'

(82) 'What, then, do you think of Quintus Metellus?' he asked. 'He saw his three sons become consuls, and one of those was a censor too and celebrated a triumph; a fourth son was praetor; he died leaving all four safe and well; his three daughters were married; and he himself had served as consul, censor and augur, and had celebrated his own triumph. Assuming that he was wise, surely he was happier than Regulus, who died in enemy hands of sleep deprivation and starvation, even if Regulus was also wise?'[58]

(83) 'Why is it me you are asking?' I replied. 'Ask the Stoics.' 'So what do you think they would reply?' 'That Metellus was in no way happier than Regulus.' 'Then our discussion should start from there', he said. 'But we are wandering off the point', I replied. 'I am not asking what is true, but what each party is committed to saying. If only the Stoics did say that one person could be happier than another – you would soon see their system in ruins! They locate goodness in virtue alone, in morality and nothing else. Neither virtue nor morality has degrees, as far as they are concerned. And the only good is that whose possession necessarily makes one happy. So since the only thing which they count for happiness cannot admit of degrees, there is no case in which one person can be happier than another.

'See how all these propositions cohere? Heavens above – I must confess what I think – the cohesion of their ideas is remarkable. Their conclusions are in agreement with their first principles, the intermediate steps are in agreement with both; indeed every part agrees with every other part. They know what follows from what, and what is inconsistent. It is like geometry, where if you grant the premises then you must grant everything. Concede that there is nothing good except what is moral, and you must concede that the happy life consists in virtue. Or look at it the other way round: concede the latter, and you have conceded the former.

'Your own system is not like this.[59] (84) Your exposition bounds easily

good; so they cannot consistently also hold the Stoic thesis. He emphasizes his point, that he is talking about the consistency of a theory rather than its truth, by criticizing Epicurus, who allegedly cannot hold that the virtuous person is happy on the rack, given that he holds that pain is the worst evil. See, however, book II, 88 and note 60.

58 Two Roman examples illustrate the virtuous person who is successful in worldly terms, and the virtuous person who meets with great misfortune. For the fate of Regulus, see book II, 65 and note 48. Quintus Caecilius Metellus Macedonicus, consul in 143, died 115, enjoyed the impressive political and military successes that Cicero lists.

59 Piso in 81 repeats his point from 71: virtue alone is sufficient for the *happy* life, but other good things can improve it to produce the *happiest* life. Cicero insists that on a Stoic understanding of virtue's sufficiency for happiness there can be no degrees of happiness (and no way that

along: "There are three classes of goods." But when it reaches its conclusion, it gets stuck in the mud. It wants to say that the wise person lacks nothing needed for a happy life – a discourse based on morality, in the style of Socrates and Plato too. "This is the position I have the courage to uphold", it is claimed. But you cannot uphold it, unless you unravel your earlier statements. If poverty is an evil, then no beggar can be happy, however wise. Zeno, by contrast, was bold enough to claim that such a person is not just happy but rich. Pain is an evil: then no one can be happy in the throes of crucifixion. Children are good: then childlessness is miserable. One's homeland is a good: then exile is miserable. Health is a good: the sick are miserable. Bodily soundness is a good: the disabled are miserable. Keen eyesight is a good: the blind are miserable. Perhaps the consolation of wisdom can alleviate each of these evils taken singly. But surely it will not be able to rise above them all taken together?

'Now imagine a wise person who is blind, disabled, suffering the gravest illness, in exile, childless, needy, and being tortured on the rack for good measure. Zeno, what do you call this person? "Happy." Even completely happy? "Absolutely", he will reply. "I have shown that happiness no more admits of degrees than does virtue, in which happiness itself consists." (85) You find it incredible that this is a state of complete happiness. Well then: is your own view credible? If you have me plead your case before an audience of ordinary people, you will never convince them that a person so afflicted is even happy. Put me before experts, and they will perhaps have doubts on two scores. Firstly, they will doubt that virtue is so powerful that those endowed with it would be happy even when inside the bull of Phalaris.[60] Secondly, they will be assured that the Stoic system is self-consistent, whereas yours is self-contradictory.'

'So are you in agreement with Theophrastus' great work *On Happiness?*' asked Piso. 'We are wandering from the point', I replied. 'To cut a long story short, Piso, I am in agreement so long as what you classify as evils really are that.' (86) 'Well, do you not think that they are evils?' he asked. 'Whichever reply I give to this question', I replied, 'is bound to leave you on the hook.' 'How so?' he asked. 'Because if they are evils then no one afflicted with them will be happy. If they are not, the whole Peripatetic system collapses.' 'I see what you are up to', said Piso with a smile. 'You are afraid that I might rob

footnote 59 (*cont.*)
    other things can contribute to happiness). Thus the Stoic position is consistent, but the position defended by Antiochus is not. Once anything but virtue is recognized as good, and so addible to virtue to produce something better (the happiest life, as opposed to the happy life) then it is impossible to hold that virtue is sufficient for happiness, for the loss of these other things will remove happiness. Hence virtue alone will not be sufficient for happiness (at least given the point nobody questions, explicitly stated at 69, that happiness is complete).

60 See book IV, 64 and note 37. Cicero claims that the Antiochean view is not even more intuitive than the Stoic one (84–5). It is no more acceptable, to people who do not already accept a theory, that the virtuous person in great misfortune is (at least) happy, than it is to hold that he has the happiest life.

you of a pupil.' 'You can take him if he will follow. By being at your side he will be at mine.'

'Then listen, Lucius', said Piso. 'I must address my remarks to you.[61] As Theophrastus says, the whole importance of philosophy lies in the question of obtaining a happy life. We all have a burning desire to live happily. (87) This much your cousin and I agree on. So we have to examine whether philosophical thought can give us this life. It certainly promises to do so. If it did not, why did Plato travel through Egypt to learn arithmetic and astronomy from foreign priests? Why did he later visit Archytas at Tarentum, and the other Pythagoreans: Echechrates, Timaeus and Arion at Locri? His intention was to combine Pythagorean doctrines with his portrayal of Socrates and take on board subjects that Socrates had scorned.[62]

'Why did Pythagoras himself cross Egypt, and visit the Persian magi? Why did he roam on foot over vast foreign lands and sail across so many seas? Why did Democritus do likewise? It is said – we do not ask whether truly or falsely – that Democritus put out his own eyes. It is certain that he neglected his father's estate and left his fields untilled to prevent as far as he could his mind being distracted from reflection. What was he in search of if not the happy life? Even if he held that happiness consisted in knowledge, still his intention in pursuing his researches was that they lead to a cheerfulness of spirit. He called the supreme good *euthumia* or (often) *athambia*, namely freedom from fear.

(88) 'This idea, however distinguished, still lacked the final polish, since Democritus said little about virtue, and said it obscurely.[63] It was later that inquiry into virtue was begun, first in this city by Socrates, and subsequently transferred to this very location. No one doubted that all hope of living well, and so also happily, lay in virtue. When Zeno had learned this from our school, he dealt with "the same matter in a different manner", as the preamble to law-suits usually puts it. In his case you approve of this technique. Obviously he escapes the charge of inconsistency by simply changing the labels, while we cannot escape! He denies that Metellus' life was happier than Regulus', but says that it was to be preferred; though not more worthy of seeking, it was more worthy of adopting; and given the choice, Metellus' life is to be selected and Regulus' rejected.

'For my part, the life that he calls preferable and more worthy of selection, I call happier, though I do not attach even the slightest extra value to this life than the Stoics do. (89) What is the difference here, except that I call familiar

---

[61] Piso fails completely to meet Cicero's objection. Instead, like a good lawyer (cf. 78) he turns the point aside with an elegant joke, ignores the issue and from here to 95 repeats various points.

[62] On the travels ascribed to Plato (and below to Pythagoras and Democritus), see below, 50 and note 35. The 'Old Academy' tradition stresses the influence on Plato of Pythagoras, who put forward his ideas authoritatively. The tradition of the sceptical Academy stresses the influence of Socrates, who argued with others to obtain understanding.

[63] See above, 23 and note 21.

things by their familiar names, whereas they look for new names with which to express the same meaning? Just as there is always someone in the Senate who demands an interpreter,[64] so too we must listen to the Stoics with an interpreter. I call good whatever is in accordance with nature, and what is against nature I call evil. So do you, Chrysippus, in day-to-day business and at home. Only in the lecture-room do you change. Why? Do you think that human beings should speak in one way, and philosophers in another? True, the educated and uneducated may differ on the value of things. But when the educated agree amongst themselves on the value of something – if they were human beings they would speak in normal ways. So long as the substance remains the same, let them invent new words as they please.

(90) 'I turn now to the charge of inconsistency, before you tell me that I am straying from the point too frequently. You locate inconsistency in words. I thought it depended on facts. Let it be well understood – and here we have the Stoics as our greatest supporters – that virtue has such power that were all other things to be weighed against it they would not register at all. Take all the things which the Stoics certainly claim are advantageous, and worthy of adoption and selection, and preferred (which they define so as to mean highly valuable): when I deal with them, bearing as they do all these Stoic names, some novel and invented, like that "promoted" and "demoted" of yours, some with identical senses – what is the difference between "seeking" and "selecting"? In fact, what is selected and has choice applied to it sounds rather more sumptuous to me. At any rate, when I call all these things good, all that matters is how good I say they are, and when I call them desirable, how much so.

'Assume that I regard them as no more worthy of seeking than you regard them as worthy of selecting, and that I, in calling them good, think that they are no more valuable than you do in calling them promoted. Then they must all alike be eclipsed and vanish when they meet the radiant sunlight of virtue. (91) But, you say, any life that has some evil in it cannot be happy. In that case, there would be no crop, however rich and abundant the corn, if you noticed a weed anywhere. No business would be in profit if it incurred a single small loss amidst enormous gains. Or does one principle apply everywhere else but a different one to life?[65] Will you not judge a life as a whole on the basis of its largest part? And is there any doubt that virtue does play the largest part in human affairs, so much so that it obliterates the rest?

---

[64] From Greek to Latin, when Greek-speaking ambassadors were addressing the Senate. By this period educated Romans were fluent in Greek; the request is a matter of attitude on the part of culturally insecure Romans.

[65] The only fresh point in Piso's recapitulation; he tries to rebut the objection that he cannot claim both that virtue is sufficient for happiness and that bodily and external goods are really good (and their loss, therefore, bad). A life, he says, can be called good even if it contains some small evils, just as we do not refuse to call a crop good because of a few weeds; on his theory the loss of bodily and external goods is as insignificant. This does not meet the point that *any* loss of genuine goods, however small, threatens the thesis that virtue is sufficient for happiness, given that happiness is complete.

'I shall therefore dare to call all the other things that are in accordance with nature "goods" and not cheat them out of their old name. This is preferable to searching for some novelty word. But I shall place virtue's mass in the other dish of the scales. (92) Believe me, it will outweigh the earth and the sea. It is always the case that a thing as a whole is called after its largest and most extensive parts. We say that someone lives a cheerful life: does one episode of gloom undermine it? At any rate such an outcome hardly applied in the case of Marcus Crassus. Lucilius says that Crassus smiled but once in his life, which did nothing to stop him calling Crassus "the Unsmiling".[66] They called Polycrates of Samos "the Fortunate". Nothing happened to him that he did not wish for except that he threw a cherished ring overboard into the sea. That one annoyance hardly made him "the Unfortunate", to be reinstated as "the Fortunate" when that same ring was found in the belly of a fish. Now if Polycrates was not wise (and being a tyrant, he certainly was not) then he was never happy. If wise, then he was never miserable, even when being crucified by Oroetes, Darius' appointee.[67] "But he suffered many evils." Who is denying it? Yet those evils were overwhelmed by the magnitude of virtue.

(93) 'Or do you even refuse to let the Peripatetics say that the life of all who are good – namely the wise – decked out as such a life is with every virtue, has altogether more good than evil? Who does say this? The Stoics, obviously. Not at all. Actually it is those very philosophers who measure everything in terms of pleasure and pain who clamour that the wise always have more of what they want than what they do not want. So this is the weight placed on virtue even by those who declare that they would not lift a finger in the cause of virtue unless pleasure was the result. What, then, are we to do, who claim that the slightest excellence of character takes such precedence over all bodily goods that the latter disappear from view? No one would dare to claim that it is appropriate for a wise person to give up virtue forever (were this possible) in exchange for complete freedom from pain. No one of our school – and we are not ashamed to call evils what the Stoics call hardships – would claim that it is better to do a pleasant but immoral act than a painful but moral one.

(94) 'We believe that it was scandalous of Dionysius of Heraclea to have seceded from the Stoics because of a painful eye condition[68] – as if he had learned from Zeno that one was in no pain when in pain! Rather, he had been told but had not learned that pain was no evil because it was not immoral, and that a brave man ought to endure it. If he had been a Peripatetic, I think he

---

[66] See book II, 57 and note 42.
[67] The story of Polycrates, ruler of Samos, as told by Herodotus in book III, 40ff. Polycrates, afraid of annoying the gods by his good fortune, threw a favourite ring into the sea, but it was returned to him by a fisherman who had found it in the stomach of a fish. Piso makes the point that the loss of the ring hardly affected Polycrates' overall good fortune, especially by contrast with his later misfortune of betrayal and crucifixion by the Persians.
[68] Dionysius of Heraclea (c. 330–c. 250), a Stoic for most of his life, suffered from an eye disease so painful that he could no longer sustain the Stoic thesis that pain is not an evil (as opposed to a rejected indifferent) and left the Stoa for a form of hedonism.

would have remained constant in his views, since they call pain an evil but teach the same requirement of staunch endurance that the Stoics do. Even your very own Arcesilaus, though he was too stubborn in debate, was really one of us, since Polemo was his teacher.[69] Once Arcesilaus' close friend Charmides, an Epicurean, visited him when Arcesilaus was racked by the pain of gout. As Charmides was leaving in consternation, Arcesilaus cried, "Stay, my dear Charmides, I beg you. The pain has not reached from here to here" – and he indicated his feet and his heart. Yet he would rather have not been in pain.

(95) 'This, then, is our system, which you think inconsistent. Virtue has a kind of heavenly excellence, a divine quality of such power that where it arises, in conjunction with the great and utterly glorious deeds that it generates, there can be no misery or sorrow. But there can still be pain and annoyance. And so I would have no hesitation in claiming that all who are wise are happy, but that one person can nevertheless be happier than another.'

'This position of yours, Piso, is in urgent need of strengthening', I said. 'But if you can defend it, I will let you steal not just my cousin Cicero but my own self.'

(96) 'In my view', said Quintus, 'the position is already quite secure. I had valued the humble furnishings of this philosophical school more highly than the opulent possessions of the others. Indeed such seemed to me its riches that I was able to obtain from it everything I had found desirable in our studies. How delighted I am that it has actually turned out to be more subtle than the rest as well, which people said was just the feature it was lacking.'

'Not as subtle as ours', teased Pomponius. 'But damn it all, I found your exposition quite wonderful. I did not imagine that such ideas could be put into Latin. Yet you found an aptness of expression and a clarity that is a match for the Greeks. But it is time to go, if you agree. Let us make straight for my place.'[70]

At this, we decided we had debated enough, and so we all headed off into town to Pomponius' house.

---

[69] Piso claims on the basis of Arcesilaus' fortitude in the face of pain that he really belongs in the tradition of his teacher Polemo – although Arcesilaus broke away from the doctrinal tradition of Platonism.

[70] Piso has won the rhetorical battle; Quintus is convinced, as well as Lucius. Cicero leaves it to the reader to judge the importance of the philosophical argument against the elegantly presented theory.

Index of names

To help those unfamiliar with Greco-Roman culture to avoid confusions and find their way round Cicero's wide range of references, I have added brief identifications for ancient figures referred to. See also the Note on Greek and Roman names (xxxiv–xxxv).

Index of subjects

Academy, history of, x, xi, and n. 5, xii, xiii, xiv, 26 and n. 4, 117 n. 2, 118, 119, 120; sceptical, *see* Scepticism, Academic

Antiochus' ethical theory (sometimes described as Peripatetic) xvi, xx, xxi, xxii, xxvii, 37 n. 26, 49, 52; criticized, 143–7; defended, 120–50

Carneades' division of ethical theories, xxiii and n. 21, xxiv, xxv, xxvi and nn. 22 and 23, xxvii, 32 n. 19, 38 and n. 27, 39 and n. 30, 40, 41, 74 and n. 18, 75, 106 and n. 26, 123 and n. 20, 124, 125 and n. 21, n. 23

Courage (one of four cardinal virtues) 18, 19, 42, 43, 46, 47, 51, 57, 58, 77, 92, 107, 137

death, attitude to, 21, 22, 23, 45, 48, 53, 59, 60, 74, 84 and n. 36, 128

definition, 10 and n. 24, 27 and n. 6, 28, 32, 36, 77, 92

desires, 17, 18 and n. 37, 20, 22, 33, 34, 35, 36, 48

dialogue form, ix, xii, xv, xvi, xvii

emotions, 76 and n. 20

Epicurus' ethical theory, xvi, xxi, 65, 100, 106, 118, 144, 145 n. 57; criticized, 8, 10, 11,12, 26–64; defended, 13–25, 28, 29, 31, 32

epistemology, Antiochus', xiv, xv and n. 8, 91, 96, 97, 129–32, 134, 135, 143 and n. 54; Epicurean, 13, 23 and n. 45; Stoic, xiv, xv and n. 8, 70, 76, 88, 89, 106, 107, 143 and n. 54

eudaimonism, *see* final end

final end or goal, ix, xvii–xxi, 13, 17, 27, 55–7, 60–3, 72–5, 79, 80, 81, 82 and n. 33, 84, 89, 95, 99, 100–108, 112, 120, 121, 125, 126, 137, 140–150

friendship, 23 and n. 46, 24, 25, 50, 52–5, 87 and n. 46, 88, 92, 127, 141

God, becoming like, as ethical goal, xxii and n. 19, xxv

good, in Stoic sense, 75 and n. 19, 76, 77, 81–3, 87, 97, 98 n. 17, 106, 109–14

happiness, *see* final end

hedonism, Cyrenaic, xviii and n. 12, 10–12, 16, 32, 33, 38–40, 63

justice, 19, 20, 42–6, 50, 54, 87, 88, 91, 92, 97, 137, 140

'logic' part of philosophy, 10, 22, 32, 65, 73 and n. 16, 74, 88, 93 , 94 and n. 11, 107, 108, 120, 121

metaphysics, *see* 'physics' part of philosophy

moral development, individual, 42, 70–3, 96, 97, 99, 101, 125 and n. 24, 126–38; towards others, 42, 84 and n. 37, 85 and n. 38, 86, 87, 91, 138–140

morality, *see* virtue

natural goods, role in happiness, xxiii, xxv, 38–40, 78 and n. 24, 79, 96–103, 108, 123, 124, 126, 140–7, 148 and n. 65, 149, 150

nature, role in ethical theory, 13, 14, 18–20, 25, 35, 37, 38, 42, 46, 56, 68, 70–2, 73 and n. 15, 75–7, 84, 86, 87, 88, 91, 95–7, 99, 100–5, 108, 109, 113, 115, 125–38, 140; human nature distinguished from nature as whole system, 128, 129

'Old Academy', x, xiii, xiv, xxvii, 91–7, 104, 109–11, 113, 114, 116, 117 n. 2, 122, 124, 125, 147 n. 62

'physics' part of philosophy, 9, 10, 12, 22, 23, 65, 88, 94, 95 and n. 13, 120, 121

Pleasure, xxiii, xxv, 10–13, 18, 19, 24, 25, 38–43, 45, 46, 48–56, 61–5, 70, 75, 80, 86, 100, 107, 108, 123, 124, 129, 130, 133, 135, 136, 141, 142; kinetic/static distinction 13 n. 31, 15

157

Cambridge texts in the history of philosophy

Titles published in the series thus far

Aristotle *Nicomachean Ethics* (edited by Roger Crisp)

Arnauld and Nicole *Logic or the Art of Thinking* (edited by Jill Vance Buroker)

Bacon *The New Organon* (edited by Lisa Jardine and Michael Silverthorne)

Boyle *A Free Enquiry into the Vulgarly Received Notion of Nature* (edited by Edward B. Davis and Michael Hunter)

Bruno *Cause, Principle and Unity* and *Essays on Magic* (edited by Richard Blackwell and Robert de Lucca with an introduction by Alfonso Ingegno)

Cavendish *Observations upon Experimental Philosophy* (edited by Eileen O'Neill)

Cicero *On Moral Ends* (edited by Julia Annas, translated by Raphael Woolf)

Clarke *A Demonstration of the Being and Attributes of God and Other Writings* (edited by Ezio Vailati)

Condillac *Essay on the Origin of Human Knowledge* (edited by Hans Aarsleff)

Conway *The Principles of the Most Ancient and Modern Philosophy* (edited by Allison P. Coudert and Taylor Corse)

Cudworth *A Treatise Concerning Eternal and Immutable Morality* with *A Treatise of Freewill* (edited by Sarah Hutton)

Descartes *Meditations on First Philosophy*, with selections from the *Objections and Replies* (edited by John Cottingham)

Descartes *The World and Other Writings* (edited by Stephen Gaukroger)

Fichte *Foundations of Natural Right* (edited by Frederick Neuhouser, translated by Michael Baur)

Hobbes and Bramhall on Liberty and Necessity (edited by Vere Chappell)

Humboldt *On Language* (edited by Michael Losonsky, translated by Peter Heath)

Kant *Critique of Practical Reason* (edited by Mary Gregor with an introduction by Andrews Reath)

Kant *Groundwork of the Metaphysics of Morals* (edited by Mary Gregor with an introduction by Christine M. Korsgaard)

Kant *The Metaphysics of Morals* (edited by Mary Gregor with an introduction by Roger Sullivan)

Kant *Prolegomena to any Future Metaphysics* (edited by Gary Hatfield)

Kant *Religion within the Boundaries of Mere Reason and Other Writings* (edited by Allen Wood and George di Giovanni with an introduction by Robert Merrihew Adams)

La Mettrie *Machine Man and Other Writings* (edited by Ann Thomson)

Leibniz *New Essays on Human Understanding* (edited by Peter Remnant and Jonathan Bennett)

Malebranche *Dialogues on Metaphysics and on Religion* (edited by Nicholas Jolley and David Scott)

Malebranche *The Search after Truth* (edited by Thomas M. Lennon and Paul J. Olscamp)

Melanchthon *Orations on Philosophy and Education* (edited by Sachiko Kusukawa, translated by Christine Salazar)

Mendelssohn *Philosophical Writings* (edited by Daniel O. Dahlstrom)

Nietzsche *The Birth of Tragedy and Other Writings* (edited by Raymond Geuss and Ronald Speirs)

Nietzsche *Daybreak* (edited by Maudemarie Clark and Brian Leiter, translated by R. J. Hollingdale)

Nietzsche *Human, All Too Human* (translated by R. J. Hollingdale with an introduction by Richard Schacht)

Nietzsche *Untimely Meditations* (edited by Daniel Breazeale, translated by R. J. Hollingdale)

Schleiermacher *Hermeneutics and Criticism* (edited by Andrew Bowie)

Schleiermacher *On Religion: Speeches to its Cultured Despisers* (edited by Richard Crouter)

Schopenhauer *Prize Essay on the Freedom of the Will* (edited by Günter Zöller)

Sextus Empiricus *Outlines of Scepticism* (edited by Julia Annas and Jonathan Barnes)

Shaftesbury, *Characteristics of Men, Manners, Opinions, Times* (edited by Lawrence Klein)

Voltaire *Treatise on Tolerance and Other Writings* (edited by Simon Harvey)

Printed in the USA
CPSIA information can be obtained
at www.ICGtesting.com
LVHW021307281223
767623LV00001B/18